L-BANDITTI assailing the SAVIOUR of INDIA.

EDMUND BURKE: A LIFE IN CARICATURE

EDMUND BURKE

A LIFE IN CARICATURE

NICHOLAS K. ROBINSON

YALE UNIVERSITY PRESS

NEW HAVEN AND LONDON

Designed by John Nicoll

Set in Bembo by SX Composing DTP, Rayleigh, Essex

Printed in Spain by KSG Elkar

Library of Congress Cataloging-in-Publication Data

Robinson, Nicholas K., 1946–
      Edmund Burke: a life in caricature / Nicholas K. Robinson.
          p.   cm.
      Includes bibliographical references (p.) and index.
      ISBN 0-300-06801-8
      1. Burke, Edmund, 1729–1797—Caricatures and cartoons.   2. Great
    Britain—Politics and government—18th century—Caricatures and
    cartoons.   3. Statesmen—Great Britain—Bibliography.   4. Political
    scientists—Great Britain—Biography.   I. Title.
    DA506.B9R63   1996
    g41.073'092—dc20
      [B]   96–9817
                                                                                                                CIP

A catalogue record for this book is available from the British Library

The right of Nicholas K. Robinson to be identified as the author of this work has been asserted by him in accordance with the Copyright, Designs and Patents Act, 1988.

FOR MARY, TESSA, WILLIAM AND AUBREY

To say truth, Madam, 'tis very vulgar to print, and as my little productions are mostly satires and lampoons on particular people, I find they circulate more by giving copies in confidence to the friends of the parties.

Sir Benjamin Backbite (in *The School for Scandal* by Richard Brinsley Sheridan, 1777)

CONTENTS

Acknowledgements   ix

Introduction   The Caricaturer's Stock in Trade   1

Chapter One   The Flowers of Oratory   10
Advisor to the Rockingham Whigs, 1770–82

Chapter Two   Paradise Lost, Paradise Regained   38
Resignation and Re-appointment to Government, 1782–83

Chapter Three   Carlo Khan   53
The India Bill and Loss of Government, 1783–85

Chapter Four   Assailing the 'Saviour of India'   79
The Pursuit of Warren Hastings, 1785–88

Chapter Five   Fighting for a Crown   118
The Regency Crisis and its Aftermath, 1788–90

Chapter Six   The Knight of the Woeful Countenance   136
Opposition to the French Revolution, 1789–93

Chapter Seven   Pity the Sorrows of a Poor Old Man   171
The Final Years, 1794–97

Conclusion   Sublime and Beautiful Reflections   190

Appendix 1   Persons most Caricatured, 1778–97   194

Appendix 2   Addresses of Printsellers and Publishers   195

Abbreviations   196

Notes   197

Index of Caricatures   206

General Index   209

Queen of hearts

Queen would be

Queen Hant

Queen Scrub

Queen of

Fox

Done by W. M.

THE CARICATURERS STOCK IN TRADE

Pub. 26 March 1786

by W. Humphrey, Lancaster Court

ACKNOWLEDGEMENTS

I own, I don't understand any of those Prints, & Burlesques; I am too dull to taste them; And, if they are not decypher'd for Me, I could not in the least guess, very often, what they mean.

Duke of Newcastle, in a letter to the Earl of Hardwicke, 30 September 1762

A political cartoonist working today hopes that his or her readers will immediately recognise the people being cartooned, and the context in which they appear. The subject matter, portentous or trivial, will have made the headlines, in the papers or on television, but whether it is an on-going saga or a passing fancy, the immediacy of the cartoonist's response makes it increasingly difficult to spot the characters and identify the incidents as time goes by. So if the Duke of Newcastle had trouble penetrating the satirical allusion of the prints of his day, then reading that ephemeral imagery so many years later can be a baffling, at times impossible, task. Fortunately a revered authority, not available to the Duke, has for many years provided an almost inexhaustible mine of information for scholars in this field. The *Catalogue of Political and Personal Satires* in the British Museum, published between 1870 and 1954 describes 17,391 prints preserved in the Department of Prints and Drawings. The first four volumes by F.G. Stephens, covering almost 5,000 prints up to 1770, are valuable. The subsequent seven volumes, 1771–1832, by M. Dorothy George, constitute a meticulous and erudite work of scholarship, extensively mined by every writer since. My debt to Dr George is enormous. I must thank as well Antony Griffiths and his colleagues in the Department of Prints and Drawings at the British Museum, from which over a third of the plates in this book have been reproduced, for their kindness over many years.

The most enjoyable part of my task has been to see at first hand not only the BM collection but other great holdings as well. In every institution I have been struck by the unfailing helpfulness and courtesy of those who look after the prints and make them accessible. It is therefore a real pleasure to acknowledge the assistance of the staff of the Lewis Walpole Library, Yale University; the Library of Congress; the Pierpont Morgan Library, New York; New York Public Library; the Huntington Library, San Marino, California; the Colonial Williamsburg Foundation; the Yale Center for British Art, Paul Mellon Collection; the John Carter Brown Library at Brown University; the British Library; the Victoria and Albert Museum; the National Portrait Gallery, London; the Collection of the Palace of Westminster; the Ashmolean Library, Oxford; the National Library of Ireland; the Library of Trinity College, Dublin; the National Gallery of Ireland; the Crawford Art Gallery, Cork; the Public Record Office, Northern Ireland; and the Linenhall Library, Belfast. Other curators and librarians, alas, will reproach me with (or tell me with glee of) the treasures I have overlooked and neglected elsewhere.

I am indebted to many writers. One cannot but be influenced by Conor Cruise O'Brien's thematic biography of Burke, *The Great Melody*, an invaluable source of information and analysis. And students of Burke owe a great deal to the editors of the

1. W. Mansell: *The Caricaturers Stock in Trade.* Published 26 March 1786, by W. Humphrey. BM 6931; private collection.
Clockwise from top (outer figures): Queen Charlotte ('Queen of hearts'), George III, Colonel George Hanger, Duchess of Devonshire ('Queen of Fox'), Duke of Richmond, Lord North, Frances Abington ('Queen Scrub'), Sarah Siddons ('Queen Rant'), Maria Fitzherbert ('Queen would be'), and the Prince of Wales; (inner figures): Charles James Fox, William Pitt the younger and Edmund Burke. By 1783 Burke's spectacles had become an almost unique accoutrement in caricature. Equally distinctive was Fox's five-o'clock shadow.

Correspondence (led by the late Thomas W. Copeland) and of the volumes so far of the *Writings and Speeches* (led by Paul Langford). In the field of caricature, helpful works, named in the Notes section, include those by Herbert M. Atherton, John Brewer, Vincent Carretta (source of the Duke of Newcastle quotation), Diana Donald, Richard Godfrey, Ernst Gombrich and Draper Hill.

With his usual generosity of spirit and scholarship Edward McParland has subjected the draft to detailed and helpful criticism, which has led to the reshaping of some chapters and the enhancement of all. I have deeply appreciated the support of John Nicoll and his colleagues at Yale University Press. My thanks are also due to Andrew Edmunds, whose knowledge of caricature and good food, gained over a lifetime of dealing and collecting, he has endeavoured to share with me over the past twenty-two years. He kindly gave me access to little-known material for research and reproduction. Rosemary Baker, a respected scholar in the field, has been untiring in her help and support. I have benefitted greatly from the advice of W.E. Vaughan, and value the encouragement I received at the outset and since from F.X. Martin, OSA. It is impossible to list all who have helped in different ways but they include: Joan Tighe Clayton and the late Harry Clayton, Anne Crookshank, David H. Davison, Edwin Davison, Brendan Dempsey, Patricia Donlon, H. George Fletcher, Nigel Glendinning, Malcolm Hay, Gabriel C. Hogan and Jacinta Hogan, Don K. Jemmy and the Jemmys of Wexford, Brian P. Kennedy, Duncan F. Kennedy, Elizabeth Kirwan, Peter Murray, Susan Naulty, Bernard Reilly, Jill Roberts, Roger Stalley and Joan H. Sussler. To others who have assisted may I offer a general expression of gratitude. I alone am responsible for errors of fact or interpretation.

For kind permission to reproduce material my thanks are due to: the Trustees of the British Museum; the Trustees of the British Library; Andrew Edmunds Esq., London; the Print Collection, Lewis Walpole Library, Yale University; the Trustees of the Pierpont Morgan Library, New York, (photography: David A. Loggie); the Library of Congress; the Huntington Library, San Marino, California; the Yale Center for British Art, Paul Mellon Collection; the House of Commons; the Board of Trinity College, Dublin; the National Gallery of Ireland; the Crawford Art Gallery, Cork; private collectors (photography by Davison & Associates). The task of coping with my spidery handwriting through various drafts has been cheerfully and expertly executed by Angela Douglas. Early drafts were similarly undertaken by Ann Lane.

Above all, I want to thank my wife Mary, the book's greatest friend, for her constant and unflagging support. I dedicate it to her, and to Tessa, William and Aubrey.

THE CARICATURER'S STOCK IN TRADE

Charles James Fox and Edmund Burke, the story goes, walked into Mrs Humphrey's print shop in St James's Street, whose window displayed a severe attack on the Irishman. 'My friend here, Mr. Burke,' said Fox 'is going to trounce you all with a vengeance.' 'No, no, my good lady,' protested Burke, 'I intend to do no such thing. Were I to prosecute you, it would be the making of your fortune.'[1]

This book is not a conventional recounting of Edmund Burke's story, but a voyage into the murky waters of propaganda and prejudice in late eighteenth-century London. It was a time when every leading figure in that close-knit society was the target of abuse, sometimes cheerful, often vitriolic, frequently laced with earthy vulgarity. They were at the mercy of a talented, cynical, opportunistic pack of what today we would call cartoonists and – because the word 'cartoon' (in the sense of a humorous drawing) was coined in the mid-nineteenth century – what this book will refer to as caricaturists.[2]

Personal caricature,[3] the joke of mock portraiture, had long been fashionable in Italy. Its inventor at the turn of the seventeenth century, Annibale Carracci, explained it, tongue in cheek, thus: 'Is not the caricaturist's task exactly the same as the classical artist's? Both see the lasting truth beneath the surface of mere outwards appearance. Both try to help nature accomplish its plan. The one may strive to visualise the perfect form and to realise it in his work, the other to grasp the perfect deformity, and thus reveal the very essence of a personality. A good caricature, like every work of art, is more true to life than reality itself.'[4] In effect – as two modern commentators note – 'the real aim of the true caricaturist is to transform the whole man into a completely new and ridiculous figure which nevertheless resembles the original in a striking and surprising way . . . With a few strokes he may unmask the public hero, belittle his pretensions, and make a laughing stock of him. Against this spell even the mightiest is powerless'.[5]

Embraced and appropriated for political use in mid-eighteenth-century London by talented amateurs like George, Viscount Townshend, 'caricature' became established as the name for satirical prints. In the process a peculiarly English weapon was forged.[6] Why should an Italian amusement borrowed by English dilettanti become so formidable a weapon? In the first place it was grafted on to an older, European tradition of print making that had taken root in London earlier in the century. Symbolism and allegory – the British lion asleep or muzzled, broken keys of the papal arms, locusts swarming over Whitehall, the cat pulling chestnuts from the fire – gave such prints their political bite, and still play their part in today's cartoon. Frequently used in conjunction with another tradition, verse satire – then a front line offensive weapon in its own right – the print was a medium that had allowed satirists (many of them Dutch) to poke fun at the stock exchange scandals of 1720 known as the South Sea Bubble. More significantly it had been a vehicle for English opposition to the statecraft of the larger than life Whig Prime Minister Robert Walpole during his long tenure of office, from 1721 to 1742.

Nor was it a weapon confined to Tories; a supporter of the political preacher Dr

Henry Sacheverell, whose sermons were declared to be seditious libels in 1710, wrote that 'the chief means by which all the lower order of that sort of men call'd Whigs, shall ever be found to act for the ruin of a potent adversary, are the following three – by the Print, the Canto or Doggrell Poem, and by the Libell, grave, calm, and cool . . .'[7]

Secondly, caricature thrived on the immunity it increasingly acquired from prosecution. Perhaps in those early days its capacity to make mischief was underestimated. It seemed too innocuous to justify suppression. Gradually the sheer scale of the material made it less susceptible to control, especially as imagery could be less explicit than the printed word.[8] Fortunately for the printsellers, *scandalum magnatum,* the old statutory offence of making defamatory statements about persons of high estate, was no longer effectual.[9] In theory the law of seditious libel – designed to protect King and government from hatred or contempt – applied equally to pictorial satire and the printed word. Yet in practice the former appeared to enjoy more tolerance. It was more difficult to curb and the authorities often found prosecution not worth the expense or effort.[10] Besides, as a writer in the weekly journal the *Craftsman* put it, 'the Sale of a Libel always rises in proportion with the Sufferings of its Author',[11] the very point made by Burke in Mrs Humphrey's print shop.

And perhaps there is another reason why caricature gained such immunity: identifying a medium through which they could publicise their own point of view, governments themselves lay behind the commissioning or 'inspiring' of some of these plates.[12]

Not everyone was amused by the activities of George Townshend and his associates. A letter to the *Public Advertiser* in June 1765 (signed mockingly George Bout-de-Ville) rounded on Townshend:

> Every Window of every Print shop is in a Manner glazed, and the Shop itself papered with Libels. One Arch-Libeller in particular has rendered himself more than a hundred Times liable to Prosecution for *Scandalum Magnatum.* There is scarce a distinguished person in the Kingdom, whom he has not exhibited in Caricature. He has dealt his grotesque Cards from House to House, and circulated his defamatory Pictures from Town's end to Town's end. Is there a great General of the highest Rank, and most eminent military Abilities, who has rescued us from the Horrors of Popery and Slavery, and delivered down to Posterity the Blessings of the Revolution? If the Size of his Person as well as Fame, should be larger than ordinary, this malicious Libeller, at three Strokes of his Pencil, scratches out his Figure in all the Ridiculous Attitudes imaginable. Is there a Nobleman distinguished for Wit, Eloquence, and Learning ? If his Person be long, and lank, and lean, and bony, he also is in the like manner exposed to Ridicule. If the Name of a Scotch Peer bears the least Resemblance to Boot, and his Christian Name be John, an huge Jack Boot serves for a Pun on Copper-Plate.[13]

One charge against the Scotch Peer in question, the much lampooned Earl of Bute, was that he bought off such opponents, and rewarded authors and satirists for their propagandist services. A print of 1762 by 'Alexander Mackenzie' that shows him distributing largesse to *The Hungry Mob of Scriblers and Etchers* (Plate 2), hits in the process Dr Samuel Johnson, who is seen at the head of the queue clutching his pension of '300£ pr.Ann.'.[14] Prominent, too, with his crutched stick is the caricaturist and printseller Matthew Darly, at whose side is a diminutive figure thought to be William Hogarth. A quotation from the Bible (Proverbs xxv, 21) is given

Scots Scourge N.º 27.

Alex.ʳ Mackenzie Inv.ᵗ et Sculp 1762 L.ᵈ Bute hired a number of writers, as Smollett, &c &c See Almoss Anecdotes L.ᵈ Bute.
Vol. II. p. 9.

The HUNGRY MOB of SCRIBLERS and Etchers

If thine Enemy be hungry give him Bread to eat;
and if he be thirsty, give him water to drink. *Proverbs 25. 21.*

2. 'Alexander Mackenzie' (pseudonym): *The Hungry Mob of Scriblers and Etchers*. Published 1762. BM 3844; British Museum.
Artists, printsellers and writers stand in line to be hired or bought off by the Earl of Bute, First Lord of the Treasury. Matthew Darly, who has defamed him with *The Screen*, is prominent, and stands beside the small figure of William Hogarth. First in the queue is Samuel Johnson, for whom Bute had secured a pension on the Irish civil list (*see* Plate 16). Bute's well turned leg had been conspicuous in a full length portrait by Allan Ramsay in 1758.

below: 'If thine Enemy be hungry give him Bread to eat, and if he be thirsty give him water to drink'. Clearly the intent is libellous rather than improving, yet how is a prosecutor to pin it down? In the face of the wounding charge that one is not able to take a joke, perhaps the wisest reaction is to treat the caricaturist's attention, however scurrilous, as a form of flattery.

This was the London in which Edmund Burke made his way. His rise to political prominence coincided with the flowering of the classic age of English caricature, a period of extraordinary licence and creativity in graphic satire. As we shall see, not just Burke's but everybody's reputation was at risk. Character assassination, the peddling of downright lies and, more dangerous, of credible half-truths, had been rife for years. Specialist print shops had joined booksellers and engravers in meeting the popular demand for plates on political and social topics alike. Now the arrival of caricaturists like James Gillray, Thomas Rowlandson, James Sayers and William Dent brought a new dimension of professionalism that laid the foundations of the modern cartoon, and established a flourishing trade in the west end of London.

Much of the caricature of the 1780s and 1790s was instinctively oppositionist, but in the propaganda battles that flared from time to time many of the satirists were guns for hire. Even Gillray was available, though he was, to develop the metaphor, a loose cannon, too independent a spirit for a mere hireling. Draper Hill has a different analogy. 'Gillray', he writes, 'seems to have had all the manners of a hungry cat in mid-spring . . . Confined like a circus panther, he was a provider of dangerous entertainment.'[15] Dorothy George, the great historian of graphic satire, describes the caricatures as 'documents in an endless discussion on politics and persons, war and diplomacy . . . They were a recognised weapon of controversy, national and sometimes international, to a degree that gives them an importance outside the scope of the modern cartoon. Crises and scandals and vendettas evoked prints and counterprints, sometimes commissioned by those concerned . . . They are history, concrete, personal, and tendentious, seen through contemporary eyes'.[16]

What were these caricatures and how did they circulate? Following a preliminary sketch (perhaps volunteered by an amateur or based on the suggestions of an insider) a copper plate was engraved or etched, and from this the print was taken and offered for sale at a typical price of sixpence 'plain' or a shilling if hand-coloured. (To put these sums in context, the first, as may be seen from the 1775 anti-recruiting satire, *Sixpence a Day*,[17] was the daily wage of a solider. The latter sum, it has been calculated, represented a month's supply of candles.)[18] In an age familiar with the triumphs of such laborious processes as mezzotint and aquatint (frequently devoted to the realistic reproduction of oil paintings) the immediacy of technique of the caricatures, both in line and colour, must have been startling. And immediacy of technique expressed an immediacy of subject matter in these political and social satires, which were rushed out while the story was fresh, to capture the mood of the moment. Writing in 1874, Robert Buss related this account by Cruikshank, who was then an old man, of Gillray at work:

> George Cruikshank knew Gillray, and has said that the bold and vigorous style of Gillray's designs and etchings was entirely owing to the degree of enthusiasm he brought to bear on his work; indeed, to a pitch painful to witness, as it exhibited a mind touched with madness. So prolific was his invention that it seemed to be inexhaustible. With no previous study or preparatory drawing, he would take a large plate and fill it entirely with figures, etching them rapidly one after the other, and contrasting their action most skilfully, so that not one appeared to be redundant. For likenesses, he referred to sketches on small pieces of card. Practice such as this can only be fully appreciated by an engraver or one accustomed to etching.[19]

And such is Gillray's technical virtuosity that the fury of execution Cruikshank describes is controlled to match the mood he seeks to create, whether it be the frenzied vision of apocalypse (*see* Plate 186) or the lethargy of an overheated drawingroom (*see* Plate 125).

The commercial value of a well conceived and executed print was protected, thanks to William Hogarth's efforts, by a Copyright Act of 1735 (8 George II *c*.13), which safeguarded original engraved designs from piracy for fourteen years. To benefit from copyright each print had to carry (to the gratification of historians) the name and address of the publisher and a publication date, 'as the Act directs'. An account in 1791 of how an 'eminent printseller' despatched prints abroad in great numbers noted that 'in Germany the words published as the Act directs were often taken to mean published by express order of parliament'.[20] Hogarth's Act did not extend to Ireland and a flourishing print trade in Dublin from the 1790s – the only one in these islands of any significance outside London – was based on piracy. Dublin printsellers were happy to volunteer their names and addresses but naturally (though to our frustration) declined to date them.

It is almost impossible to estimate how many impressions were taken from each copper plate: the print runs varied enormously from a few dozen to several thousands,[21] at which stage wear on the reworked plates could be disguised by the heavy application of colour to the print. Wearing was caused not by printing but by the constant wiping and polishing involved in removing the oily surface ink before each impression was made by forcing the paper (which had been dampened) into the engraved work of the plate. Whatever the totals achieved, the images could be printed in batches as sales demanded, hand-coloured (in varying degrees of competence) along a production line above the shop, and, if good enough, added to the window display. Edmund Burke himself, as will be seen later, helped to inspire one of the best-selling designs of the eighteenth century, on the repeal of the Stamp Act in 1766 (*see* Plate 11). It was claimed that 2,000 prints were sold in four days at a shilling each and that the total number sold amounted to a phenomenal 16,000.[22] One estimate is that the majority of political prints probably sold about 500 copies.[23]

The leading printsellers, therefore, were entrepreneurs, dealing in a luxury trade, and probably formidable characters in their own right. The fashion for caricatures drawn (and sometimes etched) by amateurs was promoted in the 1770s by Matthew and Mary Darly's print shop in the Strand, 'where Gentlemen and Ladies may have Copper plates prepared and Varnished for etching. Ladies to whom the fumes of the Aqua Fortis are Noxious may have their Plates carefully Bit, and proved, and may be attended at their own Houses'. Or, if they wished, 'Ladies and Gentlemen sending their Designs may have them neatly etch'd and printed for their own private amusement at the most reasonable rates'.[24] George Cruikshank would later say that his most profitable work, as with Rowlandson and Gillray, had been 'the washing of other people's dirty linen' by 'putting on to copper the crude designs of fashionable amateurs'.[25] Edward Topham (later to be caricatured by Gillray as editor of the *World*) was one of the amateurs published by Darly;[26] another was Richard Sheridan who designed social prints under the name 'Dicky Sneer'.

A print of 1775, *Ecce Homo* (Plate 3), which has been attributed to Francesco Bartolozzi,[27] shows Darly's print shop under attack from another engraver and drawing teacher William Austin. Suffering 'the most malicious wicked and Diabolical combinations consultations and insinuations of that most unfeeling set of Men cald printsellers' poor Austin seeks in vain to rebuke their insolence, and in his emotion drops a doctor's prescription made out by the celebrated Dr John Monro, physician to Bethlehem Hospital and expert in lunacy.

Among the printsellers who came to prominence in the 1780s was Hannah Humphrey, who operated first from Bond Street and later established premises in St James's Street. From about 1794 her monopoly of the publication of Gillray's work made her pre-eminent, and she looked after Gillray attentively, who lodged above her shop and with whom she may have had a liaison. William Holland of Drury Lane, and later Oxford Street, opened his establishment in 1782 and seven years later could inform his customers that 'Caricature Collectors may now be supplied with the greatest variety in London of political and other humorous prints, bound in volumes

3. Anon.: *Ecce Homo.* (1775). BM 5318; British Museum.

A copy of this very print is prominent in the window of Matthew Darly's print shop (top left), and labels William Austin as a patient of the Bethlehem hospital for insanity. The title, 'Behold the Man' (John XIX, 5) mocks Austin that such persecution is his crown of thorns. Austin, using his own portfolio as a shield, cries 'Damn your foolish Caricatures'.

4. Richard Newton: *Holland's Caricature Exhibition*. Watercolour drawing (*c.* 1794); British Museum. Not just the Royal Academy but caricature itself is caricatured by Newton, who satirises the clientele of William Holland's exhibition rooms enjoying Newton's own work. One of the exhibits is his *Promenade in the State Side of Newgate* (top, second from left), reminding customers that Holland had done time for seditious libel.

and ornamented with an engraved title and a characteristic vignette: one hundred prints in a Volume, Five Guineas Plain or Seven Guineas Coloured'.[28] (The cost in the 1790s of James Malton's *Dublin* was only a few pounds more: ten guineas for a bound set of twenty-five elaborate aquatint views, hand-coloured, and accompanying text, all vastly expensive to prepare and produce and a most luxurious object.) Holland, who was also a caricaturist and book publisher, was imprisoned in Newgate Gaol in 1793 for a seditious publication. His obituary in the *Gentleman's Magazine* in 1816 records that he was 'an eminent publisher of caricatures and a patron of Woodward, Rowlandson, Newton, Buck and other artists, was himself a man of genius and wrote many popular songs and a volume of poetry, besides being the author of the pointed and epigrammatic words which accompanied most of his caricatures'.[29]

Holland occasionally extended the publication line in his prints to advertise his wares: 'Published by William Holland, No. 50 Oxford Street, in whose rooms may be seen the largest Collection in Europe of Caricatures. Admit[tance] 1 sh[illing].'[30] That shilling gained entrance to one of London's more diverting resorts for the *bon ton,* to judge from Richard Newton's drawing *c.*1794 of 'Holland's Caricature Exhibition', an affair almost as fashionable as the shows at the Royal Academy it sought to lampoon (Plate 4).[31]

VERY SLIPPY WEATHER

5. Anon. after James Gillray: *Very Slippy Weather.* Undated. Published (after February 1808) by J. Sidebotham, Dublin; private collection.
The print shop display helped to bring material to a wider audience, occasionally at the risk of broken windows (*see* p. 72). A clergyman inside the shop smirks at a print on Catholic emancipation.

Another leading dealer was Samuel William Fores who opened premises at No. 3 Piccadilly in 1784. He, too, charged a shilling for admission to his lounge, while a rival, James Aitken, offered free entry, reminding his readers in May 1789 that 'Aitken's Exhibition Room in Castle Street, Leicester Fields, is now open'd for the inspection of the Nobility, & the Public in general, containing the only compleat assortment of Satire, Humorous & Caricature productions now extant – Admittance Gratis'.[32] Fores charged 2s.6d a day to hire out folios for the amusement of house guests, with a deposit of £1 for their safe return.[33] For the general public who could not afford admittance to the lounges of Holland or Fores, the printsellers' windows were their ever-changing picture galleries, and crowds assembled outside Mrs Humphrey's to view Gillray's latest offerings, as he himself records in a print of 1808.[34] Unconstrained by the Copyright Act, James Sidebotham happily filched the image for his Dublin audience (Plate 5).

By this time Thomas Tegg had come on the scene, selling inexpensive social caricatures at 111 Cheapside. He advertised that 'Noblemen, Gentlemen, etc. wishing to ornament their Billiard or other Rooms, with Caricatures may be supplied 100 percent cheaper at Tegg's Caricature Warehouse. Merchants and Captains of Ships supplied Wholesale for Exportation'.[35] This reflected a long-standing trade. As early as 1721 William Price was advertising in the *Boston Gazette* his 'Choice parcel of the best sort of Prints & Maps lately brought from London, all in Good Frames well black'd',[36] and by the 1770s the print shop was to be found in most cosmopolitan cities in America.[37]

The print shop usually offered the first sight of these caricatures, and Gillray's print of 1808 captured the stir they could cause when displayed in the shop window. We can, perhaps, grasp a little more of this initial impact if we try to reconstruct the setting. We know from *Sayer and Bennett's Catalogue of Prints for 1775* that mezzotints after Reynolds (many of them portraits) accounted for about a quarter of the stock, and were offered for sale alongside political satires and 'droll, humorous and entertaining prints'.[38] The vogue for portrait prints and caricatures must have lent something of the air of a portrait gallery, if not physiognomical museum, to the print shops. Certainly a satire of Lord Thurlow (Lord Chancellor, 1778–83 and 1783–92), such as Plate 106 or Plate 108, would have been sharpened if on display in the shop alongside it was Bartolozzi's print of the Lord Chancellor, after Reynolds's *Portrait of a Nobleman*, in all his grandeur.[39]

It has been observed that the diverse character of satirical prints in circulation points to an audience at many social levels.[40] Some prints reached a mass market; others, being fashionable commodities, must have been in demand in the provinces as well as overseas. But from the contents of most surviving political prints we may judge their intended audience to be well educated and politically informed. This was London society enjoying the foibles and scandals and misadventures of its own. It comprised, as the historian Sir George Trevelyan has described it, 'a few thousand people who thought that the world was made for them and that all outside their own fraternity were unworthy of notice or criticism'. Yet it should not be forgotten that beyond this intended (and purchasing) audience was a wider public who would not have bought prints, yet saw them in shop windows, taverns and coffee houses.[41]

Who were the main targets? Of the seventy or so figures most caricatured between 1778 and 1797, the last twenty years of Burke's life, the dubious honour goes to Charles James Fox. As son of the controversial Henry Fox, he made his first appearance in caricature at the age of eight.[42] His personality, politics and lifestyle were irresistible, inspiring an astonishing stream of squibs and mockeries, double in volume those of the next most popular subjects: William Pitt, George III, Lord North and the Prince of Wales. Hard on the Prince's heels comes Burke in sixth place, followed by another Irishman, Richard Brinsley Sheridan, and the brooding Lord Chancellor Thurlow. Thereafter aristocrats and admirals, monarchs and mistresses join demagogues, hangers-on, politicians and placemen in creating an intricate and racy survey of the period.[43] Many plates with little or no political content are happy to spread the fame, and retail the gossip, of those who are making the headlines. An example is *The Caricaturers Stock in Trade*, a print by W. Mansell in 1786 that reflects the fashionable interest in physiognomy – the science of judging character from facial characteristics – and reveals some of the artist's devices (Plate 1). Fox, appropriately, is at the heart of it, with great black eyebrows and a jaw of five o'clock shadow. Beneath him, with backs to each other, are Burke and William Pitt. Burke is wearing what could be a turban (signifying his preoccupation at the time with Indian affairs) or – more likely – a 'pudding' or cushioned cap used to protect the heads of toddlers. Since a 'pudding headed fellow' was one whose brains were all in confusion, the use of this cap is nicely ambiguous.[44] It is not, as we shall see, Burke's stock-in-trade headgear, but he is almost unique in prints of this period as a wearer of spectacles.[45] Moving clockwise from the top, Queen Charlotte is 'Queen of hearts' (though in a contemporary print she becomes *The Queen of Hearts Cover'd with Diamonds*, in a whiff of scandal that will be considered later).[46] She is pictured beside her husband George III, whose features are echoed in the Prince of Wales's face opposite. The hook-nosed George Hanger, his tricorn hat adorned with Prince of Wales feathers, is that young man's crony. The 'Queen of Fox' is the Duchess of Devonshire, unchivalrously abused in the prints for canvassing on behalf of the Whig leader with whom she is said to have had an affair.[47] The bald head of the Duke of Richmond, Master General of the Ordnance, 1782–95, was a boon to the caricaturists, and one may speculate as to whether those who are readily identified in caricature (even in today's editorial cartoon) get more exposure than otherwise, and with what result. Lord North, at the very heart of politics for twenty years – twelve of them, 1770–82, as premier – and losing America *en passant*, has had more than his share of exposure, and can be recognised even from behind, by his ample shape and (again, stock-in-trade) blue riband of the Garter. 'Queen Scrub' identifies by labelling – a common feature of these prints – the actress Frances Abington, in the news for playing the male role of Scrub in Farquhar's *Beaux' Stratagem* and causing a furore.[48] Above her, and placed beside Burke to suggest a pair with histrionic powers, the great Shakespearian actress Sarah Siddons is dubbed 'Queen Rant'. As for 'Queen Would Be' with her Prince of Wales feathers, Maria Fitzherbert is the talk of the town. A respectable and twice widowed Roman Catholic, her sense of propriety has induced the headstrong young heir to the throne to contract a secret marriage ceremony, in defiance of the Act of Settlement (which laid down that the heir to the throne should not marry a Catholic), thus inspiring a host of wicked satires. Finally we come to her companion, the Prince, whose handsome features already hint at traits of character that the artist, playing the physiognomy game, lets his readers decipher for themselves. This was precisely what Johann Lavater the celebrated Swiss physiognomist feared for his science: 'What passes in the mind should be traceable in the face which is the mirror of it. But these traits, these amiable movements are frequently so delicate, and, in faces which have in other respects a strong expression, they are so little perceptible . . . that neither the crayon nor the graver is able to catch them; especially in the hand of an artist who deals in caricature'.[49]

Literary allusions abound in the prints, to Shakespeare or Milton, to the characters in *The Beggar's Opera,* to Don Quixote or Hudibras. Famous paintings are parodied: Reynolds and Fuseli are mocked; Burke will feature in more than one travesty of the fashionable historical painter Benjamin West. And be they allegory, mythology or emblematical allusion, the references have to be recognisable to the customer, for this is a commercial trade responding to popular taste and the passions and fashions of the moment. The prints themselves helped to cultivate that taste, to mould opinion, to break – and make – reputations. It could be argued, for instance, that Sheridan's importance as a political figure has been exaggerated by them. As Richard Godfrey has observed, 'to be caricatured, however brutally, was at least to be noticed; the ambitious George Canning recorded in his diary for 21 August 1795 that "Mr Gillray the caricaturist has been much solicited to publish a caricature of me and intends doing so" '.[50] Even Samuel Johnson, reacting earlier to *Apollo and the Muses Inflicting Pennance on Dr Pomposo Around Parnassus,* hoped 'the day will never arrive when I shall neither be the object of calumny or ridicule, for then I shall be neglected and forgotten'.[51]

I rather doubt that Burke saw it that way. And by the time young Canning was eagerly awaiting the caricaturist's attention Burke was reflecting bitterly on 'the hunt of obloquy, which has ever pursued me with a full cry through life'.[52] Part of that hunt is described in the following pages.

CHAPTER ONE

THE FLOWERS OF ORATORY

Advisor to the Rockingham Whigs, 1770–82

We first come across Edmund Burke in caricature in February 1770 when he was forty-one years old. His path to such notice may be summarised briefly. Second son of Richard Burke, a Protestant attorney practising in Dublin, and of a Roman Catholic from County Cork whose maiden name was Mary Nagle, Burke was educated at an Irish Quaker school and at Trinity College, Dublin, and came to London in 1750 to study for the bar. Finding literary work more to his taste than law, he set about making his reputation as a writer at the cost of having the allowance from his father discontinued. In 1756 he published anonymously an elegant satire, *A Vindication of Natural Society*, which proved so artful an imitation of the style of the late Henry St John, Viscount Bolingbroke, that many took it to be a posthumous work, and missed the irony that began with the title itself. Burke felt it necessary to preface the second edition with an explanation that the book was in fact designed to show that 'without the exertion of any considerable forces, the same engines which were employed for the destruction of religion, might be employed with equal success for the subversion of government'.[1] His charge, that Bolingbroke was importing French ideas – from the unnamed Voltaire – that were tantamount to a pre-revolutionary process, abhorrent and dangerous, would be repeated against Richard Price and others thirty-four years later in his famous *Reflections on the Revolution in France*.[2]

Burke's next work, *A Philosophical Inquiry into the origin of our Ideas of the Sublime and Beautiful*, which he had started in his undergraduate days at Trinity College and now completed in 1757, was an important contribution to a debate on the theories of aesthetics carried on throughout the eighteenth century, and secured him a considerable intellectual reputation. For some years the words 'Sublime and Beautiful' (offered as an alternative to phrases like 'arrah' and 'by Jasus' and the depiction of that Irish icon, the potato) would suffice to identify him in caricature. Nor would this reference be intended as flattering; there was a strong anti-intellectual element in society which would see such pretentious flights of fancy as adding to Burke's crimes of Irishness and adventurism. The sublime, said Burke, is what excites a particular kind of delight, which we feel when we are given ideas of pain or danger without ourselves being exposed to either. Among the sources of the sublime he instanced are darkness, power, vastness, surprise and terror. Beauty, on the other hand, 'is a name I shall apply to all such qualities in things as induce in us a sense of affection and tenderness, or some other passion the most nearly resembling these'.[3] So beauty is characterised by smallness, smoothness, delicacy and, in colours, clearness and brightness. His analysis of these aesthetic categories was of fundamental importance in the mid-century and later. His protégé James Barry, writing of his perception of Ghiberti does so in Burke's terms: he speaks of Ghiberti's 'ideas of true beauty and perfection on the one hand, and of real grandeur and sublimity on the other'.[4] David Berman sees the *Philosophical Inquiry* as drawing 'heavily on, what is distinctively Irish in philosophy'[5] though the tag 'Sublime and Beautiful' so often pinpointing Burke in caricature was hardly intended to operate on the same level as the 'arrahs' and the potatoes. Richard Payne Knight, the theorist of the picturesque (and, appropriately as it happens, of the priapic) demurred, declaring that whatever *astonishment* or *terror* one might feel on seeing Burke in St James's without his breeches and armed with a blunderbuss, the sight could scarcely be called sublime.[6] But the fifteen editions of the *Philosophical Inquiry* published in Burke's lifetime are evidence of the importance and fame of 'the last great work of Irish philosophy'.[7] Following the immediate success of the book he was commissioned in 1758 by Dodsley the publisher to edit the new *Annual Register*. It soon became an influential and widely respected review of politics and literature, of which Burke would hold the editorship for some thirty years.

This literary output was giving him stature, and winning him influential friends, but his finances were precarious. He sought a job that would bring him into public life and provide for his new circumstances, having married in 1757 Jane Nugent of Bath, daughter of an Irish Catholic physician. Accordingly, in 1759 he became private secretary to William Hamilton, a Commissioner of the Board of Trade nicknamed 'Single-speech' for a celebrated maiden speech in parliament, which some believe was written by Samuel Johnson. Appointed Chief Secretary for Ireland in 1761, Hamilton took Burke with him. When he lost the post in 1764, and subsequently lost Burke, their quarrel was bitter and may have caused the rumours spread about Burke, alleging Catholic subversion. Although one historian believes that Hamilton would have looked a fool to start such rumours, his role – almost as damaging – may have been, if asked, to confirm them.[8]

Extricating himself from Hamilton with some honour (giving up in the process a pension of £300 Hamilton had found for him on the Irish civil list), Burke was taken on as private secretary by the Marquis of Rockingham, parliamentary leader of the Rockingham Whigs, who in 1765 had been asked to form a government. Although the administration remained in place for only a year, Burke's job brought him to the centre of national affairs as Rockingham's principal advisor, with an influence that the caricaturists in due course would note. He was brought into parliament, initially for the pocket borough of Wendover, and sought to adapt to his new life by becoming an enthusiastic gentleman farmer. He borrowed heavily to buy a substantial country estate at Beaconsfield in Buckinghamshire, with a Palladian house complete with collection of paintings. The cost of Beaconsfield, coupled with disastrous stock investments made with his brother Richard and others, was to burden him with financial difficulties into old age.

These problems, for the most part, lay ahead. Meanwhile, in early 1770, circulating within the Rockingham party, and about to be published,[9] was his *Thoughts on the Cause of the Present Discontents,* designed to show where the party stood, and 'how different its constitution, as well as the persons who compose it are from the Bedfords, and Grenvilles, and other knots, who are combined for no publick purpose; but only as a means of furthering with joint strength, their private and individual advantage'.[10] 'The publick in general', wrote Rockingham to the Duke of Portland, 'have never as yet had a fair State of our Principles laid before them. In my opinion they will like them'.[11]

Yet as Burke achieved success he began to pay a price for it. Racism, malice and anti-intellectual sentiment can be detected in the spiteful campaign being waged against him by elements of the London press. The *Public Advertiser* taunted him as 'Edmund Bonnyclabber' (a word derived from the Irish language, denoting milk naturally clotted on souring) and 'Whiteboy' (probably because one of his Nagle

6. T. Bonnor: *Junius*. Published (February 1770) for the *London Magazine*, XXXIX. BM 4314; private collection. The *London Magazine* joins in the popular game of trying to identify the author or authors of the celebrated *Letters*: Burke (left) and Lord George Sackville (right) were among the many suspects, while the central figure is thought to be Sir Philip Francis, unmasked as 'Junius' generations later.

relatives, James of Garnavilla, County Tipperary, had been tried and acquitted in 1767 on a charge of high treason for being concerned with that secret agrarian association).[12] It enviously derided 'these *Liberty Boys*' who 'have lately appeared among us, who have acquired (God knows how) a small property in the Country, and now take the Lead in every Thing'.[13]

It was his writing that first attracted the attention of the caricaturists. Between January 1769 and January 1772 the *Public Advertiser* published a series of brilliantly written satirical *Letters* under the pseudonym 'Junius',[14] attacking the governments of the Duke of Grafton and Lord North and the political influences of George III. Junius was clever, venomous, and dangerously well informed, and speculation about the authorship of the *Letters* was intense. In February 1770, the *London Magazine* joined in this popular game by publishing a plate offering three suspects, bracketed together by the title *Junius*[15] to suggest a cabal (Plate 6). On the left is Burke, identified by the book on which he leans, *Sublime and Beautifull*. The figure on the right is similarly identified by a letter before him, 'To L[or]d G[eorg]e S[ac]k[vi]lle'. The central figure, quill poised above a letter 'To the King', resembles Sir Philip Francis.[16] Few at this time suspected the younger Francis of being Junius. Some contemporaries thought Junius was William Hamilton; one antagonist, Sir William Draper, believed him to be either Sackville or Burke and many believed the *Letters* were written by more than one, as the caricaturist here implies. There is an Irish connection between his candidates. Francis was born in Dublin. Sackville, Vice-Treasurer of Ireland and son of the Duke of Dorset, a lord lieutenant, was a graduate of Trinity College, Dublin; so, too, was Francis's father,[17] who was from Dublin and (it was a small world) as Lady Caroline Fox's private chaplain had taught Charles James Fox to read. And some commentators found an Irishness in Junius's style which, wrote James Prior in 1824, 'bears little resemblance to that of any English author, but partakes much of the wit, the irritability, the pride, the bitterness of invective, the imagery, the almost morbid jealousy and animosity, which marked some of the political contentions of the sister country'.[18]

Burke did write occasionally during this period under pseudonyms, for example in the spring of 1768 as 'Mnemon' to the *Public Advertiser* about the *nullum tempus* affair (discussed at page 15); and it is interesting that the response to 'Mnemon' in that paper on 11 March was signed *Anti-Vox Teague* ('Teague' being a colloquialism for Irishman). He wrote another piece to the *Public Advertiser* in August 1768 as 'Tandem', on the divisions between Rockingham and Grenville.[19]

Suspicions about Burke arose in part from the position he took in the Middlesex election dispute of 1768. In this he opposed the exclusion of the demagogue, John Wilkes (convicted of blasphemy and seditious libel) from the House of Commons, and thus supported the voters of Middlesex, who continued to return him as a member. And suspicions that Burke was Junius were bound to have been raised by his brilliant parody of Lord Bolingbroke. But Burke's friend Dr William Markham (Bishop of Chester 1771–77 and later Archbishop of York) warned him that the Junius suspicions were also based, in part, on a widespread feeling that Burke's overweening ambitions were leading him to attack his natural superiors, and advised him to remember his place.[20] Boswell records Samuel Johnson's shrewd observation in 1779: 'I should have believed Burke to be Junius, because I know no man but Burke who is capable of writing these letters; but Burke spontaneously denied it to me. The case would have been different had I asked him if he was the author; a man so questioned, as to an anonymous publication may think he has a right to deny it.'[21]

If, as seems likely, the central figure is Sir Philip Francis, it is something of a scoop for the caricaturist, T. Bonnor,[22] to have identified him (albeit with others) in so celebrated a concealment and one that was not finally resolved until the 1960s.[23] The print has a curiosity value in two other respects. First, the notion that Burke was Junius, was one put about by Francis himself, in order to put people off the scent. Secondly, if (as Conor Cruise O'Brien has cogently argued) the inducement for Junius to go out of business was that Francis would obtain a lucrative post in India on the Supreme Council of Bengal,[24] the print has the added interest that Francis's bitter clash with the new Governor General, Warren Hastings, would later bring Junius into close collaboration with Burke in Hastings's impeachment. However, the print has a far greater significance: the imputation that Burke is Junius, or part of Junius, will stick, and will confirm the prejudices of the inner circle that he is an impudent, dangerous fellow.

That being said, Burke is next cast supportively – as Cicero – in a complex print of 1770, *Political Electricity* (Plate 7).[25] The print takes its name from recent demonstrations in electrical science by Benjamin Franklin. Its theme is of an electrified chain which sends a charge through the various components of the elaborate, old-fashioned design. (Between 1770 and Burke's death in 1797, the nature of caricature was to evolve dramatically. Prints such as this with complicated emblems and hieroglyphics were on the way out and would be replaced by a form which both laid the foundation of the modern newspaper's editorial cartoon and, with its captions, anticipated the tabloid headline.) Prominent in this design is a large pair of scales, each side laden with political figures. 'The Opposition Scale' – though upheld by the ropes of constitutional liberty – weighs lighter than the 'Great State Scale', despite the presence in the balance of six opposition orators, the first of whom is Burke. A description below the image explains that 'Ye Acts of Magna Charta[,] against General Warrants, Habeas Corpus, Ye Bill of Rights & Ye Nullum Tempus Bill &c are hung upon ye Scale Ropes to make weight but all wont do. Ye Scale of Virtue is outweigh'd by that of Vice, & thy speech O Cicero availeth thee Nothing'.[26]

These fundamentals of the constitution had been invoked in recent events, notably

in the affair of John Wilkes. The Habeas Corpus Act (which prevented suspects being held without trial) secured Wilkes's release when arrested for seditious libel. The dubious procedures adopted in the case were then challenged, in particular the legality of issuing general warrants, which were not directed at a named person but ordered the arrest of all concerned with the offending production of Wilkes's paper, the *North Briton*. The Court of Common Pleas determined the illegality of general warrants in

7. Anon.: *Political Electricity* (detail). (1770). BM 4422; British Museum.
Of the figures surmounting the state scales vice triumphs over virtue, and the administration (helped by money bags from the Treasury) weighs heavier: Lord North, Sir Fletcher Norton (Speaker), William de Grey (Attorney General), Jeremiah Dyson and George Onslow (lords of the Treasury) and Lord Cl–e (either Lord Clare or Lord Clive). Outweighed are Edmund Burke (right), William Dowdeswell (former Chancellor of the Exchequer), Colonel Isaac Barré (here thought to be 'Junius'), Charles Cornwall (later Speaker), Lord John Cavendish (later Chancellor of the Exchequer) and Richard Whitworth MP, an anti-ministerial writer.

a series of cases in 1763, while the short-lived Rockingham administration also persuaded the Commons to pass a resolution against general warrants on 25 April 1766, following a resolution which three days earlier condemned as illegal the seizure of papers of the supposed author, printer or publisher of a libel.[27] The Act of Nullum Tempus in 1769 removed a different grievance, rectifying a defect in the Duke of Portland's title to lands granted by the Crown, which was being exploited shamelessly by Sir James Lowther, son-in-law of the Earl of Bute, with the connivance of the Treasury. The postponement of the bill in 1768 had led to a national outcry, Burke denouncing as 'the Disgrace of our Law' the maxim *nullum tempus occurrit Regi*: that no length of time in possession (in this case of lands) may be pleaded against the claims of the Crown. 'The Truth is,' wrote Burke, 'this Prerogative has hitherto owed its Existence principally to its Disuse. It was an Engine, at once so formidable to the People, and so dangerous to those who should attempt to handle it, that it never was considered amongst the Instruments of a *wise Minister*. It remained like an old Piece of Cannon I have heard of somewhere of an enormous Size, which stood upon a ruinous Bastion, and which was seldom or never fired for fear of bringing down the Fortification for whose Defence it was intended.'[28] A scroll beneath Burke, referring to 'The Injur'd Ghost of Liberty at the Bar of the H[ouse] of C[ommons]', points to Burke's honourable role in opposing the rejection of Wilkes as MP for Middlesex. Burke and his companions[29] are outweighed by 'ye leaders in Ad[ministratio]n', Lord North and his colleagues, seated on the Treasury Bench. George Grenville, the former First Lord of the Treasury, lies across the beam of the balance, 'Doubtfull which will preponderate'.

When Mrs Hardcastle, the garrulous country wife in Oliver Goldsmith's *She Stoops to Conquer*, seeks to reassure her guests that she is no rural bumpkin she boasts: 'I take care to know every tête-à-tête from the Scandalous Magazine'. The name of this notorious monthly periodical was, in fact, the *Town and Country Magazine*, which started publication in 1769 and continued for about twenty years. Each issue invariably included a more-or-less salacious story under the guise of a moral tale, and a pair of the celebrated tête-à-tête portraits, which provided much of its appeal. By 1771 it could claim that it sold 12,000 copies a month and that . . . 'The Tête-à-Têtes which give universal satisfaction to all readers, always excepting the parties concerned, will invariably form an object of the greatest attention.'[30]

In March 1774, the *Town and Country Magazine* published, as part of this series, an

8. Anon. (perhaps Archibald Hamilton junior): *Miss S–r. The Hibernian Demosthenes*. Published 1 March 1774, for the *Town and Country Magazine* by Archibald Hamilton junior. BM 5251; British Library, London.
A scurrilous attempt to link Burke, married since 1757, to a Miss S–r, 'the daughter of an American Merchant'. That month he had opposed the coercive measures introduced in the Commons after the Boston Tea Party.

engraving of *Miss S–r* and *The Hibernian Demosthenes* (Plate 8). This illustrates a scabrous piece retailing scandals about Burke, ranging from his supposed Jesuit education at St Omer in France (a taunt that the caricaturists will later peddle remorselessly) to an alleged mistress, Miss S–r, 'the daughter of an American Merchant'. Burke had been since 1770 agent in London for the Colony of New York, and in March 1774 had opposed the coercive measures introduced in the Commons after the Boston Tea Party. There is no evidence that he conducted any extra-marital liaisons and the allegation seems to have been advanced scurrilously to explain the position he took on the American issue. 'Be content to bind America by laws of trade', he said (on 19 April 1774), 'you have always done it . . . Do not burthen them with taxes'.[31] As agent for New York he received a respectable salary and it is this which led (in the words of his biographer Prior) to 'an illiberal surmise that his advice might not be wholly disinterested'. As for a roving eye, there is, it may be noted, a curious print by William Dent published in July 1783 (*see* Plate 36) in which Burke, dressed as a Jesuit, holds to his bosom a small female figure. But, far from being sexual innuendo, this depiction refers to the story of Little Red Ridinghood, and taunts him as the wolf in sheep's clothing. It recalls, perhaps, a speech he made on 9 July 1782 on Fox's resignation, where he likened the Earl of Shelburne to the wolf.[32] Apart from one or two prints (*see*, for example, Plate 150) mocking his suggested infatuation with Marie Antoinette[33] (which were clearly not intended to be taken seriously) there are no other caricatures, in an age when such material was seized on with relish, to suggest he was anything but a devoted husband. Boswell, not noted for them himself, commended his 'orderly and amiable domestic habits'.[34]

It is frustrating that the caricaturists do not oblige us with more prints to celebrate – however one-sidedly – some of Burke's principal activities before the 1780s, particularly those on behalf of the colonists. Perhaps, unidentified, he winks at us from

9. Anon.: *The Congress or The Necessary Politicians.* (*c.* 1775). BM 5297; British Museum. Burke (right) and his companion in the latrine respond differently to the resolutions of the American Congress on taxation. In the background two prints decorate the 'necessary house'; one a portrait of John Wilkes as Lord Mayor of London, popular with the colonists; in the other William Pitt the elder is tarred and feathered for his pro-American stance (parodying an incident when this happened to an unpopular commissioner of customs at Boston), and ruefully recalls the Latin of Horace: I am turned into a white bird.

prints of this period. For instance, in *The Congress or The Necessary Politicians* (Plate 9), it is reasonable to surmise that Burke is the bespectacled politician so assiduously reading [*An*] *Answer to a P*[*amphlet*] [*en*]*titled Taxation* [*no*] *Tir*[*anny*], as he sits in the 'necessary house'. His friend Samuel Johnson, who disagreed with him on the American question, had written his pamphlet *Taxation no Tyranny* (February 1775) in answer to the resolutions and address of the American Congress which sat from 5 September to 29 October 1774. Here the 'Resolutions of the [C]ongress' are being put to necessary, if unsavoury, purposes by Burke's companion. Burke's speech opposing American taxation − the *London Evening Post* described it as 'the most excellent speech that has perhaps been ever uttered in a public Assembly' − was delivered on 19 April 1774, and published on 10 January 1775.[35]

If Burke appears rarely in caricature before 1780, he is, however, known to have inspired (with Grey Cooper, secretary to the Treasury) Benjamin Wilson's *The Repeal, Or the Funeral of Miss Ame-Stamp*, one of the best-selling designs of the century,[36] published anonymously in March 1766 and, indeed, to have had a hand in inspiring Rockingham's repeal of the Stamp Act itself, immediately before that.[37] This whole episode illustrates the use made of satirical prints by politicians − in this case Burke and the Rockingham party − and also the phenomenal popularity and dispersal of the prints themselves. *The Repeal* was not the first print they promoted. We know from the artist's manuscript autobiography[38] that Wilson produced *The Tomb-Stone* in February 1766 'In order to please Lord Rockingham . . . who had promised to take care of him'. This phrase indicates that Wilson, one of the leading portrait painters of the day, had struck an agreeable bargain, and would be guided as to the contents of the plate. Nobody was better placed than Burke to provide such guidance. *The Tomb-Stone* proved 'very successful in its object' so that 'Mr Edmund Burke and Grey Cooper pressed him much to try another political print', which was *The Repeal. The Tomb-Stone* (Plate 10) laments the death in October 1765 of the Duke of Cumberland who, according to the mortuary inscription, had saved his country twice, at Culloden, 'and after by selecting a Ministry, out of those virtuous few, who gloriously withstood General Warrants, American Stamps, Extensions of Excise − &c &c &c'. But while Britannia and America weep at such a loss Grenville, Bute and the Duke of Bedford dance on the lid of the sarcophagus to the pipes of a demon and the encouragement of others including the Earl of Halifax, whose pocket is stuffed with 'Gen[eral] Warrants' to remind us that it was he who signed the warrant against the 'authors, printers, and publishers' of Wilkes's *North Briton*. As with *The Repeal*, the publication of the print was much promoted in the *Public Advertiser*, no doubt as part of the effort 'to please Lord Rockingham'.

In 1765, George Grenville's government had induced parliament to pass a Stamp Act imposing stamp duties in America on legal transactions and on newspapers, provoking the great outcry that Americans were being taxed without representation. When shortly afterwards Grenville lost favour with George III Rockingham formed the new administration (13 July 1765) and immediately had to cope with the crisis. Drawing on the advice of Burke, his private secretary, he repealed the Act but at the same time affirmed parliamentary supremacy over the colonies in a Declaratory Act. *The Repeal* (Plate 11) describes a funeral procession, in which George Grenville carries to its tomb the coffin of his 'favourite child', 'Miss Ame-Stamp B.1765 died 1766', followed by Lord Bute and other mourners. Skulls fixed above (and dated 1715, 1745) associate the 'Family Vault' with the Jacobite rebellions.

But, nearby, American business has returned to the warehouses on the Thames, thanks to three ships, the *Grafton*, the *Rockingham* and the *Conway* (eponymously

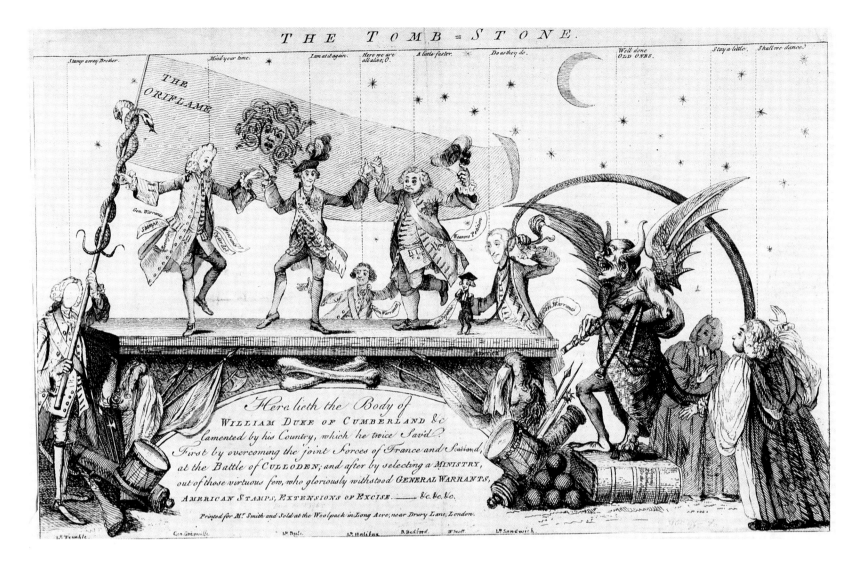

Stamp away Brother.   *Mind your time.*   *I am at it again.*   *Here we are all alive, O.*   *A little faster.*   *Do as they do.*   *Well done OLD ONES.*   *Stay a little.*   *Shall we dance?*

THE ORIFLAME

Here lieth the Body of
WILLIAM DUKE OF CUMBERLAND &c
lamented by his Country, which he twice Sav'd
First by overcoming the joint Forces of France and Scotland,
at the Battle of CULLODEN; *and after by selecting a* MINISTRY,
out of those virtuous few, who gloriously withstood GENERAL WARRANTS,
AMERICAN STAMPS, EXTENSIONS OF EXCISE. —— *&c. &c. &c.*

Printed for Mr. Smith and Sold at the Woolpack in Long Acre, near Drury Lane, London.

E. Temple.   Geo Grenville.   Ld Bute.   Ld Halifax.   D. Bedford.   Dr Scott.   Ld Sandwich.

10. [Benjamin Wilson]: *The Tomb-Stone.* [25 February 1766]. BM 4124; British Museum. 'Printed for Mr Smith', it cost sixpence.

On the left, Earl Temple – his face blank to mock his covert support for the demagogue Wilkes, waves the *Oriflame*, ancient banner of the Kings of France. On Cumberland's tomb, dance George Grenville, the Earl of Bute and the Duke of Bedford, to the music of a bagpipe-playing demon.

representing opponents of the Act), and two large bales containing black cloth and 'Stamps from America' have been returned and unloaded, no longer required.

Five days before its publication on 18 March 1766, the appearance of the caricature was promoted in the *Public Advertiser*: 'THE PRINT called THE REPEAL will certainly be published in a few Days, notwithstanding the many Endeavours to prevent its Appearance.' Its commercial success was phenomenal. On 21 March, records the *Public Advertiser*, 'The extraordinary Demand for the Print . . . being greater than is in the Power of one Workman to supply, Mr. Smith begs Leave of those who are pleased to honour him with their Commands to any large Quantities, that he may be indulged with as much Time as can possibly be allowed, in order to take off a proper Number to answer the Demand'. And, in the *Gazeteer and New Daily Advertiser* of 27 March, 'Mr. Smith begs leave to advertise the public, that there is a spurious and Grub-street print copied from the celebrated REPEAL, which is calculated to hurt the sale of the original print. He therefore hopes they will not encourage so unfair and vile a performance, but continue to favour him with their commands when, for the future, a separate and printed explanation will be given along with each print'. Business being business, however, the *Gazeteer* is happy to publish immediately below Mr Smith's entreaty, a promotion of the piracy in question: 'This Day is published, A new Carectura Print, price only sixpence. THE REPEAL. The great demand for this print has induced the proprietor to lower the price. Sold by J. Pridden, at the Feathers, in Fleet-street.' Did Benjamin Wilson invoke the Copyright Act and pursue Pridden

THE Hero of this Print is the gentle Mr. *Stamper*, who is carrying to the Family Vault his favourite Child, in a Coffin, Miss AME-STAMP, about 12 Months old. *Anti-Sejanus*, who reads the Burial Service, is the first in the Procession.—After him follow Two Pillars of the Law, supporting Two Black Flags: on which are the usual Stamps, consisting of the *White Rose* united with the *Thistle*, supposed to have been originally contrived on the *Tenth of June*. The expressive Motto of *Semper eadem* is reserved: but the Price of the Stamp is changed to *Three Farthings*, which the

Budget explains: and the *small Numbers*, which are pointed at, are too contemptible to deserve Notice *by the Majority*. The Chief Mourner, *Sejanus*, follows Mr. *Stamper*. Then Two remarkable Personages, the celebrated *Weaver* and Lord *Gawkee*: after them *Jemmy Twitcher*, with his Friend and Partner, Lord H——. Two B——s conclude the Procession. Upon the Fore Ground are two large Bales of Black Cloth and Stamps returned from *America*.

The unhappy Gang are separated from the joyous Scene that is opposite, on the other Side of the River *Thames*: where, along the Shore, are Open Warehouses for the Goods of different Manufacturing Towns now shipping for *America*. In the River are three First-rate Ships, the *Rockingham*, the *Grafton*, and the *Conway*. Among the Goods shipping off, is a large Case, which is wrote upon a Statue of Mr. *Pitt* : this is heaving on board a Boat *Number* 250. There is another Boat *nearer* the First-rates, taking Goods in also ; and is *numbered* 105.—— N. B. The two Skeleton Heads, upon the Vault were Monsters born in the Rebellions of the Years 1715 and 1745.

11. [Benjamin Wilson]: *The Repeal or The Funeral of Miss Ame-Stamp.* [18 March 1766]. BM 4140; British Museum.

Dr Scott, author of 'Anti-Sejanus', leads supporters of the Stamp Act in a funeral procession: the lawyers Wedderburn and Norton are followed by Grenville (holding the coffin) and Lord Bute, said to be chief mourner, to whom a grim Bedford gesticulates and is in turn restrained by Earl Temple. Lords Halifax and Sandwich bring up the rear with two bishops.

for his audacity or were the originators simply happy to see their opinions circulate so profitably? Six versions of varying size, four of them piracies, are recorded in the British Museum holdings.

This instance of the use made of satirical artists by Burke and the Rockingham Whigs leads us to wonder how much 'inspiring' of prints Burke did at this stage as a young and energetic promulgator of Rockinghamite opinions.[39] Was such activity confined to the brief period of Rockingham's administration from July 1765 to July 1766? If he is quietly feeding lines to the printmakers does that keep him out of their prints? Hardly, for what sells a political print is its handling of an affair or event that has caught the public attention and the customer's ready recognition of the players and issues involved. In other words, caricatures reflect the public perception of who is important and, by this yardstick, Burke has not yet arrived. As for Benjamin

Wilson's talents as etcher, they did not stop at political caricature; his fake Rembrandts tricked 'certain artists and amateurs who imagined themselves to be connoisseurs'.[40]

A caricature in pen and ink by John Hamilton Mortimer, *c.*1776, of *Literary Characters Assembled Around a Medallion of Shakespeare* is thought to include Burke in the company of Samuel Johnson (who since 1764 had been at the heart of 'The Club', the celebrated dining and conversational group), along with Johnson's friend and fellow lexicographer, Giuseppi Baretti, and others.[41] Mortimer, a Royal Academician, whose bold style and admirable draughtsmanship influenced Rowlandson and Gillray, may be in the caricature himself. Burke and Johnson testified as character witnesses for the Italian writer in his trial for murder in 1769, as did Reynolds and Goldsmith, other founders of The Club, and David Garrick the actor. Baretti was acquitted,[42] though in his *Journal* of April 1776 Boswell is still disputing the outcome, while adding Johnson's verdict: 'that it was not for crimes such as murder or robbery that he would be hanged, but for some political daring writings'.[43] In The Club, that sparkled with such diverse talents, Burke was a dominant figure, intimate from the 1750s with Johnson (who admired him hugely), and frequently referred to anonymously as 'a celebrated friend' or 'an eminent person' in Boswell's *Life*.[44]

It is 1779 before Burke is spotted again, in one of a dozen tableaux in *The Political Raree-Show: or a Picture of Parties and Politics, during and at the close of the Last Session of Parliament* (Plate 12). It is instructive to note from the various scenes what some of the national issues are perceived to be. The cost of war with America is driving the premier Lord North, 'The Distressed Financier', to float high interest loans with Jewish moneylenders and the devil. Sir William Howe and John Burgoyne are 'The Generals in America' doing nothing (Howe drinking and playing cards), or 'worse than nothing', as Burgoyne surrenders to the Americans at Saratoga. The First Lord of the Admiralty, Lord Sandwich, nicknamed Jemmy Twitcher in the prints (after a character in the *Beggar's Opera*) for splitting on John Wilkes, is here implicated in abuses of management of the Royal Hospital for Seamen at Greenwich. The Catholic Relief Act of 1778 is behind 'The English Papists laughing at ye Protestants', while plans to extend the Act to Scotland have incited 'No Popery' riots, with 'The Scotch Presbyterians pulling down the Papists Houses'. Continuing restrictions on Irish trade have provoked 'A Picture of Irish Resolution', by Protestants and Catholics alike, not to buy British goods, and at the Custom House in London, the female figure of Commerce, as distressed as Hibernia, lies in a faint. In a scene entitled *The Opposition Pudding-makers* (Plate 13) the cooks are: 'Mr Burke wid the flowers of oratory, and de Millers Rockingham, Shelburne, &c wid de flour to make de pudding'.[45] But more than oratory is indicated by Burke's body language: it is no accident that he is at Rockingham's side, and he appears to be prescribing the recipe as the opposition's dish is prepared, and Rockingham begins to stir.

As his influence became more widely recognised, Burke was increasingly targeted by the caricaturists. A crucial development was his speech on economical reform, delivered on 11 February 1780 from the opposition ranks. It was a time when groups on both sides of the House coalesced or manoeuvred to wield parliamentary power, with fluctuating support from among the large number of independent members. Four main parties supported North's government: followers of the Crown itself, and the followers of Lord North, the Earl of Sandwich, and Earl Gower. In opposition Rockingham's larger party (itself comprising the Marquis's connections with those of the Duke of Portland and the Duke of Devonshire, and Charles James Fox's circle) combined with two smaller ones, Shelburne's and Sir James Lowther's, and was

12. Anon.: *The Political Raree-Show*. Published 1 July 1779, by Fielding & Walker. BM 5548; private collection.

Tableaux in a peep-show (from top, from left to right) encapsulate political preoccupations: government borrowings at high interest (1); continuing reverses in America (2 and 3); maladministration at the naval hospital for Greenwich pensioners (4 and 5); the island of Jersey repelling a French expeditionary force (8); Catholic relief and no-popery riots (9 and 10); Irish resolutions against British goods and commercial recession (11 and 12).

13. Detail of Plate 12. Burke 'wid the flowers of oratory', is Lord Rockingham's right-hand man.

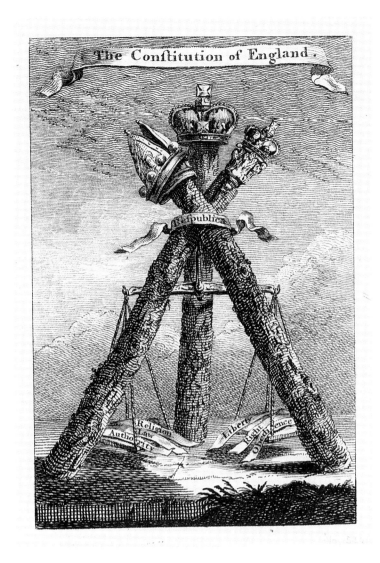

14. Anon.: *The Constitution of England.* [*c.* 1774]. BM 5240; British Museum.
The scales of justice, nicely balancing religion, law and authority in one pan with liberty, right and obedience in the other, is suspended from a stable tripod of King, Lords and Commons.

15. Anon.: *The Constitution* [1770]. BM 4430; British Library.
Lord Bute, again displaying a well turned leg (*see* Plate 2), abuses his position to make the King's influence outweigh the fundamental laws of the constitution.

supported by a growing number of independents, weary of the disastrous and expensive war in America.[46] (These were arrangements of convenience and Burke, for example, did his best to distance the Rockinghams from Shelburne whom he detested). 'In the elections of 1780', writes John Ehrman, 'it has been reckoned that Government returned twenty-four Members to Parliament, and that another 221 seats lay more or less at the disposal of 119 private persons. If the Crown was to be certain of providing the basis of a Government party in the Commons, it could therefore do so only in co-operation with other interests'.[47]

The opposition's proposals for reform overlapped. Some, like Shelburne who had inherited Chatham's mantle, sought reform of parliament itself and its representation; for them economical reform was just a first step. The Foxites were also enthusiastic supporters of both economical and parliamentary reform. But for Burke and the Rockinghams further steps beyond economical reform were not desirable; if the balance between Crown, aristocracy and people had been upset in recent years the constitution – epitomised by the undated print, *c.*1774, *The Constitution of England* (Plate 14) – was nonetheless sound, and economical reform would restore the balance by tackling the inordinate expense of government and the political influence of the Crown.[48] (The metaphor of three sturdy oak trunks, representing King, Lords and

16. Anon.: *The Irish Stubble alia[s] Bubble Goose.*
(*c.* November 1763). BM 4068; private collection.
The Irish civil list is a goose, blindfolded by Bute, and
plucked naked by Henry Fox (Lord Holland) and
others, despite the efforts of the Earl of
Northumberland, Lord Lieutenant of Ireland, to
restore her sight. Samuel Johnson (above) is taunted as
a hypocrite for his earlier condemnation of pensioners.
Meanwhile, a Frenchman threatens that 'De English
get de feders I vill gett de goose'.

Commons and bound together by the *Respublica*, would have appealed to Burke.
From this structure the artist hangs the balance of justice weighing evenly, on one
side, *Religion, Law, Authority,* and on the other *Liberty, Right, Obedience.*) The perils
of undue royal influence, when manipulated by one such as Bute, had been
graphically demonstrated in a print of 1770, *The Constitution* (Plate 15). In such
circumstances, it was alleged, the King's little finger could be made to outweigh even
'Magna Charta' and the 'Bill of Rights'.

The civil list, a fixed annual income voted by parliament for the King, enabled him
to provide for the civil and foreign services as well as his court. But payments overran
the income and from time to time parliament had come to the King's assistance to
deal with accumulated debts. Cynicism about the excessive demands of politicians and
placemen (appointed to positions without regard to their fitness) is illustrated in the
case of the Irish civil list (Plate 16), which in 1763 was represented as *The Irish Stubble*

alia[s] Bubble Goose, plucked naked of its feathers by Fox's father, Lord Holland and other pensioners, and weighed down with a burden of £74,000. Samuel Johnson deplores the scene below:

> Here let those reign whom Pensions can Incite
> To vote a PATRIOT black a COURTIER white
> Explain their COUNTRYS dear bought rights away
> And plead for Tyrants in the face of day.

Yet, placed behind Johnson's ear, his own quill turns out to be a feather from the same goose, worth £300 a year.

In England, parliament had settled an accumulated debt of £600,000 in 1777, and had increased the civil list to £900,000 a year.[49] Better management, it was thought, would curb the problem and help rein in the influence wielded through holders of sinecures. Now Burke rose to present to the House 'A Plan of Reform in the Constitution of Several Parts of the Public Economy'.[50] To tackle the public finances comprehensively was a thankless, even invidious task: 'I risk odium if I succeed, and contempt if I fail', but he pointed to the example of France, with whom Britain was at war:

> When I look to the other side of the water, I cannot help recollecting what Pyrrhus said, on reconnoitring the Roman camp: – "These barbarians have nothing barbarous in their discipline" . . . Principle, method, regularity, economy, frugality, justice to individuals, and care of the people, are the resources with which France makes war upon Great Britain. God avert the omen! But if we should see any genius in war and politics arise in France to second what is done in the bureau! – I turn my eyes from the consequences.[51]

He proposed to start with the King's own household with its multiplicity of redundant offices and anomalous jurisdictions:

> Cross a brook [he mocked] and you lose the King of England; but you have some comfort in coming again under his Majesty, though 'shorn of his beams', and no more than Prince of Wales. Go to the north, and you find him dwindled to a Duke of Lancaster; turn to the west of that north, and he pops upon you in the humble character of Earl of Chester. Travel a few miles on, the Earl of Chester disappears; and the king surprises you again as Count Palatine of Lancaster. If you travel beyond Mount Edgecombe, you find him once more in his incognito, and he is Duke of Cornwall. So that, quite fatigued and satiated with this dull variety, you are infinitely refreshed when you return to the sphere of his proper splendour, and behold your amiable sovereign in his true, amiable, undignified, native character of Majesty. [Burke drives his point home.] As his Majesty submits to appear in this state of subordination to himself, his loyal peers and faithful commons attend his royal transformations, and are not so nice as to refuse to nibble at those crumbs of emoluments which console their petty metamorphoses.[52]

For someone rated 'nought out of twenty' for humour by the splenetic Mrs Thrale, Burke here – and elsewhere – displays a witty line in ridicule.[53] And, of course, the issue he addresses is as much of constitutional as it is of economic concern.

As for the royal household, 'exceedingly abusive in its constitution', Burke's review takes him back to old feudal practices long discarded by all but the monarchy.[54] 'If my memory does not deceive me, a person of no slight consideration held the office of patent hereditary cook to an Earl of Warwick: the Earl of Warwick's soups, I fear, were not the better for the dignity of his kitchen'.[55] He takes aim at a variety of offices such as the Board of Works ('For all this expense we do not see a building of the size and importance of a pigeon-house') and the Secretary of State for the Colonies: 'this department has not been shunned upon account of the weight of its duties, but on the contrary, much sought on account of its patronage. Indeed, he must be poorly acquainted with the history of office who does not know how very lightly the American functions have always leaned on the shoulders of the ministerial *Atlas* who has upheld that side of the sphere'.[56] He proposes to regulate the pay offices for army, navy and pensions. His plans for the civil list would require it not to carry forward unpaid salaries as debt to each succeeding year and would rank the most powerful offices of the state as last claimants on the list, so that claims most at risk to be 'lapsed, sunk and lost' would be the salaries and pensions of the First Lord of the Treasury himself, the Chancellor of the Exchequer, and the other commissioners of the Treasury. Next at risk would be the offices nearest to the King such as masters of the horse, grooms of the stole, lords of the bed-chamber. Burke conjures up the consequences for the poor minister responsible for any shortfall: 'Bless me! what a clattering of white sticks and yellow sticks would be about his head! what a storm of gold keys would fly about the ears of the minister! what a shower of Georges, and thistles, and medals, and collars of SS would assail him at his first entrance into the antechamber, after an insolvent Christmas quarter!'[57]

Burke's speech led (11 July 1782) to the temporary abolition of the Board of Trade[58] which he had rounded on scathingly: 'This board is a sort of temperate bed of influence, a sort of gently ripening hothouse, where eight members of Parliament receive salaries of a thousand a year for certain given time, in order to mature, at a proper season, a claim to two thousand, granted for doing less, and on the credit of having toiled so long in that inferior, laborious department.'[59] Behind this sarcasm lies his main point, quoted down the years as a canon of conservatism, 'that Commerce, the principal object of that office, flourishes most when it is left to itself'.[60] One to lose his place by the suppression of the Board of Trade was Edward Gibbon, with the happy outcome that from being a Lord Commissioner of the Board he retired to Lausanne and completed *The Decline and Fall of the Roman Empire* in 1787. Burke had foreseen this, describing it as the release of a nightingale to sing in freedom, and not at the public charge. This, then, is the background to the caricaturists' sharpening focus on Burke.

A pro-government print published two weeks later (27 February 1780) describes the *Opposition Defeated* by Lord North astride John Bull (Plate 17). America, France and Spain, adversaries in the war, have been trampled by the bull which now dispatches Shelburne into the arms of the devil and his 'trusty servants', the controversial Unitarian theologians Dr Richard Price and Dr Joseph Priestley, both friends of Shelburne. Another friend, here cast as his faithful dog *Poli[phemus]*, laments: 'then my Jewel its all over I should have worried him if you had got him down'. 'My Jewel' always indicates an Irishman, and in this case he is Colonel Isaac Barré who fought at the side of General Wolfe at Quebec and lost his sight, like Polyphemus the cyclops blinded by Ulysses. The triumphant North (nicknamed Boreas after the North Wind) blows against a tavern sign painted with the royal crown, so that it eludes the grasp of the young Prince of Wales swaying on the shoulders of Charles James Fox. Significantly this is the first caricature to associate the Prince with the opposition. 'Borias', he complains, 'thou hast blasted all my attempts at the Crown'. Burke, seeing an opportunity to intrigue, leads Lord Rockingham by the nose towards the rout. 'Arrah,' he says, 'make haste or we shall not be in at The

OPPOSITION. DEFEATED.

17. Anon.: *Opposition Defeated*. Published 27 February 1780, by W. Macintosh. BM 5644; British Museum. Rockingham, left, is being led by the nose to the fray by his advisor Burke, who wears a lorgnette and is identified as an Irishman by the stock-in-trade 'arrah'. The dog beside him is also Irish, using the phrase 'my jewel' to address its master, Shelburne. Its collar *Poli-[phemus]* – after the cyclops blinded by Ulysses – identifies Colonel Isaac Barré MP, who lost his sight serving in action under General Wolfe.

Death.' Rockingham stumbles, muttering 'Teague and ambition will be my downfall.'[61] Burke, identified by a paper as 'Junius', is in turn being urged on by an old crone with a stick, perhaps representing Famine, and an allusion to his plan of economical reform.[62] At times, Burke despaired of the languor and passivity of his leaders, and 'their want of the stimulus of ambition'.[63] The question, he once put to Rockingham, 'is whether your Lordship chooses to lead or to be led; to lay down proper ground yourself, or stand in an awkward and distressing situation on the ground which will be prepared for you'.[64] A few days later in *The Bull Broke Loose*,[65] John Bull reverts to his more usual oppositionist role and breaking free from his tethers and egged on by opposition leaders, charges at Lord North. Inciting the bull, Burke calls out 'Extravagant Emoluments, Places & Pensions'.

Becoming better known to the public, Burke was still at the stage where the printsellers identified him for their customers by labels such as 'Sublime and Beautiful' or 'Oeconomical Reform';[66] James Sayers had yet to apply to him, and James Gillray yet to perfect'[67] those characteristics that would place him immediately: long nose, spectacles and (Gillray's enduring taunt) Jesuit soutane and biretta. Like other Irishmen and women he gave clues to the reader with phrases of such subtlety as 'arrah', and 'by Jasus'. Earlier, in 1769, the *Public Advertiser* had ridiculed him as one who 'thunders down upon us all those *by Jasus* threats that are peculiar to Cowards in Politics as well as in the Field'.[68] So a problem of identification can arise where more

26

than one Irishman is featured. Such a print is *Patriotic Song for Poor Old England*, another satire on the opposition dating from March 1780.[69] Two of those adding ingredients to a large cauldron are probably intended for Burke and his compatriot Barré, the MP for Calne. One, most likely the financially embarrassed Burke, puts in a potato, muttering 'G[o]d fire me now if I've a Potatoe left'; the other, about to throw in some meat, exclaims: 'by Jasus nothing makes better Mutton Broth than a good Cow heel'. This is a peculiarly apt example of an Irish Bull, the name given to an expression involving (as the *Oxford English Dictionary* puts it) 'a ludicrous inconsistency unperceived by the speaker', and for which the Irish were much teased in caricature.[70]

England declared war on Holland in December 1780. Several opposition leaders criticised the violent break in relations. There was an important debate on 14 May 1781 on Burke's motion inquiring into the conduct of Admiral Rodney and General Vaughan in attacking the Dutch West Indian island of St Eustatius. Rodney's justification for the seizure of booty, which included the property of Dutch, American, French and Spanish nationals, was that much of it belonged to British subjects. Unfortunately, what was sent home was captured *en route* by the French. Burke strongly attacked the confiscation, earning the soubriquet, in a print by Thomas Colley, of *Don Volaseo The Famous Spanish Partizan,* a bespectacled and quixotic cavalry officer mounted and with sabre drawn (Plate 18). Perhaps the caricaturist is recalling the Spanish hero Velasco, who died defending the Cuban fortress of Castillo del Morro in 1762 against the much larger forces of an English squadron.[71] Though the building outlined in the distance seems more ecclesiastical than domestic it is conceivable that it represents the central block of Burke's country house at Beaconsfield.[72]

It was inevitable that in caricature, as in life, Burke was to clash many times with

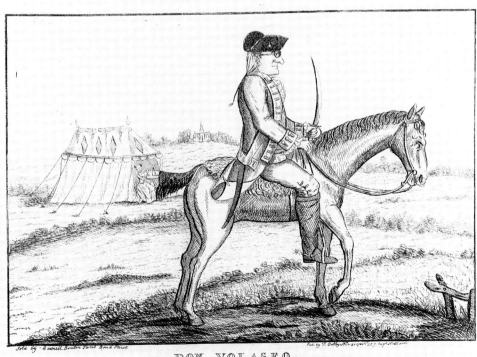

DON VOLASEO.
The Famous Spanish Partizan.

18. [Thomas Colley]: *Don Volaseo*. Published 21 November 1781, by T. Colley. BM 5854; British Museum.
Burke is mocked for attacking in parliament the widescale seizure of booty – the property of Spanish and other nationals – by Admiral Rodney and General Vaughan in their capture, 1781, of the island of St Eustatius. Burke as a quixotic figure would later be a recurrent theme in caricature: *see* Plates 86, 148-51, 155 and 183.

George III. Burke's *Thoughts on the Cause of the Present Discontents* published in 1770 had outlined a plan of parliamentary resistance to the manoeuvres of the King whose power, 'almost dead and rotten as Prerogative, has grown up anew, with much more strength and far less odium, under the name of Influence'.[73] The King was himself no stranger to caricature; since his accession in 1760, at the age of twenty-two, he had been subjected to a barrage of satirical abuse, despite Charles Churchill's warning in 1763:

> For if we Majesty expose
> To vulgar eyes, too cheap it grows,
> The force is lost, and free from awe,
> We spy and censure ev'ry flaw.[74]

In 1773, for instance, the *Westminster Magazine* ridiculed him not for exerting undue influence as King, but as the puppet of his ministers in cabinet, where 'six grey-headed Statesmen sit round a green-headed King, now amusing him with rattles, now feeding him with Court-pap, while they follow the heady current of their own humours'.[75] Burke's first, rather indirect, encounter comes in *The Royal Hunt, or a Prospect of the Year 1782* (Plate 19). He and other opposition members watch in anger as the Temple of Fame is razed by the enemies of Britain, while ministers carouse with their *filles-de-joie*. 'Wont even Destruction move ye[?]' cries Burke as *America* and other pillars of the temple lie in heaps at their feet. The engraving, published on 16 February 1782, was soon reissued with verses beneath called *The Chase*, in which the King brushes aside national disaster provided he can still go a-hunting. Verse VI runs:

> If Fox and Burke and Barré still
> Should circumscribe our space
> Leave me but round sweet W[in]d[so]r's hill,
> Sufficient for the Chase.

In the print, the King's administration is being harried not only by Fox, Burke and Barré but by a new opposition figure, demanding that ministers 'Shake off this Indolence': William Pitt, who had entered parliament in January 1781, gravitating towards his father's small party now led by Shelburne. A few days after this print was first published the 22-year-old would make a brilliant *ex tempore* maiden speech on Burke's motion to reintroduce his bill for economical reform, drawing from Burke the famous verdict: 'He is not a chip of the old block: he is the old block itself.'[76]

The surrender to General Washington at Yorktown in the autumn of 1781 effectively brought the American war to an end. It doomed as well the long administration of Lord North, who had been in power since 1770 and was now increasingly abandoned by the independent country MPs. The King, however, resisted the inevitable and it was not until the end of February 1782 that a motion in the House of Commons was carried formally concluding the war, and almost another month before North was allowed to resign. With great reluctance on the King's part, Rockingham, after sixteen years, returned to power on 27 March 1782 in liaison with, or, perhaps it would be fairer to say, encumbered by, Shelburne. In *Banco to the Knave*[77] Gillray took artistic licence in satirising the ministerial changes, thinking it more fun to have Charles James Fox, inveterate gambler, assume the faro bank from Lord North, and perhaps indicating that the new Foreign Secretary would dominate the administration. One man looking on with a thin smile was Burke, the new Paymaster General of the forces.

The ROYAL HUNT, or a PROSPECT of the YEAR 1782.

Published according to Act of Parliament by R. Owen, in Fleet Street Febr. 16.th 1782.

10 The Temple of Fame, formerly the Wonder of the World, but now in Ruins.

19. Anon.: *The Royal Hunt, or a Prospect of the Year 1782*. Published 16 February 1782, by R. Owen. BM 5961; British Museum.
The First Lord of the Admiralty, Sandwich, a courtesan on each side, plays catches and glees while Britain's enemies destroy the Temple of Fame. Lord North (bottom left) yawns at it all (*see* note 49, p. 202), but opposition members protest angrily: behind Sandwich, William Pitt the younger appears, for possibly the first time in caricature, next to Keppel, Burke and Richmond.

The first print of Rockingham's government brings home George III's plight. *The Captive Prince – or – Liberty run Mad*, published on 23 April 1782,[78] shows the hapless monarch being shackled by ministers: Fox, Admiral Keppel, the Duke of Richmond and Lord John Cavendish, Chancellor of the Exchequer (Plate 20). Rockingham has removed the Crown, saying 'Dispose of these Jewels for the Publick Use', an allegation of republicanism against the new ministry that is to recur in these prints. Beside the Commander-in-Chief, General Conway (who does not know which way to turn) Burke muses: 'The best of Ministers the best of K[ings]' a reference to the King's reluctant message recommending the 'effectual Plan of Oeconomy' devised by Burke. 'It was', said Burke, 'the best of messages to the best of people from the best of Kings.'[79] Burke's features are taken from an engraving after Sir Joshua Reynolds,[80] as are those of Rockingham[81] (the process of etching has reversed the image) and Keppel.[82] During his brief term in the office of the Paymaster (March–July 1782) Burke did achieve a measure of economical reform, though not as much as he had proposed from the opposition benches in 1780. Nonetheless, he abolished by Act of Parliament 134 offices in the royal household and in civil administration of which he

The CAPTIVE PRINCE — or — LIBERTY run MAD. *Pub. 23d. Apl. 1782 by T. Grant Oxford St.*

20. Anon.: *The Captive Prince – or – Liberty run Mad.* Published 23 April 1782, by T. Grant. BM 5979; private collection.

For customers of caricature a new administration meant getting to grips with some unfamiliar faces. Here several clues to identity are given. The heads of Burke (left), Conway and Keppel are taken from Reynolds portraits, as is Rockingham's (right).

Burke is labelled 'Pay Master' and quotes from an eulogy he had given a week previously. General Conway is in uniform as Commander-in-Chief. Keppel, in naval uniform, says, 'I command the Fleet', and Richmond, new Master General of the Ordnance, 'I command the ordnance', allowing Fox (identified in traditional fashion) to trump them: 'I command the mob'. Rockingham wears aristocratic robe and hose as he seeks to dispose of the crown 'for the Publick Use'. Only the figure shackling the King's left foot, resembling Lord John Cavendish, is offered without further guidance.

thought more than forty were 'considerable employments'.[83] Early in 1783 we meet a victim of Burke's Civil List Act: Basil Feilding, Earl of Denbigh, Master of the Royal Harriers and Foxhounds from 1762 until the post disappeared as a result of economical reform. 'It is not proper', said Burke, 'that great noblemen should be keepers of dogs, though they were the King's dogs.'[84] Lord Denbigh, seen in *Wonders Wonders & Wonders*,[85] says to Fox:

> Through you & Burke I lost my Place
> Yet I forgive the sad Disgrace.

He was, said Walpole, 'the lowest and most officious of the Court-tools'.[86]

Despite Burke's efforts the civil list did not achieve solvency and for years afterwards debts continued to pile up. For all his care in tying down expenditure under various headings, Burke miscalculated in omitting provision for unforeseen occasional payments for special purposes. When these cropped up – as frequently happened – they had to be paid for by special parliamentary grants, and the Act was quickly undermined.[87] Furthermore, by reducing the number of places in the royal household, his Act did nothing to diminish the King's influence, for the value of

30

honours (such as the creation of peerages) which were still in the King's gift increased correspondingly.

Elsewhere he made valuable reforms in the Paymaster's office: henceforth the office's funds would be kept at the Bank of England in an official account separate from the Paymaster's private cash. He would no longer be able to earn income on the accumulation of large balances in the account (as former Paymasters had done – with the conspicuous exception of the elder Pitt). Even as he was struggling personally to make ends meet he could announce to the Commons that the Pay Office was now, at £4,000 a year, worth £23,000 a year less to its head.[88] Judging by the fortunes of some earlier incumbents this was, if anything, a conservative calculation. To appreciate just what Burke was turning down (and, incidentally, how Fox's father Henry, Lord Holland, had attained such widespread unpopularity) it should be remembered that the Paymaster General was, in effect, sole banker to the army. His was the task, much sought after, to receive the very considerable sums voted by parliament for the needs of the army – sums much swollen in time of war – and to disburse them when authorised to do so. The burden he carried was to be liable for all sums received until a long-drawn-out audit procedure had been completed and, years after leaving office, he was given a formal *quietus* or final discharge. Complicated book-keeping and legal requirements caused great delay – 'rigour, as usual, defeats itself' said Burke.[89] Collecting expenditure vouchers, for instance, during a hard-fought overseas campaign was a recipe for chaos. Burke put it nicely: 'As the extent of our wars has scattered the accountants under the paymaster into every part of the globe, the grand and sure paymaster, Death, in all his shapes, calls these accountants to another reckoning'.[90] Meanwhile, the burden of accountability often remained long after the Paymaster had left office and, if necessary, attached to his legal representatives after death.

If that was the burden, what made the office such a political plum was the entitlement of the Paymaster by law and custom to invest the balances in hand for his private enrichment.[91] Here archaic practices worked in his favour: as the monies voted were for specific purposes the Paymaster's bank account was not legally a consolidated fund and the large balance lying idle under one heading could not be employed under another heading where the money issued had been spent. The result was that larger balances were held than was strictly necessary. It was a matter for the Paymaster's discretion as to when to apply for money, and how much to apply for.[92] In time of war, and with a good innings as Paymaster, vast sums were available to turn to private profit. Such a Paymaster was Henry Fox. Created Baron Holland in 1763, he held the post from 1757 to 1765 and made a spectacular fortune from investments in stocks, real estate, speculative coups, and loans to jobbers and brokers, mortgagors of great landed estates, and friends.[93] This fortune would have been even more remarkable but for his promiscuous spending and the still greater extravagance of his elder sons Stephen and Charles, and, though within the bounds of contemporary practice, it aroused deep public resentment. The Lord Mayor of London gave vent to feelings in the city in an address to the King in 1769 when he denounced Holland as the 'Public Defaulter of unaccounted millions', an attack which would occasion numerous prints and squibs, such as Plate 21.

Even by 1769, no accounts – even for 1756–57, his first year in office – had been finally audited, yet, as Lucy Sutherland and John Binney point out, 'Fox was not a defaulter, if that implies that he had retarded the submission of his accounts and vouchers to the auditors; and if subsequent delays in passing the accounts could have been diminished, the blame (if any) appears to rest rather upon the Audit Office, or

21. Anon.: *Renard Stating his Accounts*. [5 July 1769]. *Oxford Magazine*. BM 4299; British Museum. Lord Holland is asked by his young son, probably Charles James Fox, to take care of his cubs. The Paymaster General's ambitions to become an earl are thrown into doubt by a future holder of that office: Viscount Barrington (third from left) fears 'he must continue a Baron for he'll never come to a Count'. James Mansfield (right), later Chief Justice of Common Pleas, thinks Ayliffe's ghost will help Fox out (a nasty dig, alluding to Fox's old steward caught forging his master's name and hanged at Tyburn, 1759). But the former Attorney General, Sir Fletcher Norton KC, offers a practical solution: 'What Signifies £400 000 00 rub a Spunge on the 4 and the Account is Settled'.

Renard Stating his Accounts.

22. James Sayers: [*Edmund Burke*]. Published 6 April 1782, by C. Bretherton. BM 6055; private collection. Sayers, an attorney who took up caricature, may have lacked the drafting skills of Gillray and others but as a Pittite propagandist he attacked the Whigs with political effectiveness and a distinctive scratchy style. Here he is the first to offer a distinctive Burke in caricature.

the Treasury'.[94] Nonetheless public sentiment was no longer prepared to condone such rapacity especially after the huge costs and miserable outcome of the American war.

This was the background to Burke's reform of the Pay Office. James Sayers, an attorney embarking on another career as satirical artist, caricatures the reforming Burke in action, in an untitled print – the first of what will be increasingly hostile encounters – on 6 April 1782 (Plate 22). At first glance, it seems an insignificant etching: Burke waving before him his 'Plan Oecon' and declaiming combatively but, taken almost certainly from a sketch made in the House, it is the first good caricature of Burke's features. Long nose, thin pouting lips, pointed chin jutting forward are added to the spectacles that will become famous and are in themselves a symbol of eccentricity. The couplet beneath enviously mocks Burke's great gifts of figurative language:

> For Rhetoric he could not ope
> His Mouth but out there flew a Trope.

Sayers may have captured the first good caricature likeness but Burke had been strikingly portrayed, notably by his protégé James Barry in or about 1771 (Frontispiece). One of the earliest members of the Royal Academy, Barry had followed Reynolds as professor of painting and would be buried next to him in St Paul's Cathedral, achieving in between these events the distinction of being the only member ever expelled from the Academy. Burke (with his kinsman William) had generously financed the Irishman's artistic training in Italy and, knowing him well, feared his quarrelsome and anti-social temperament would have disastrous consequences when he set up in London:

You will come here; you will observe what the artists are doing, and you will sometimes speak a disapprobation in plain words, and sometimes in a no less expressive silence. By degrees you will produce some of your own works. They will be variously criticised; you will defend them; you will abuse those that have attacked you; expostulations, discussions, letters, possibly challenges, will go forward; you will shun your brethren, they will shun you. In the mean time gentlemen will avoid your friendship, for fear of being engaged in your quarrels; you will fall into distresses, which will only aggravate your disposition for further quarrels; you will be obliged for maintenance to do any thing for any body; your very talents will depart, for want of hope and encouragement, and you will go out of the world fretted, disappointed and ruined.[95]

A painter in the 'grand manner' (and another Irishman of Catholic background who sought by his intellectual prowess to rise above his origins to the top rank in London) the melancholic Barry was to fulfil Burke's prophecy. His resentment of the exaggerated importance accorded – he felt – to these portrait painters was heightened by Burke's admiration for Sir Joshua Reynolds.[96] He later wrote of his sorrow that his quarrels with Reynolds were to lose him Burke's friendship.[97] Meanwhile in 1776, in what William Pressly calls 'a virtuoso display of how portraiture and history could be mixed without either losing its separate identity', Barry painted Burke and himself as *Ulysses and a Companion fleeing from the Cave of Polyphemus* in an episode from Homer's *Odyssey* (Plate 23). 'Burke' writes Pressly,[98] 'is shown as a good shepherd leading his flock from danger, and his cautionary gesture recalls his frequent admonishments to the artist to moderate his conduct.' Also in 1776, Barry executed a bold political print, *The Phoenix or the Resurrection of Freedom,*[99] lamenting the demise of liberty in Britain

23. James Barry: *Ulysses and a Companion fleeing from the Cave of Polyphemus*. Oil on canvas, 1776; Crawford Art Gallery, Cork.
Barry's portrayal of himself and Burke as classical figures, Ulysses and a companion, was executed in the same year as his bold etching on the passing of liberty from England to America, *The Phoenix or the Resurrection of Freedom*, which he signed 'U & C fecit'.

while taking comfort in its flight to America, 'a new people of manners simple & untainted' (whose Declaration of Independence was signed in July 1776). He signed the plate 'U & C fecit' which, if it is taken as Ulysses & Companion (i.e. Burke & Barry) must have claimed to reflect Burke's views in a way that Burke may have felt to be less than helpful.

But if Barry saw the printed image as a medium by which to promulgate his radical views he despised the caricaturist's art: 'Better, better far, there had been no art', he complained, 'than thus to pervert and employ it to purposes so base, and so subversive of everything interesting to society'.[100]

Unlike Barry's most obvious targets of disparagement, Gillray and Rowlandson, James Sayers (1748–1823) was not so much an artist perverting his calling as a shrewd – and partisan – political observer, a lawyer who knew how to score against the other

24. Anon.: *The Political Mirror.* (c. April 1782). BM
5982; British Museum.
The pit of oblivion beckons for North's old
administration as new ministers declaim importantly.

side, and with enough talent to execute designs accordingly. This he did in a
distinctive old fashioned manner that filled the plate with a thin and spidery line and
eschewed hand colouring. His likenesses were good and were borrowed by Dent and
other contemporaries (*see* Plates 94 and 95). From the accuracy of these likenesses, and
the contents of his plates, it may be assumed that he attended regularly at
parliamentary debates. Thomas Wright the nineteenth-century historian of caricature
was inclined to dismiss him ('Gillray was not a hired libeller, like Sayer and some of
the lower caricaturists of that time . . .')[101] and recounted how Pitt had advanced his
legal career by awarding him 'the not unlucrative offices of marshall of the court of
exchequer, receiver of the sixpenny duties, and cursitor' [a clerk of the court of
chancery].[102] But that is to underestimate not only Gillray's availability but Sayers's
caricaturing skills of observation and ridicule and his keen political grasp. He had that
ability alluded to by Ernst Gombrich writing of 'the satisfaction the successful cartoon
gives us simply by its neat summing up'[103] (*see*, for instance, Plates 39 and 72).
According to Lord Eldon, Fox felt that Sayers's prints 'had done him more mischief
than the debates in parliament and the works of the press'.[104]

The contrast between the cynicism of an administration too long in power, and the

34

reforming – if priggish – zeal of Rockingham's new ministry is illustrated in an anonymous print of April 1782 (Plate 24), in which members of the old government, blinded by the 'Mirror of Truth', stumble into the pit of oblivion. Among those to fall is Lord Mansfield (whose exclamation 'This Truth is a most cruel Libel on us all' parodies his directions to the jury in Junius libel cases). Another is Lord North, who holds a paper advertising his taxes on soap, salt and small beer; his explanation for taxing soap, that it would not burden the poor since their consumption was very small, had not been well received.[105] Rigby the Paymaster General (who died in 1788 leaving 'near half a million of public money')[106] is toppling over, as is the unrepentant Lord Sandwich, First Lord of the Admiralty: 'Damn the Navy give me a whore & a Bottle'. The new ministers, an upstanding body of men, are declaiming self-righteously. 'Your crimes stink stronger than all the Foxes in England', cries Fox. 'Honest Yorkshire will be true to the last', says Rockingham, thus identified as the Lord Lieutenant of the West Riding. 'Their duplicity as Ministers is beyond Parallel', clucks Richmond. Burke, affecting his orator's pose, declares 'You have denied GOD deceiv'd your King & Plundered your [blank]'. The artist has not found it necessary to add an 'arrah' to Burke's pronouncement, nor indeed to Barré's beside him. 'Your Army expenditures have been enormous & Shameful' he calls, and holds aloft a 'Bill for the Examination of Accounts'. Predictable lawyerly sentiments are voiced by Lords Camden and Thurlow. Between them General Conway asserts 'Your War with America I allways condemned', and a relieved Britannia sums it all up: 'They would have ruined me if they had staid in Power'. Even though the Earl of Bute was long out of power – having retired from the King's business in 1765 – he is still seen as a baleful presence; falling from the back of a witch on broomstick he is 'England's Evil Genius unhorsed or the downfall of Witchcraft.'

The theme of sweeping reform is taken up in a print by Thomas Colley on 1 May,

25. Anon.: *The late Bombardment of Government Castle.* Published 1 May 1782, by J. Barrow. BM 5985; British Museum.
The combatants are poorly characterised and Burke, with his spectacles, is one of the few who can be identified with confidence. Beyond him one can guess at Keppel, Dunning, Conway and possibly Fox, and (on his right) Barré. On the upper parapet Lord North, a cleric who may be Archbishop Markham of York, and Lord George Germain (formerly Sackville) lead the resistance. George III presides over the castle entrance, while Speaker Cornwall calls for order. The ambivalence of the figure in the foreground, who thinks it 'hot work for both parties' prompts speculation that it is the courtier Shelburne.

The late BOMBARDMENT *of* GOVERNMENT CASTLE.
Pub.ᵈ May 1ˢᵗ 1782. by J Barrow. Sold by E. Rich at the little Print Shop facing Anderton's Coffee House Fleet Street, And at Mʳ Turner's Frame maker and Print Seller, Nᵒ 40. Snow hill.

BRITANIA'S ASSASSINATION.
or ──── The Republicans Amusement.

Publ. May 10.th 1782. by E. D'Archery S.t James's Street

26. [James Gillray]: *Britania's Assassination*. Published 10 May 1782, by E. D'Archery. BM 5987; private collection.

In this early Gillray plate Whig ministers and supporters are depicted as republican assassins of Britannia, acting for the benefit of her enemies, America, France, Spain and Holland who run off with booty. Burke, waving a copy of the '[Economical] Reformation Bill' is second from the right in this group which is being restrained by Lords Thurlow and Mansfield. Gillray has not yet studied Burke's features and copies an engraving after Reynolds.

that shows the new ministers (with the help of a devil) drive their predecessors into the jaws of hell, Burke proclaiming 'Pay the Taxes by Oeconomy'.[107] Economy is also on Burke's mind in a pair of prints published by J. Barrow further attacking North's old administration. In *The late Bombardment of Government Castle* (Plate 25) Burke is one of a number of protagonists to score hits. 'The war hath cost 100 000 000 £', he says. 'You have lost us America', cries another. *The Surrender of Government Castle, in March 1782, to the late besieging Minority*[108] is explained by the sub-title: 'The old Garrison and Placemen are marching out, The new Garrison and new Placemen are marching in'. One of those marching in is Burke, who declares, 'There must be much better Oeconomy' while a newcomer further down the line responds, 'We shall do pretty well with half their salary', and another new minister says 'I hope we shall reconcile America'. The Burkean metaphor of Government Castle brings to mind his denunciation of the court faction in *Thoughts on the Cause of the Present Discontents*: 'Government may in a great measure be restored,' he wrote, 'if any considerable bodies of men have honesty and resolution enough never to accept administration, unless this garrison of *king's men*, which is stationed, as in a citadel, to control and enslave it, be entirely broken and disbanded, and every work they have thrown up be levelled with the ground'.[109] Thus the King, with every reason to fear the worst from the new administration, calls out to the departing ministers: 'To lose you, Sirs, concerns me more / Than all I lost by you before.' Gillray is quick to make the King's point in *Britania's Assassination or – The Republicans Amusement* (Plate 26). As an allegorical representation of the nation, exhorter of patriotism and virtue, Britannia had long been persecuted and abused in graphic prints.[110] The *Morning Chronicle* of 15 May 1782 drew the attention of readers to this 'very extraordinary caricature . . . Since the Newcastle administration there has not been seen a bolder satire in caricature stile against ministers'.[111] In it, Gillray depicts the destruction of an already headless statue of Britannia by members of the new ministry. Burke prepares to strike with a rolled-up copy of the 'Reformation Bill', while Britain's enemies Spain, Holland and America (pursued for a share by France) run off with pieces they have pillaged. America, a native Indian, has taken Britannia's head and left arm. 'Leave not a Wreck behind', says the Duke of Richmond. Gillray continues the theme of republicanism with Fox as *Guy Vaux* [i.e., Fawkes] conspiring with Shelburne, Burke and others against George III while he, with ass's head, sleeps on his throne.[112] In *Evacuation Before Resignation* (Plate 27) published on 21 May 1782, another Gillray print which demonstrates the earthy vulgarity so often found in prints of this period, Rockingham crouches over a close stool. Behind him stands a country MP, Thomas Powys, saying 'This is really for the Landed Interest' while holding in both hands – as the BM Catalogue notes – 'a hat with steaming and unsavoury contents'. Poor Rockingham is simultaneously retching into a hat held before him by Burke, who (in parody of his bill of economical reform) insists 'We must save everything'. Gillray may be pandering to the crude humour of his customers but he is doing more than that, for he uses such scenes to degrade both politician and principle alike. While we cannot accuse Gillray of knowingly caricaturing a dying man – for Rockingham's death shortly afterwards (at the beginning of July 1782) was unexpected – Gillray's later treatment of the dangerously ill Fox in 1806 suggests that little in the print would have been altered had he known that Rockingham was close to death.[113] For Burke, the death of Rockingham was painful, and the consequences would be dramatic.

EVACUATION before RESIGNATION.

27. [James Gillray]: *Evacuation before Resignation.* Published 21 May 1782, by H. Humphrey. BM 5990; British Museum.
Gillray knew that his customers enjoyed the crude and vulgar every bit as much as the erudite and allegorical: in this parody of Burke's plan of economical reform the poor Marquis of Rockingham is both adding to the 'Publick reservoir' and throwing up more, 'all for the Public Good'. 'We must save every thing', insists Burke. Thomas Powys, representing the country members of parliament, seems happy with his share: 'This is really for the Landed Interest' he smiles, while the Chancellor of the Exchequer, Lord John Cavendish, marvels at the minister's efforts: 'Oh how he strains every Nerve for the Publick Good. He does my business, 'tis I who should cast up the Accounts'. Rockingham died unexpectedly on 1 July 1782, some weeks after this print was published.

CHAPTER TWO

PARADISE LOST, PARADISE REGAINED

Resignation and Re-appointment to Government, 1782–83

Rockingham's death on 1 July 1782 was a double blow to Burke. Through his friend and leader he had exercised commanding influence; now, with the King's appointment of the Home Secretary, Shelburne, as head of the administration, he faced a man whom he despised. He and Fox resigned (as did some others, Lord John Cavendish and Sheridan among them, though most of the Rockinghams remained in office). A furious Burke in his resignation speech of 9 July declared that 'If Lord Shelburne was not a Cataline or a Borgia in morals, it must not be ascribed to anything but his understanding'. In other words, as Conor Cruise O'Brien puts it, 'Shelburne was too stupid to be a first-class villain'.[1]

Although, to be fair, Shelburne had an impressive intellectual range, the contrast between these two Irishmen could hardly have been greater. William Petty, Earl of Shelburne, had inherited vast Cromwellian estates in Ireland, his 'anti-Papistical sentiments' were evidently well enough known to ensure he was not mobbed during the Gordon riots in 1780, and he was happy to be an instrument of that very royal influence Burke sought to curtail. A smooth and practised courtier given to intrigue and widely distrusted, we do not see his words in caricature punctuated with 'arrahs'.

A young German visitor, Carl Philip Moritz, was in the House to hear the resignation speeches, and wrote to a friend in Berlin on 14 July:

> Then Burke rose to make a flowery speech in praise of the late Marquis of Rockingham. In the course of it, he found that some members were not listening and that a good deal of private chatter was audible. 'This is no way to treat a member of such long standing as mine!' he declared forcibly and in a voice charged with emotion: 'I will be heard!' And at once they all became quiet.[2]

This was not the first time Burke had been upset by noise in the House and the tactic of talking during his speeches would be used increasingly against him. During a speech on the Middlesex election dispute he shamed the Speaker and others into silence by threatening to 'throw open the doors and tell the people of England that when a man is addressing the chair in their behalf the attention of the Speaker is engaged'.

The resignation of Fox and Burke occasioned much ridicule. As Moritz's letter notes:

> Twelve or more newspapers are brought out daily in London – some siding with the Government, some with the Opposition. It is shocking how they seize every opportunity for personal abuse. Only yesterday it was stated that after his fall from office in favour of the youthful Pitt, Fox remarked, 'O hateful sight!' – as Satan did in *Paradise Lost* when he looked upon the being God approved – man![3]

A newspaper account that caught the public attention was ideal fodder for the printmakers, so a caricature by Sayers referring to Satan and *Paradise Lost* has Fox and

28. James Sayers: *Paradise lost*. Published 17 July 1782, by Charles Bretherton. BM 6011; private collection. Fox and Burke are expelled from the paradise of government: Sayers provided a caption from Milton's *Paradise Lost*, Book XII, which contained some consolation. 'Some natural Tears they dropt but wiped them soon; The World was all before them . . .'

Burke turning away disconsolately from the gates of Paradise (Plate 28). Carved on the keystone of the arch is the gloating head of Shelburne, and to each side are the heads of his followers John Dunning and Isaac Barré for whom he had arranged pensions for life. (It was Dunning, their legal luminary, who had galvanised the opposition by moving his famous resolution in 1780, 'that the influence of the Crown has increased, is increasing, and ought to be diminished'.)

Gillray, in one of his most celebrated early prints, depicts Burke as *Cincinnatus in Retirement/falsely supposed to represent Jesuit-Pad driven back to his native Potatoes* (Plate 29). If Sayers offered the first good satirical likeness, Gillray creates here the enduring image of Burke in caricature: the thin, astringent, bespectacled Jesuit will appear in dozens of plates over the coming years, rosary at his waist and – very shortly – head clad in a great biretta. And how tellingly Gillray evokes the heroes of antiquity with which to taunt his prey: this time it is the great Roman dictator who, delivering his country from peril in a matter of weeks, has modestly returned to his plough. Seated

CINCINNATUS *in Retirement.*
falsely supposed to represent Jesuit-Pad *driven back to his native Potatoes.* see Romish Common-Wealth.

Pub.d Aug.t 23.d 1782. by E.D.Achery St James's Street.

29. [James Gillray]: *Cincinnatus in Retirement.* Published 23 August 1782, by E. D'Achery [*sic*]. BM 6026; private collection.

If James Sayers (Plate 22) offered the first good satirical likeness, Gillray creates here the enduring image of Burke in caricature, based on scurrilous rumours that he was a Jesuit who had been educated at St Omer in France. Seated at his impoverished table he fastidiously peels a steaming potato, symbol of the penurious Irish, which he has taken from a chamber pot, 'Relick No. 1 used by St Peter'. Influenced perhaps by Sayers's print, Gillray now gives Burke spectacles and begins to elongate his nose.

at his impoverished table he fastidiously peels a steaming potato, symbol of the penurious Irish, which he has taken from a chamber pot, 'Relick No. 1 used by St. Peter'. Ironically, the gibe of 'Jesuit' he shared with his compatriot Shelburne, though for different reasons. Shelburne, for his duplicity, had been dubbed 'Malagrida' after the Portuguese Jesuit of that name, prompting another Irishman, Oliver Goldsmith, to pay the back-handed compliment: 'I never could conceive why they call you Malagrida, for Malagrida was a very good sort of man'.[4] A few years later (in 1787) Gillray would accuse him of lining his pockets by using inside information on the timing of the 1783 Franco-British peace preliminaries, by which he was supposed to have refurbished his mansion in Berkeley Square.[5] Gillray's characterisation of Burke as a Jesuit comes from rumours which first surfaced when Burke became private secretary to Rockingham back in 1765. The story is well known, and was recounted in Lord Charlemont's *Memoirs*: Burke had no sooner been appointed than the old Duke of Newcastle, primed perhaps by the malicious William Hamilton from whose service Burke had resigned,[6] urged Rockingham to reconsider: he had unwittingly taken on a most unsuitable Irish adventurer, a dangerous Papist spy secretly educated by the Jesuits at St Omer in France. Rockingham put the story frankly to Burke, accepted his refutation (taking comfort, no doubt, in Burke's graduation from that stronghold of Protestant Ireland, Trinity College, Dublin) and refused his offer to resign. Newcastle's specific allegations were quite unfounded but, as Conor Cruise O'Brien puts it, 'Rockingham might not have been so easily satisfied if he had understood the full extent, the strength and depth, of Burke's connection with Catholic Ireland . . . Burke may not actually have been a crypto-Catholic, but in the eyes of strong Protestants in eighteenth-century Britain and Ireland, he was as near to being a crypto-Catholic as made no difference'.[7]

'In our century,' notes Colin Haydon, 'McCarthyism delineated what it meant to be American by reference to 'un-American' activities; anti-Popery operated in the same way in Georgian times.'[8] The fear had long existed (and had been so much played upon to be deeply ingrained) that England, protectress of European Protestantism, was being secretly infiltrated by clandestine Papists, 'entryists', whose long term ambition when they had wormed their way into positions of influence, was to restore Catholicism. Souls were at risk; but worse, as John Locke had argued back in 1689 in his first *Letter on Toleration,* the Catholic church was 'so constituted that all who enter it *ipso facto* pass into the allegiance and service of another prince'.[9] Subjects of the Pope, and cat's paw of France and Spain, they were obliged – said the polemicists – to persecute those they regarded as heretics.[10]

Even George III occasionally outraged 'strong' Protestants. 'James II lost his Crown for such enormities', protested Horace Walpole as the King gave his royal assent to the Quebec Act in 1774, a measure granting relief to Catholic subjects in newly acquired Canada.[11] Worse, the King was caricatured in 1780 as *A Priest at his Private Devotion*[12] (Plate 30) in the immediate aftermath of the no-popery riots fomented by Lord George Gordon and his followers, perhaps for his assent to the Catholic Relief Act.

The beauty of a good conspiracy theory is that it is impossible to disprove, and therefore self-sustaining. These subversives, it was said, and particularly the Jesuits with their dispensation to lie and dissimulate, were almost undetectable. And what might lie in store for God-fearing Protestant people was emphasised by Paul Wright who in about 1785 put together a *New and Complete Book of Martyrs,* updating John Foxe's much reissued work of 1570, and giving a graphic account of past sufferings. Wright had no doubt that, next to the Bible, this book 'will be the most valuable Legacy you can leave your Children'.[13]

The rumours against Burke were revived, indeed embellished, as he courageously sought to remove Catholic disabilities, incurring the wrath of Gordon and his mob, and the displeasure of his electors in Bristol, and, whatever the sources of his inspiration, Gillray would continue to use the theme to brilliant and cruel effect, others joining in the fun. Prior's *Life of Burke,* published in 1824, refers to such rumours reaching Bristol, 'of his being a Roman Catholic, of being educated at St Omer's, and others of the same stamp'. According to Prior, Burke discouraged one of his supporters at Bristol, a Mr Noble, from seeking a formal contradiction from Burke's Quaker friend Richard Shackleton: 'To people who can believe such stories, it will be in vain to offer explanations', he said and, when pressed, 'if I cannot live down these contemptible calumnies, my dear friend, I shall never deign to contradict them in any other manner'.[14] However, Burke's brother Richard was worried enough as his election agent to get just such a letter from Shackleton, commending Burke as 'a firm and staunch Protestant'.[15] In fairness to the voters of Bristol it was his

30. Anon.: *A Priest at his Private Devotion.* 10 June 1780. BM 5680; British Museum.
Published in the aftermath of the no-popery riots (2–7 June), and on the date of Lord George Gordon's arrest, the print mocks George III as a priest. Lords Sandwich and North, above the altar, have also incurred the artist's wrath, and a special place has been found for a papal portrait, at the entrance to the latrine. There the Protestant petitions (like the resolutions of the American Congress in Plate 9) will be put to 'necessary uses', joined, it would appear, by the portrait of Luther. The caricature is inscribed 'Protestant sculpt'.

"CRUMBS of COMFORT".
or — Old-Orthodox, restoring Consolation to his Fallen Children.

31. [James Gillray]: *Crumbs of Comfort*. (*c.* August 1782). BM 6027; British Museum.
'Old-Orthodox' the devil gives consolation to his 'fallen children' on their loss of office: to Fox the habitual gambler it comes in the form of dice-box and dice; to Burke it is scourge and rosary, taunting him as a concealed Roman Catholic.

neglect of the constituency, as a Whig occupying a traditionally Tory seat in a great commercial city, as well as his independence of mind, that ultimately perfected his unpopularity; he had not visited it for four years before the dissolution of parliament in autumn 1780. Despite an eloquent speech in defence of his position on such delicate matters as Irish trade and Roman Catholic relief he accepted that defeat was inevitable and, declining the hustings, moved instead to the borough of Malton.

Now, following the resignation of Fox and Burke from office, *Crumbs of Comfort* (Plate 31) are offered to the 'fallen children' in another Gillray print of around August 1782, as they kneel at the feet of the devil, 'Old-Orthodox'. Fox receives a dice-box and dice, and Burke, calculatedly dressed in civilian clothes (to emphasise the covert nature of his Catholicism), a scourge and rosary. Equally calculated is Old-Orthodox's apparel, a 'sober Quaker drab'.[16]

We have seen how Burke's drive for economical reform, directed against the King's influence over parliament through the holders of sinecures, led to charges of republicanism against Rockingham's administration. *Raising the Royal George* (Plate 32)[17] – the title alludes to the loss of the *Royal George* with about one thousand lives

Raising the Royal George.

32. Anon.: *Raising the Royal George*. Published 5 December 1782, by J. Langham, 'print Coulourer' [*sic*]. BM 6042; British Museum.
Shelburne (second from left) and his fellow ministers Sandwich, Dunning (Baron Ashburton) and Richmond, seek to restore the royal influence. Richmond reassures a judge, probably Lord Thurlow, it is safe to dive: 'that's Born to be hang'd will never be Drown'd', while Burke, at Fox's side, ponders on the mischief they could make if joined by Boreas, the north wind.

on 29 August 1782 – shows Shelburne and his ministry at the end of 1782 endeavouring to restore the royal influence, while Fox and Burke look on. Burke may be contemplating the unthinkable when he invokes the nickname of their former antagonist Lord North:

> if boreas was here he woul'd much Swell
> and prevent the efects of the Diving Bell.

The diving bell in question is a judge, and is likely to be the Lord Chancellor, Edward Thurlow. He floats behind the King whose head emerges above the water. Thurlow, a conservative, menacing figure, was very much the King's Chancellor and a formidable presence, of whom Fox gibed: 'No one could *be* as wise as Thurlow *looks*'.[18] The wreck of the *Royal George* was a macabre spectacle that attracted, amongst others, the caricaturists Henry Wigstead and Thomas Rowlandson who journeyed to Spithead in the autumn of 1782 to view it.[19]

Fox and Burke were bent on removing Shelburne from office and their effort is shown in *A Long Pull, Strong Pull and A Pull All Together*.[20] They are joined by

Admiral Keppel and the Duke of Richmond (whose defection is anticipated) in attempting to drag Shelburne by a rope out of the Treasury. The *Rambler's Magazine* deliberately misconstrues the situation in a satire in the issue for February 1783, entitled *The F[o]x, Goose and Primier*.[21] Kneeling in supplication with Fox at the feet of Shelburne, Burke exclaims 'By Ja[su]s what a fool was I to turn myself out before I got in – That d-m'd F[o]x has made a Goose of me' to which Shelburne responds 'Very sublime and beautiful! but you are fallen like Lucifar never to hope again'. In fact Shelburne did resign, on 24 February 1783, owing to the combined attacks of Fox and North. After a brief interregnum a Fox–North coalition, nominally headed by the Duke of Portland, took over on 2 April.

Maybe the caricaturist of *The Royal George* had shrewdly anticipated matters, for Burke played a crucial role in the formation of the coalition.[22] In March an artist recalling how Fox for years had been unremitting in his condemnation of North, attacks this reconciliation as rank opportunism. Etched at the suggestion of the younger George Dance, architect and amateur caricaturist, who had supplied preliminary sketches, two companion prints (Plate 33) were published by Hannah Humphrey and have often been attributed to Gillray.[23] In the first, Fox and Burke rail against North. Fox exclaims, 'I should hold myself Infamous if I ever form'd a connection with him!' and goes on to denounce North thus: 'Disgrace! infamy! shame! incapacity, blunders, wants, weaknesses, gross stupidity, hardly conceivable that to[o] much Pride, Vice and Folly Can Exist in the same Animal'. Burke gesticulates in support. North, for his part, appeals to the Speaker: 'want of candor, Illiberality our misfortunes entirely owing to Opposition'. All is changed in the sequel, and North has joined 'the astonishing Coalition' in an attack on Shelburne and his 'Preliminary Articles of Peace'.[24] To make things worse, the articles of peace so abused were in fact substantially accepted by the new coalition ministry: in *Puke-ation in Answer to the Late State of the Nation*,[25] Shelburne notes with grim satisfaction, as he watches the prospective ministers throw up, 'I have sickend them all'. Burke says: 'This Peace sticks in my Throat'. (George Dance went on to become an influential professor at the Royal Academy, and was active in the expulsion of James Barry in 1799. Perhaps he, too, was in Barry's mind when the latter denounced caricaturists and all their works.)

Opportunism is the theme, too, of *The Loaves and Fishes*[26] published just before the coalition's appointment. Members of the rival factions sit at a table presided over by the King. Burke is one of those clutching a loaf in one hand, a fish in the other. 'Rhetorick is no use here!' he declares, ''tis catch that catch can'. On Burke's return to office as Paymaster in April 1783 he reinstated two clerks (Powell and Bembridge) who had been dismissed by Barré for malversation, for which he was attacked in parliament. Powell subsequently committed suicide; Bembridge was convicted. Either this print anticipates the affair or else the British Museum impression is later and has been amended, for two dogs laden with money bags – inscribed '£200,000' and '£100,000' respectively – are running off. Later, in 1786, Burke's attack on Warren Hastings would be contrasted with his support for, and reinstatement of, Powell.[27]

The Monster[28] was published on 2 April 1783 to celebrate the new ministry formed that day. Burke's is one head of an eight-headed fox. A rhyme below the design concludes:

> Each different Mouth bawls loudly for itself,
> Yet all agree in one thing, Snack the Pelf

33. Anon. [after George Dance the younger]: *War*. Published 9 March 1783 by H. Humphrey. BM 6187; private collection. *Neithe[r] War nor Peace!* Published 9 March 1783, by H. Humphrey. BM 6188; private collection. These have often been attributed to Gillray.

COALITION - DANCE.

"Let us Dance & Sing, — God bless the King, — For he has made us merry Men all."

Publ.^d April 5.th 1783. by W. Humphrey, 227, Strand.

34. [James Gillray]: *Coalition Dance.* Published 5 April 1783, by W. Humphrey. BM 6205; private collection. By adding a tall biretta to his costume, Gillray completes Burke's transformation into the supposed Jesuit, seen here carrying 'Little Red Ridinghood'. This probably mocks his likening of Shelburne to the wolf in sheep's clothing; as a 'concealed Catholic' Burke would be considered equally lupine.

Share out the booty! Gillray is quick to join in the fun. Burke dressed as a Jesuit – and Gillray here introduces what will become the stock-in-trade biretta – joins with Fox and North in a *Coalition Dance* (Plate 34) around a term, or bust, of George III to the fiddle music of a grinning demon. Gillray gives further enjoyment to those who spot that he is parodying Reynolds's grand painting of the Montgomery sisters, *Three Ladies adorning a Term of Hymen*, exhibited in the Royal Academy in 1774 and popularised in mezzotint by Thomas Watson. Hymen, appropriately, was the Roman god of marriage. The King's face has been obscured by Richard Allestree's influential conduct book, *The Whole Duty of Man*. After prolonged defiance the King has surrendered to the coalition. In correspondence on 7 March 1783 he was still contemplating resistance to what he called 'a desperate Faction in whose hands I will never throw myself'.[29] He prepared two draft messages to the House of Commons (conjecturally dated 28 March), one calling on 'those who feel for the spirit of the Constitution to stand forth to his Assistance' against the coalition, the other announcing his intention to resign the crown to the Prince of Wales and retire to

The Holy Benidiction.

35. [Thomas Colley]: *The Holy Benidiction*. Published 6 June 1783, by T. Colley. Not in the BM Cat. Lewis Walpole Library, Yale University.

The leaders of His Majesty's new government seek absolution from Burke, their moral guide: Fox begs 'some indulgence for our sins not yett committed', while North, in his anxiety to share office, is prepared to 'submit to thy holy Injunctions & drink Small Beer all my life time'.

Hanover. Below the design is engraved: 'Let us Dance & Sing, – God bless the King, – For he has made us merry Men all', but though he dances Burke does not look altogether happy; in one hand (the other is clutched by Fox) he holds a copy of 'Little Red Ridinghood', to show he is the wolf in sheep's clothing, and probably alluding to his resignation speech of 9 July 1782 in which he compared Shelburne with the wolf (*see* page 16). Gillray was not alone in seeking inspiration from the work of others; Reynolds himself had done so and, as Diana Donald puts it, 'The decorousness with which the Montgomery sisters paid homage to marriage . . . gained a more subtle frisson for whose who recognised the compositional source in a scene of pagan drunkenness',[30] (and, to emphasise the small world they lived in, one of the Montgomery girls painted by Reynolds was Lady Townshend, wife of the caricaturist.) A Thomas Colley print of 6 June 1783 happily peddles the Jesuit smear. Fox and North, on their knees, seek *The Holy Benidiction*[31] (Plate 35) from Fox's mentor. 'Most Holy Father grant us some indulgence for our sins not yett committed!' prays Fox. North is clearly a new convert: 'I have been a wicked fellow

47

36. William Dent: *A Learned Coalition*. Published 11 July 1783, by W. Dent. BM 6249 (that impression untitled); private collection.
Accused of covert Catholicism, Burke is cast as the wolf in the nursery story of Little Red Ridinghood.

A LEARNED COALITION.

S.ᵗ Omer, preferring sense to food,
Wisely hugs little Red Riding Hood.

my Sins are Manifold & grievous. I'll submit to thy holy Injunctions & drink Small Beer all my life time'. 'Go & Sin no More', responds Burke, 'renounce thy duplicity and become as Men deserving the Confidence of thy Sover[eig]n'. And the image of Jesuit as wolf in sheep's clothing is helped on its way by William Dent (Plate 36).[32] Gathered in his arms, Little Red Ridinghood innocently embraces a smiling Burke, whose regalia include a belt of 'friendship', a rosary made of guineas and, instead of a crucifix, a dagger. Earlier in the century Bishop Willis of Gloucester had used the analogy of the wolf to warn of the dangers of Catholicism: 'The business of a Wolf is

48

not to feed and protect, but to tear and devour: And is not this the business of Popery, whenever it has Power over Protestants?'[33]

Burke is no sooner back in office than his plan of economical reform is again to the fore. Viscount Townshend is thought to have designed *The Blessings of Peace*[34] wherein George III poses the question 'My Lords and Gentlemen, what should I do' and elicits Burke's unpopular response that 'nothing but deminishing your Expences and discarding old Servants, Will Save this Kingdom'. These caricatures are full of passing references and ephemeral detail immediately recognisable to their audience. In this print Richard Brinsley Sheridan makes his first appearance with Burke; turning to Pitt he says 'The next play I write [I] intend giving you a place in the Character of the Angry School Boy'. Pitt, outgoing Chancellor of the Exchequer, had crossed swords with Sheridan by admiring 'the elegant sallies of his mind, the pleasing effusions of his fancy, his dramatic turns, and his epigrammatic allusions' if they were only reserved for the theatre, to which Sheridan responded that 'should I ever again engage in the occupations to which he alludes, I may, by an act of presumption, attempt to improve on one of Ben Jonson's best characters, the Angry Boy in *The Alchemist*'.[35] (Angry boy was slang for a 'blood', a fast or foppish man, or a 'vaporer', a boaster or braggart). Now, so many years later, much of the witty detail must pass over our heads, undeciphered.

Sheridan's altercation with Pitt reminds us that the parliamentary intake of 1780 had brought to prominence these two young men of precocious talent and natural antipathy. Wholly different in background and temperament, they would clash combatively for the next quarter of a century. If Pitt was bred to politics and high office, Sheridan, like Burke, had made his way from a relatively humble Irish background. His sister Alicia Lefanu thought that too much was being made of these modest origins, and sought to put the record straight when she wrote of 'a family of equal antiquity and respectability in Ireland . . . which, though at the beginning of the last century it no longer possessed the large estates that the ancient geographers of the kingdom assigned to the Sheridans, yet never fell from its rank among the respectable gentry of the county of Cavan'.[36] There, at Quilca, his grandfather Thomas entertained his friend and fellow clergyman, Swift, who recalled a dank and tumbledown residence, and a chair 'that collapsed and let him down on his Reverend Deanship's bum'.[37]

Thomas's son, also Thomas, was Swift's godson and took to the boards, becoming manager of the Theatre Royal in Smock Alley, Dublin, and marrying Frances Chamberlaine, a woman of literary gifts. Their son Richard, born in 1751, was sent to school at Harrow, where he was taunted as a poor player's son. Yet, without a shilling to his name, Sheridan had achieved celebrity by his mid-twenties. Along with a string of dramatic successes (*The Rivals* (1775), *The Duenna* (1775), *The School for Scandal* (1777), *The Critic* (1779)) he negotiated the purchase from David Garrick of his share of the Drury Lane Theatre, in a typically complicated and hazardous financial manoeuvre. Drury Lane's valuable patent under the Licensing Act of 1737 gave it, with Covent Garden, a monopoly of London's theatrical business and when Sheridan became its manager in 1776, not yet twenty-five, fame beckoned.[38] Sheridan's – and the theatre's – impecunity would become notorious, and much alluded to in caricature. In later years, Byron would sympathise with Sheridan's plight of never having had any money of his own, but would note he had had a good deal of other people's.[39] Meanwhile the young dramatist and impresario, having made friends and allies in the Whig party, turned his attention to Westminster and won a seat for the

37. [I. or J.] Porter: *A Joint Motion or the Honey-Moon of the Coalition*. Published (*c.* April 1783) by W. Richardson. BM 6222; private collection.
Some members of the new coalition appear not to enjoy the medicine they advocated in opposition: Cavendish attempts to persuade one minister to swop the medicament 'Office' for that in his hand, 'Reform', while Burke has applied the enema of 'Oeconomy' to a reluctant North.

A JOINT MOTION OR THE HONEY-MOON OF THE COALITION.

Staffordshire constituency. Now, like Burke, he held a non-cabinet post in the Fox-North coalition.

Burke's difficulty in pressing on with reform is reflected in a scatological print, *c.*April 1783. In *A Joint Motion or the Honey-Moon of the Coalition* (Plate 37) he stands grimly over Fox and North, wielding a great clyster that dispenses the enema of 'Oeconomy'. A reluctant North defecates with pained expression. From the furrowing of his eyebrows one supposes Fox, too, is straining in discomfort – or is he just coaxing his coalition partner? Together they hold the [Peace] 'Preliminaries' – proposals they had denounced so vehemently a few months previously. Lord John Cavendish, Chancellor of the Exchequer, presses a medicine bottle, 'Reform', on another apprehensive office holder whose old-fashioned court dress indicates his conservatism. Lines from *Macbeth* embellish the scene:

> What Rhubarb Senna or What Purgative Drug
> Will scower these English hence?

In his speech on economical reform in 1780 Burke had anticipated the thankless nature of his task: 'the cold commendation of a public advantage never was,and never will be, a match for the quick sensibility of a private loss'.[40]

The Up & Down or Wheel of Admi-ration (a play on administration and admiration)[41] reminds us, however scurrilous its intent, of the heavy financial loss suffered by Burke in having resigned office the previous July. Burke blurts out, as he runs towards Fox and North, 'Zooks I can no longer suffer Hungary Guts & Empty Purse fol de rol'. But Sayers has Burke frowning as if dissatisfied with his place, in *Razor's Levee*.[42] Horace Walpole felt this caricature – the interior of a barber's shop – was 'better composed than ordinary and has several circumstances well imagined'. One circumstance which might cause Burke's frown is the depiction over the fireplace of

A BLOCK for the WIGS ___ or, the new State Whirligig.

38. [James Gillray]: *A Block for the Wigs*. Published 5 May 1783, by W. Humphrey. BM 6227; British Museum.

George III is reduced to wig-block for the new coalition: to the King's discomfiture the Whigs are in control, encircling him on the 'State Whirligig' or merry-go-round, while the John Bull inn, behind, is being plundered. Following Fox and his loot is North, whose falling headpiece suggests he has difficulty – as a newcomer – in carrying the role of Whig. Burke comes next, his skeletal form pointing to obsessive observance of his own plans of economical reform (or, perhaps, to his impecunity). Admiral Keppel is taunted for his court martial after the Battle of Ushant (27 July 1778): 'Dam'd rough Sailing this. I shall never be able to keep my Seat till the 27th July'. The whole apparatus is kept in place by other blocks – 'Treasury', 'Navy' and 'Army'.

'A new Map of Great Britain and Ireland'; it has been ripped and Ireland hangs down, almost torn off.

The wig/Whig motif is taken up by Gillray who represents George III as *A Block for the Wigs* (Plate 38) in a merry-go-round on which the Whigs are riding, called the 'New State Whirligig'. The puns are manifold: a block was the wood on which criminals were beheaded, as well as the piece of wood on which wigs or hats were formed. Of course a blockhead was also a stupid fellow and one of the many epithets used so indiscreetly by Fox in his denunciations of the King. ('It is intolerable', wrote Fox in 1781, 'that it should be in the power of one blockhead to do so much mischief').[43] One can over-analyse from this distance but Gillray is a master of delicious ambiguity. Dressed as a Jesuit, Burke reads from *Sublime and Beautiful* as he speeds around, but it is his leg, represented in skeletal form, that catches the eye – is it intended simply to indicate the character of his 'economical reform', or does it allude, as well, to his pressing personal financial problems? This parody of Burke's reform policy is taken to its logical conclusion in *All Alive or the Political Churchyard*[44], a collection of tombstone epitaphs.

> Here Lieth Ed^d Burke [reads one], Oeconomist Extraordinary to his Majesty,
> To Save his breath He welcom'd death.

In the 1780s parsimony would not have been a particularly popular virtue in a London that was thriving on new wealth, technical innovation and the steady growth of a consumer society. Indeed, George III's frugal habits were satirised as penny-pinching and tight. A writer to the *Town and Country Magazine* in 1781, arguing that luxury was needed to promote industry and support labour, rejoiced that 'the coffers of departed misers are opened, and their contents circulated'.[45] A sneaking admiration for the big earners, the big spenders may be detected in the nearby memorial suggested for Henry Dundas, then Lord Advocate of Scotland:

> The cause of damnation he gained with such ease
> He is gone to the Devil to ask for his fees.

The Oeconomist Extraordinary to his Majesty is seen by the *Rambler's Magazine* as a monkey clipping the nails of the imperial lion's paw.[46] Worse, he is one of the *Portland Sharks*[47] pillaging the stranded ship *Britannia* at the direction of Lord North, and exclaiming, 'By my Shoul, [another form of 'arrah'] these are true flowers of Rhetoric'. (Portland, though he headed the coalition, acknowledges: 'I am but a make weight amongst you'.) And a print published by J. Barrow, characterising ministers as the *Golden-Pippin Boys, on the Branches of State*[48] casts Burke as their apologist: 'Apple Stealing began at old Adam, and will only die with old Time'. The reality was quite the reverse. Burke, widely read on Indian affairs and a leading member of the House of Commons select committee, was already moving to confront one of the great apple-gatherers, the Governor General of India, and preparing what history would call 'Fox's East India Bill' to bring under public control the wealthy and powerfully connected East India Company: not, it would seem, the action of a placeman seeking to secure his own golden pippins.

One whose golden pippins had been gathered was Sir Philip Francis. Probably bought off as 'Junius'[49] with a post worth £10,000 a year, Francis had gone to India in 1774 as one of the newly appointed members of the supreme council in Bengal, where his violent quarrels with the Governor General culminated in his being shot and wounded in a duel in 1780. Returning to England with a large fortune he became a superb, if dangerous, source of information for Burke[50] and his select committee, whose remit was widened to consider how 'the greatest Security and Advantage to this Country, and . . . the Happiness of the Native Inhabitants may be best promoted'.[51]

On 17 April 1783 in the House of Commons Burke 'pledged himself to God, to his country, to that House and to the unfortunate people of India, to bring to justice as far as in him lay, the greatest delinquent that India ever saw'.[52]

CHAPTER THREE

CARLO KHAN

The India Bill, and Loss of Government, 1783–85

Shortly before he died, Burke wrote of his contribution to Indian affairs: 'Let everything I have done, said or written, be forgotten but this'.[1] His industry over many years in mastering this subject in all its scale and complexity was remarkable. As P.J. Marshall notes, 'The sources of his knowledge may in some cases have been tainted, but Burke brought much experience of public affairs, a powerful mind, an unyielding conscience, and a decisive if, his critics might add, a somewhat erratic judgement to bear on all that he learnt'.[2]

His deliberations led him by 1783 to the belief that the East India Company was so corrupt as to be unfit to run its own affairs, and that the directors and general court of the company should be replaced by commissioners appointed under statute to oversee its conduct and manage its commerce. Fox was persuaded of the necessity for this course, though only too aware of the strength of the private interests they were taking on: for at issue was the enormous wealth and patronage of India. And he knew the opposition would seize it as 'a most tempting opportunity'.[3] What he underestimated was the extent to which the King, in his determination to destroy the coalition he detested, would be prepared to intervene in the parliamentary contest. When Fox moved the East India bill in the House of Commons in November 1783 he was embarking on a course that would bring down the administration.[4] Throughout, the caricaturists were on hand to gloat.

Sayers did most of the damage, damning the proposals as *A Transfer of East India Stock*.[5] Fox carrying off on his shoulders the great prize of East India House was a skilfully wounding accusation that he had wrested it from the directors and shareholders for the enrichment instead of his own nominees. *Carlo Khan's triumphal Entry into Leadenhall Street* (Plate 39) is probably Sayers's most famous satire. Fox called it the most effective blow at the India bill, while Nathaniel Wraxall wrote of this and *A Transfer of East India Stock* 'it is difficult to conceive the moral operation and wide diffusion of these caricatures through every part of the country'.[6] Fox, a triumphant oriental prince (who for years to come will be dubbed Carlo Khan) rides into Leadenhall Street, headquarters of the company, on the back of the great elephant North. A flag which had proclaimed 'The Man of the People' has been altered to pronounce him (in Greek) 'King of Kings'. Leading the elephant is the draughtsman of the bill, Edmund Burke; his Jesuit's garb has been abandoned in favour of oriental costume, and he blows strenuously on a trumpet. But perched on a chimney pot above, a raven – bird of ill omen – croaks forebodingly.

Of fifteen prints on Burke and the East India bill, only two show sympathy for the coalition. One is *Confucius the Second; or, a New Sun Rising in the Asiatic World*[7] and is based on Burke's account (in his speech of 1 December 1783) of the wrongs perpetrated against the begums of the Indian state of Oudh and against Chait Singh, the Rajah of Benares. The begums, grandmother and mother of the vizier of Oudh, who was deeply indebted to the East India Company, had suffered the seizure of their

53

Carlo Khan's triumphal Entry into Leadenhall Street.

Plate 2.   Published 5th Dec 1783 by Thomas Cornell Bruton Street.

39. James Sayers: *Carlo Khan's triumphal Entry into Leadenhall Street*. Published 5 December 1783, by Thomas Cornell. BM 6276; private collection.
In this celebrated print Sayers represents the coalition leaders as a circus troupe triumphantly taking over Leadenhall Street, headquarters of the East India Company. The lumbering Lord North carries a relaxed Fox, and is led on by Burke who – the most active of the three – publicises their presence.

40. [John Boyne]: *The Retreat of Carlo Khan from Leadenhall St*. Published 24 December 1783, by E. Hedges. BM 6285; private collection.
All is changed from Plate 39. Lord North has been transformed from elephant to donkey, and his bridle is now held by the City of London who wields the lash of Public Resentment. The clouds are rolling away from India House which is inscribed 'Business done as usual'.

41. Anon.: *The Fall of Carlo Khan*. Published 24 December 1783, by D. Brown. BM 6286; private collection.
Carlo Khan's triumphal entry of Plate 39 has turned into a rout. Fox complains of 'Secret Influence' as he tumbles to the ground, while Burke is about to trip over his own 'Plans of Oeconomy'.

property and treasures on the authorisation of Hastings to make good the vizier's obligations. In the caricature, Burke and North on elephants – North's is inscribed 'Plunder Restored 1[7]83' – approach 'the unfortunate prince, Cheit Sing' and 'the plundered Princesses, the begums of Oude'. Burke, dressed as a Jesuit, points to the rising sun, which is Fox; while pillagers from the East India Company are to be seen on the far side of the Ganges river.

Most prints, however, take the other side in what has all the signs of a propaganda offensive. Typical is the representation of the members of the coalition as *East India Reformers*[8] who have taken over the committee room of India House: Fox excretes on the company's charter, while North gathers for himself a bundle of valuable stocks, and Burke boots out two directors, exclaiming 'I will direct ye'. Elsewhere they are the *S[ta]te Miners*,[9] undermining King, Britannia and the rock of the Constitution, Burke beating the muzzled British lion with a scourge, or they are *Banditti* around a table: North and Fox drinking and others sharing out the spoils, though a rather prim Burke seems oblivious to all this and lost in his 'Plan of Oeconomy'.[10] This last print, by John Boyne, was published on 22 December 1783, four days after the coalition fell. After an easy passage through the Commons the bill had been stopped in its tracks when Earl Temple circulated a written statement he had gained from the King:

> His Majesty allowed Earl Temple to say, that whoever voted for the India Bill was not only not his friend, but would be considered by him as an enemy; and if these words were not strong enough, Earl Temple might use whatever words he might deem stronger and more to the purpose.[11]

The Lords got the message, the bill was defeated and the King despatched officials to take from North and Fox their seals of office. A few days later Boyne, paying homage to Sayers's famous print, depicts *The Retreat of Carlo Khan from Leadenhall Str* (Plate 40). Seated back to front on North – now reduced to an ass – Fox retches into his turban. Using the King's bridle, North is led away by a young woman representing the city of London and brandishing the lash of 'Public Resentment'. A penitent Burke (his first appearance baldheaded) trails behind, his nose buried in the 'Sinners Guide'. From an upstairs window in India House ('Business Done as Usual') the King waves triumphantly. Also published on 24 December is *The Fall of Carlo Khan* (Plate 41) in

GENERAL BLACKBEARD *wounded at the Battle of* LEADENHALL

42. [Thomas Rowlandson] after John Nixon: *The Pit of Acheron.* [January] 1784. BM 6364; private collection. Acheron, here represented as the Thames at Westminster, was the river which the souls of the dead had to cross in order to reach Hades. There the shades of Fox, North and Burke are conjured up from a pot of unsavoury contents. Other ingredients available for the brew include the diminutive figures of Thomas Erskine MP (a future Lord Chancellor) and John Lee, Attorney General in the Fox–North coalition.

43. John Boyne: *General Blackbeard wounded at the Battle of Leadenhall.* Published 5 January [1784], by E . Hedges. BM 6367; private collection.
A parody by the Irish artist John Boyne of Benjamin West's most famous painting, *The Death of Wolfe,* supposes Fox to have been mortally wounded by the defeat of his India Bill. Burke, author of the bill, anxiously proffers a restorative while the actress Perdita Robinson applies smelling salts. She had been Fox's mistress (he moved on, as we shall see, to the Duchess of Devonshire) and, before that, the Prince's; the latter wistfully kisses her hand. Concern shows on the faces of Keppel, Portland, North, Sheridan (kneeling theatrically) and Cavendish. Leadenhall Street was the headquarters of the East India Company.

a style imitative of (and remarkably close to that of) Sayers, and a sequel to his *Triumphal Entry.* Lord North the elephant, prodded and tormented by opponents of the bill, causes Fox to tumble off, while Burke, who has dropped his rein and trumpet, flees before the goaded animal and is about to trip over his 'Plans of Oeconomy'. Pitt in the background shores up India House.

In desperation the King had turned to the 24-year-old Pitt, appointing him Prime Minister on 22 December. But with a majority in the Commons for Fox and North, the 'Mince Pie' administration was not expected to survive much beyond Christmas.[12] The title of a print signed 'Yerac' (attributed to W.P. Carey) sums up the awkward political situation facing the King: *To Day Disliked, and yet perhaps Tomorrow Again in favour. So Fickle is the mind of R[o]y[a]lty!!!*[13] The King has hurled Fox, North and Burke to the ground where they are admonished by the devil: 'So perish all who seek to disturb my empire'. In Burke's hand a paper inscribed 'Fall of Longinus The Sublim[e]' reminds readers that in the first century the Greek writer Longinus had pioneered philosophical studies on the sublime, and implies, perhaps, plagiarism on Burke's part.

To Rowlandson, in a print after the Irish artist John Nixon, (Plate 42) Fox, North and Burke are the plagues of England, conjured up by hags who bring the regicide Macbeth to mind. For Boyne (Plate 43), here anticipating Gillray's great parody of the same picture, Benjamin West's *Death of [General] Wolfe* is the inspiration for showing Fox as *General Blackbeard wounded at the Battle of Leadenhall,*[14] indicating, perhaps, the enormity of the débâcle. As Burke anxiously offers one kind of comfort to the fallen leader, another more congenial to Fox is offered by 'Perdita' Robinson. Her expression at once tender and world-weary, she proffers smelling salts, and copes simultaneously with the attentions of the Prince of Wales, who kisses her hand. (The actress's affairs with both the Prince and Fox had been the subject of earlier prints.)[15]

Another artist, thought to be Samuel Collings, chooses to parody Samuel Butler's *Hudibras:* Fox as the fat hunchback, and Burke as his sectarian squire Ralpho find themselves, like common criminals, in the stocks and contemplating the whipping post, with its wry notice *Otium Cum Dignitate,* leisure with dignity.[16]

As the youthful Prime Minister, Pitt, prepared to offer a more palatable East India bill, Fox's position – as his traducers would have it – is summed up in *The Tryumph of Pitt, or the Man of the People in the Dumps* (Plate 44):

> My Indian Schemes of Wealth & I must fall
> But that this Boy should ride me's Worst of all.

while Burke the Jesuit prays: 'The Lords have pull'd you down may the Lord raise you up again.' Verses printed beneath the title are to be sung to the tune 'an Ass in the Chaplet': whether this is the coronal wreath Fox aspires to, or the rosary in Burke's hand, is a matter for conjecture. The choice of Pitt as Chatham's heir is acclaimed:

> Like the Father the Son does in excellence rise
>   In Eloquence, Honor & Wit,
> Then let us all selfish designers despise
>   But high lift the Bumper to Pitt.

The ensuing parliamentary struggle between Pitt and Fox offered the satirists full scope for theatrical confrontation. There is the spectacle of *The Rival Quacks* in which Fox – together with his zany, 'Burkobus' – and Pitt harangue the mob outside parliament as rival mountebanks.[17] And *The Battle Royal, or who wears the Breeches*, (Plate 45) is a tug of war between the two parties for the Kings's trousers. Deprived of this attire, and missing one half of his crown, the King yet maintains some dignity in the pose of Justice, blindfolded and with sword and scales. Adding his weight to the efforts of Fox, North and Burke is a slight figure thought to be the General (and caricaturist) Viscount Townshend,[18] competing for the post of Master General of the Ordnance. This office is jealously guarded by Richmond on the other side, who peers over his colleagues Pitt, Shelburne and possibly Lord Sydney. Richmond was Fox's uncle, and his passion for fortification earned him the nickname 'Uncle Toby' after the chief character in Sterne's *Tristram Shandy*. The artist does not know the outcome, but forecasts trouble in either event: one picture in the background depicts a scene of 'chaos', the other shows North, Fox and the devil enjoying a game of shuttlecock

44. Anon.: *The Tryumph of Pitt.* 13 January 1784. BM 6374; British Museum.
With India House propped up by the Lords, the city of London and 'Wickham' (either Lord Mahon, MP for Wycombe who opposed Fox's bill or the Earl of Shelburne, who was Baron Wycombe), Pitt sits astride Fox, triumphantly brandishing his 'more palatable East India Bill', while Burke prays for his leader's recovery from such a humiliating fall.

45. Anon.: *The Battle Royal, or who wears the Breeches.* Published 15 January 1784, by W. Humphrey. BM 6375; British Museum. A tug of war for the 'breeches' of government likely to result in their being ripped. The pictures on the wall offer an equally bleak alternative, between chaos, and a game of shuttlecock with the crown.

Satan's officers are characters from Milton's *Paradise Lost*. Keppel's standard proclaims him Asmodeus, the evil demon. Its reference to July 27th again recalls the unfortunate battle of Ushant. Burke is Moloch, the idol to whom children were sacrificed. As Mammon, North personifies the evils of wealth and miserliness, while the Duke of Portland (nominally head of the coalition) bears the standard of Belial, the wicked one.

with the crown, which has been adapted for play with the Prince of Wales's feathers. The bathos of a battle royal over a pair of breeches is all the more pointed in its contrast with the Miltonic *mise-en-scène* of 22 June 1784 (Plate 46), with its suggestions that the Prince of Wales has been making mischief. The satanic Fox (discarding for the moment his mask of geniality) urges the ranks of the majority not to 'bend the supple knee'. He is joined in the review by the Prince. Brimming with self-importance, his love for dressing up has been captured in a splendidly theatrical pose as he tramples under foot his motto 'Ich Dien', I serve. Burke, 'Moleck the Sublime & BEAUTIFULL' wears the grim smile of a zealot.[19]

A Prince who will not serve, Fox as Satan, Burke as Moloch: the constitutional implications of this abuse are serious. And this line of attack is sustained by an anonymous caricaturist who shows the crowned British lion being chained and blindfolded by Fox, North and Burke (Plate 47), usurpers of the royal prerogative.[20] To another, etching anonymously, Fox is *Cromwell ye 2nd Exalted* on a gallows (Plate 48), his two companions below him,[21] and in what may be more a play on names than real constitutional charge, Fox (assisted by Burke and other conspirators) is *Guy Vaux*, and blows up Pitt's India bill.[22]

The King's prominent role, too, is the subject of satire. He is St George, slayer of the three-headed dragon.[23] He is Hercules (Plate 49).[24] He is Jove (Plate 50), victorious over *The British Titans*, Fox, Burke and North. But in a print supportive of the trio (Plate 51) he is Nebuchadnezzar – a traditional archetype of the royal tyrant[25] – to their Shadrach, Meshach and Abednego, and receives the due response: 'Know O King that we *will not* worship ye Golden Image'. The golden image is Pitt, placed on a pedestal of 'Family Presumption' and described below:

> Not all that glitter's Gold, alass,
> Your baby's but a thing of Brass.

A motley assortment make obeisance, including representatives from Burke's old constituency of Bristol, while His Majesty soars above the scene on a balloon of

47. Anon.: *Frontispiece* [16 February 1784], from *The Beauties and Deformities of Fox, North and Burke.* BM 6411; British Museum.

While North blindfolds, and Fox chains, the British lion, here symbol of the King, Burke retains custody of the lock and key. Britannia, meanwhile, turns for help to her new champion William Pitt, suitably irradiated by the rising sun.

48. Anon.: *Cromwell ye 2nd Exalted*. Published 1 March 1784, by S. Fores. BM 6432; private collection.

North (right) and Burke intone the Anglican prayer of general confession beneath their hanged companion, Fox, charged in propaganda as another Cromwell. The poison bag refers to an incident in which a leather bag with noxious contents was thrown into Fox's face on 14 February in Westminster Hall.

49. Anon.: *The Royal Hercules Destroying The Dragon Python*. Published April [1784], by [J.] Hedges. Not in BM Cat.: The Pierpont Morgan Library, New York. Peel Collection No. 107.
The King crushes a creature with the heads of Fox, North and Burke. Burke spews out a turban, symbol of the untold wealth that might have accrued from the East India Bill, and jeeringly labelled 'Oeconomy'.

50. [Samuel Collings]: *The British Titans*. Published 23 Feb 1784, by W. Wells. BM 6419; British Museum. George III is Jove, and Fox Typhon, despatched from the heavens by a mighty thunderbolt to join other Titans, Burke, Lord John Cavendish and North in the infernal regions below. While the King's actions are being guided by Thurlow, prominence is given to the boyish Pitt nearby. His irradiated head is covered in a laurel wreath that vies with the royal crown of prerogative. Isaac Barré, grateful for favours done, rests his hand supportingly on Pitt's shoulder.

'Prerogative' that emits suggestively a gas labelled 'Gracious Answer'. In another image, armed with his sword of 'Prerogative' he is shown trying to drag *The Unfortunate Ass*,[26] the people, down the road of absolute monarchy. Fox is restraining him, saying 'I humbly Insist upon the management or else will not grant any Supplys'. (In an attempt to displace Pitt, Fox had moved that the payment of money for public services be cut off after the prorogation or dissolution of parliament, for which Sayers portrayed him as Cromwell.)[27] Elsewhere the monarch's action is more favourably received: in one print, though surrounded and threatened by serpents with the heads of Burke ('Deceit'), Fox ('Ambition') and North ('Envy')[28] he vows from his seat of 'Preroga[tive]' that 'I will maintain my dignity tho' I have but Half a Crown left'. Fox's confidence of success is illustrated by a Rowlandson print in which he, Burke and other 'robbers' have taken over 'the Old House in Little Brittain', George III's tavern, while the sleeping landlord is being bundled off to Hanover.[29]

But the tide was turning against the Whigs, and Fox's majority began to ebb away. *The Fox & Badger Hunting the Ki[n]g's Hounds* (Plate 52) lampoons 'Rat Catcher' John Robinson, the former Treasury Secretary, and his rats, the MPs he induced to desert

THE ROYAL HERCULES *Destroying* THE DRAGON
PYTHON

THE BRITISH
TITANS.

THE GOLDEN IMAGE

that NEBUCHADNEZZAR THE KING had set up.

A Gilded Image - & before it -
A Mob on Marrow-bones adore it
That immemorial time have sold
All conscience to his God-ship Gold'. -

Look ere you leap & scan the PIT',
Your sapient worships may be bit
Not all that glitter'd Gold, alas,
Your baby's but a thing of Brass.

51. 'Annibal Scratch' [attributed to Samuel Collings]:
*The Golden Image that Nebuchadnezzar the King had set
up.* Published 11 March 1784, by W. Wells. BM 6445;
British Museum.
'Annibal Scratch', thought to be the pseudonym of
Collings, is an appropriate nod to the inventor of
caricature at the beginning of the seventeenth century,
Annibale Carracci.

52. Anon.: *The Fox & Badger Hunting The K[in]g's
Hounds.* Published 28 February 1784, by W.
Humphrey. BM 6428; British Museum.
Three rats have been induced to join John Robinson
and the King's supporters in parliament, shown in the
background as 'St Stephen's Kennell'.

THE FOX & BADGER HUNTING THE K — G'S HOUNDS.

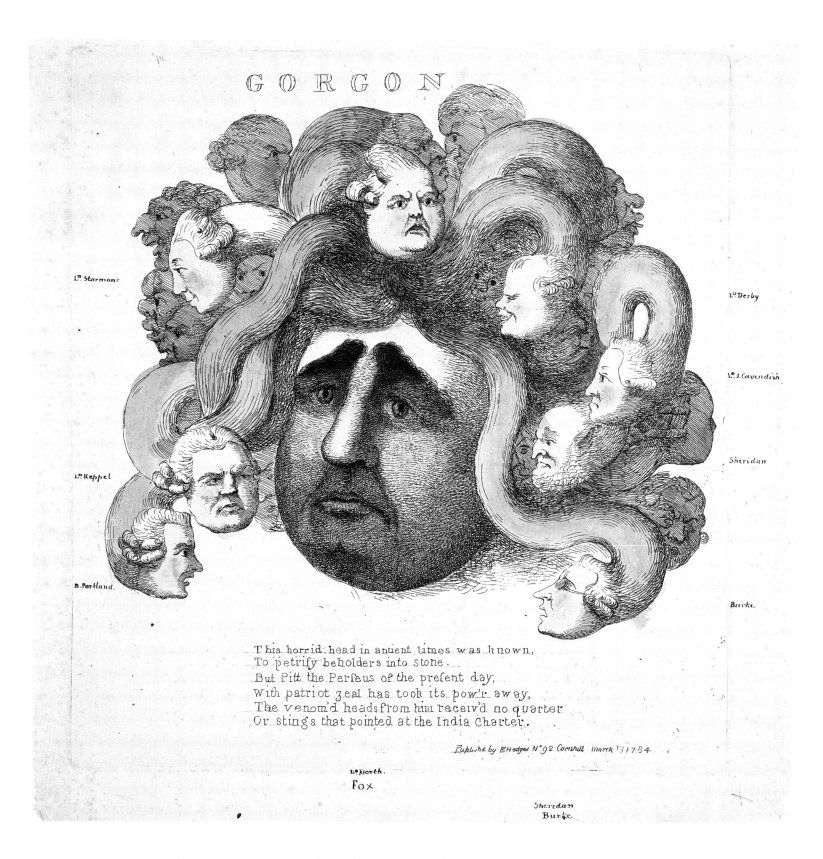

GORGON

Lᵈ Starmont

Lᵈ Derby

Lᵈ J.Cavendish

Sheridan

Lᵈ Keppel

D. Portland.

Burke

This horrid head in antient times was known,
To petrify beholders into stone,
But Pitt the Perseus of the present day,
With patriot zeal has took its pow'r away,
The venom'd heads from him receiv'd no quarter
Or stings that pointed at the India Charter.

Publish'd by E Hedges Nᵒ 92 Cornhill March 13.17.84.

Lᵈ North.

Fox

Sheridan
Burke

53. Anon.: *Gorgon*. Published 13 March 1784, by E. Hedges. BM 6450; British Museum.
Fox is one of the Gorgons of classical mythology whose head, covered with ministerial serpents, is a trophy to be claimed by Pitt, 'the Perseus of the present day'.

to Pitt with prospects of pensions and places (*see* page 23).[30] Chased by Fox, North and Burke (in biretta, and blowing a horn as if again calling the tune) Robinson runs behind Pitt and other hounds who have been joined by three rats. The quick-witted Sheridan put an old phrase to use when denouncing 'a certain member' employed to corrupt MPs by buying votes; on cries of 'name him!' he declined, saying it would be invidious, but added 'I could do that Sir, as soon as you could say Jack Robinson'.[31]

By 8 March 1784, Fox's majority was reduced to one. In one of the prints that reflect the impending defeat he is portrayed as the *Gorgon* (Plate 53) among whose hair of ministerial serpents Burke is prominent. Beneath are the lines:

> This horrid head in antient times was known
> To petrify beholders into stone.
> But Pitt the Perseus of the present day,
> With patriot zeal has took its pow'r away.
> The venom'd heads from him receiv'd no quarter
> Or stings that pointed at the India Charter.

Burke's spectacles, it seems, are by now so well known that in an illustrated broadside their magical properties can be offered for the use of the King. *The Ganders addressing the Lion*[32] are supporters of the coalition anxious for the removal of the 'stripling Elephant', Pitt, in favour of their 'noble Bear and Fox':

> Besides our noble Renard has
> A pair of Spectacles of glass,
> which if your Majesty but chose,
> to let him place upon your nose,
> h'ed make you see in darkest night
> whatever he thinks wrong or right.

The response is polite and to the point:

> For Spectacles we have no need,
> But thank ye as much, as if we did.

Burke's spectacles will often be used to point up his peculiar or exaggerated vision of the world (sometimes explicitly, as here, or in Plates 76, 113, 161; more often implicitly, as, for instance in Plate 152).

In another publication, the youthful Pitt, on a pedestal over the bodies of North and Fox, embodies *The Triumph of Virtue*[33] as his foot traps a serpent, Burke. The print is described below the design: 'The Pitt is raised, the Fox is fallen, The North-wind ceases, and Edmund Reassumes his Native Self'.

Puns abound. Fox, inevitably, is *Reynard caught at last or the [Fox] in a Pitt*[34] and wails from the hole: 'I shall be lost for ever in the depth of this terrible Pitt'. Burke, dressed not as a Jesuit but in deep mourning, observes (in a complete travesty of his position): 'I think as matters are now it will be my wisest way not to assist you any longer'. He and North had, in fact, offered to forgo office if a coalition of Pitt and Fox could be thus secured.[35] Country gentlemen meeting at the St Alban's tavern – among their number were Thomas Powys and Charles Marsham, MP for Kent – mooted such a coalition and William Dent renders this as *The Countryman's Dream of Coalescing Virtue and Vice* (Plate 54). Powys, asleep in his chair, imagines the happy scene. To the pipe and drum of the Prince of Wales, Pitt's angelic supporters Richmond, Shelburne, and Thurlow, haloes shining, dance around the maypole of George III with Burke, Fox and Portland given devils' horns. North, also with horns but dressed as a nanny, hugs an infant Pitt to his bosom. Such a coalition, negotiations for which had been approved with utmost reluctance by the King, would be seen as victory for Fox. The King watches *A Race for a Crown* (Plate 55) with the weeping Queen, and resigns himself to present the coveted prize to Fox's connections, but it was Pitt (here just a steward at the winning post) who prevailed in the struggle. Parliament was dissolved on 25 March 1784 and, in a design published next day, Pitt

THE COUNTRYMAN'S DREAM OF COALESCING VIRTUE AND VICE.

Round about the Maypole see how we trot, hot pot, hot, brown Ale we have got — — — — — — — — Midas.

54. William Dent: *The Countryman's Dream of Coalescing Virtue And Vice.* Published 20 March 1784, by J. Ridgway. BM 6457; private collection. Thomas Powys (left) nods off to sleep, dreaming of a new coalition involving Pitt, while his colleague Charles Marsham has drafted a resolution 'That Union may be effected without Principil'. As 'Messrs. Powass and Mash'em, Dealers in British Spirits' they have become proprietors of St Alban's tavern.

is shown to eclipse Fox, and his 'Fiends of Darkness'.[36] One of the verses below runs thus:

> Let Reynard delight in his Cards and [h]is Dice,
> Lord N[orth] and B[urke] both may Glory in Vice,
> But the Virtues of Pitt tho he is but a Youth,
> Shines with Lustre Supreme for Speaking the Truth.

Another artist drapes Burke and Sheridan in heavy mourning worthy of a theatrical costumier, to weep over the great marble tomb of North and Fox (Plate 56). Gallows nooses, dangling from the head of the monument, indicate their fate, 'The True Reward of Such Virtues'.

The King's obvious pleasure at the outcome of events is the subject of *Solomon in the Clouds*.[37] Held aloft in the air by Thurlow, Pitt and Temple, he excretes a great blast inscribed 'Proclamation for Dissolution from a Broad Bottom'. It had been a hazardous affair. Writing to Pitt on 23 December 1783 George had described himself as 'on the Edge of a Precipice'[38] and a print in early February suggests the King in his zeal could well follow Fox, North and Burke into the abyss to which – as mighty

55. Anon.: *A Race for a Crown*. Published 20 March 1784, by G. Humphrey. BM 6459; British Museum. The crown itself is depicted as being at stake in the general election of 1784. Pitt, who actually won the election, looks on from the winning post as Fox (right) and North lead the field. If the royal party appears distressed, the response of the racegoers is more likely to reflect the outcome of their wagers.

56. Anon.: *The Tombs of the Worthies*. Published 27 March 1784, by M. Smith. BM 6470; British Museum. Fox and North, recumbent under a pair of nooses, are mourned by Burke ('Sublime & Beautifull') and Sheridan ('Theatrical Justice' and 'The Critic'). They are interred in the company of Wat Tyler, the leader of the Peasants' Revolt of 1381 and Jonathan Wild, the notorious thief and informer hanged at Tyburn in 1725. And an ironic memorial (left) has been erected to the 'virtues of Jemmy Twitcher', the nickname for Lord Sandwich, who had retired in 1782 as First Lord of the Admiralty.

57. Anon.: *Dissolution*. Published 6 February 1784, by
B. Walwyn. BM 6404; British Museum.
From the edge of the precipice, George III, as Jupiter –
driven by Pitt, Temple, Richmond and Sydney – hurls
his thunderbolts at Burke, North and Fox, whose rival
crown has been lost.

Jupiter – he hurls thunderbolts of *Dissolution* (Plate 57). If Jupiter determines the
course of human affairs, it is his ministers, Pitt, Temple, Richmond, and Sydney who
have propelled his chariot to the edge.

For the King's opponents, the longer-term consequences of the 'back-stairs'
intriguing by Earl Temple and the court were viewed with apprehension:

> The *book* of the *generations* of *parliament*: – Charles Fox *begat* the India Bill, and the
> India Bill *begat* Opposition; Opposition *begat* Lord Temple, and Lord Temple *begat*
> Secret Advice; Secret Advice *begat* the Back-stairs, and the Back-stairs *begat* the
> Dismission; the Dismission *begat* a new Ministry, and a new Ministry *begat* a
> Dissolution; a Dissolution *begat* a General Election, and a General Election *begat*
> D–n–d Lies; D–n–d Lies *begat* a Majority, and a Majority will *beget* what they
> please.[39]

The ensuing general election was bitterly contested and prompted many satires,
especially on Fox's own campaign in the two-seat Westminster constituency. The
British Museum catalogue for 1784 records about 150 prints on the dissolution and
election. Of these, two-thirds are anti-Foxite, a fifth against Fox's constituency
opponent Sir Cecil Wray, and only a tiny handful attack Pitt himself. Rowlandson
(perhaps commissioned to work up plates from sketched suggestions) seems to have
been happy to row in on both sides. Dent and Boyne were for Pitt, as (more often
than not) were the artists tentatively identified as Barrow, Collings and Phillips. Only
one print is attributed to Gillray;[40] he will be recruited by the government in the
following Westminster contest in 1788. The Irish artist W.P. Carey seems to have
been on Fox's side as was, occasionally, Isaac Cruikshank. Another admirer was the
drawing master and caricaturist William Austin (*see* Plate 3), mocked by Paul Sandby
as *Fox's Fool*,[41] but no British Museum prints of this period are attributed to him.

Representing Fox as quack, or devil, or plague, and Burke as Jesuit, or serpent, or
personified deceit, illustrates the expressive range of the satire, which was

supplemented by all the cruelties of personal caricature. And in the election struggle, the caricaturist's efforts were only part of a broader propaganda battle. It was one of unprecedented scale, waged in newspaper accounts and advertisements, real and parodied, in ballads, and squibs and mock elegies.

Contesting for the government side against Fox were Samuel Hood, a celebrated naval commander, and Wray, a former yeomanry captain, less distinguished. Hood, who had been given the freedom of the city of London in 1782 and made a baron in the Irish peerage, headed the poll from the third day and always looked certain to take the first seat. Wray, on the other hand, had been brought in by Fox at a by-election and now, to keep his seat, was changing sides. Opposition propagandists quickly had him in their sights, denouncing him as a Judas and mocking infelicitous proposals he had made recently in parliament. One was to demolish Chelsea Hospital which housed – uneconomically, he felt – elderly and incapacitated army pensioners:

> Whilst such men as Sir Cecil were quarrelling in the house of commons about the distribution of political loaves and fishes . . . they [the troops] allow themselves to be shot at for about fourpence threefarthings per day for the good of their country, and the prospect of being *amply* provided for in *Chelsea Hospital* with a pitcher of broth and a flannel night-cap.[42]

Votes were cheerfully extorted by both sides. A Foxite paragraph claimed that 'The Pages of the Back Stairs have been hard at work in favour of the Court candidates all over the kingdom: How do you vote Mr Dip? Their Majesties admire your candles amazingly. Mr Putty, you'll give Sir – a plumper . . . Upon my honour their Majesties mean to have all their windows new glazed'.[43]

Voting in the two-seat Westminster constituency was confined to householders, i.e. those who were liable to pay poor-rates. The scope for cheating was plain as was the scope for partisan reporting. One account notes that 'after having exhausted the Royal Kitchen, the Scullery, the Buttery, the Mews, military renegadoes, and civil raggamuffins, the creatures of the Court were forced to attempt the gross fraud of passing garreteers and inhabitants of cellars as honest voters in the poll of yesterday'.[44] Not everything went according to plan, so when 'the noble itinerant' Lord Mountmorres, an Irish peer, was rejected by the High Bailiff, Wray's devoted supporter Mrs Hobart, 'in all her fatness, foeculence and phlegm, hung her head in shame and sorrow'.[45]

The vote of Lloyd Kenyon, former Attorney General and now Master of the Rolls, was noted with sarcasm. 'His house is in the parish of St Giles, but he voted for a little *back-room* which projects into Portugal Street . . . That a man of his rank, and who lately filled the first law office of the Crown, should descend to vote as the *occupier* of a *back-room,* three yards square, in a city w[h]ere the right of election is in *housekeepers,* shows to what shifts the Court is driven in the present struggle.'[46] Or, as another wit put it, 'that new *luminary* of the *legal hemisphere* Sir H. Lloyd Kenyon, Master of the Rolls, having only a *stable* in Westminster, gave the suffrages of his two *dock'd coach horses* by *proxy,* to Lord Hood and Sir Cecil Wray.'[47]

Fox was receiving similar treatment at the hands of the *Morning Post* and the *Public Advertiser* and his supporters were said to be 'pimps, brothel-keepers, quack doctors, uncertificated bankrupts, blacklegs, and blackguards of all denominations'.[48] Thus a scrutiny of the ballots was forecast if Fox succeeded, for 'It is certain, that the majority of those who have hitherto polled for that Gentleman, had a most suspicious appearance. Their *drapery,* and other circumstances about, renders the validity of their votes extremely questionable'.[49] And heaven forbid that Fox might yet form an

administration, for then the Prince's cook, Mr Weltje, 'and two or three of the head waiters [at Brooks's Club] are certainly to be brought into parliament; and, perhaps, made Bank or India Directors'.[50]

Meanwhile a wag reveals the contents of Pitt's 'Secret Service Ledger', showing payments liberally dispersed to the proprietors of 'the M[ornin]g P[os]t', 'the P[ubli]c A[dvertise]r' and other unnamed papers, 'several print shops', ' Mr – for his indecent engravings', 'Mr P[itt]'s paragraph puffers,' 'the porter-house brawlers' and so on.[51]

One source of support for Fox raised eyebrows. At a dinner given by his committee for nearly five hundred electors Lord George Gordon addressed the company, 'and in a speech of near half an hour (full of good sense) strongly exhorted every true friend of religion, and the laws of his country, to support Mr Fox'.[52] It was Gordon, fanatical and unbalanced, whose petition against the Catholic Relief Act of 1778 had sparked off the no-popery riots of June 1780. For a few days London had appeared to be out of control and Burke's house had been one of those threatened by the violent mob. Gordon's support of Fox must have made Burke queasy, at the very least, and it was seized upon by Fox's detractors: 'Nothing can be more ridiculous, nor more unlikely than that Lord George Gordon has given his interest in Westminster to Mr Fox: it surely would be the height of inconsistency in that nobleman to support one who has already polled 300 Catholics [illegal votes], and whose warmest advocates are among the friends to popery'.[53] Warming to the theme, a later paragraph invokes a persona familiar in the caricatures and accuses *The Jesuit of St Omer's* of contemptuously throwing the Bible away on the hustings at Covent Garden, the day he took the election oath.[54] And for the purpose of satire another child is invented for Burke: 'A treaty of marriage is said to be on foot between the Right Honourable Lord George Gordon and Miss B. daughter of Edmund B. Esq. *Lord Rector of Glasgow*! This unexpected coalition of parties will, it is thought, be productive of much public benefit; for, by moderating *fanaticism* on the one side, and flexifying *bigotry* on the other, who knows but that a *mass and a meeting house* may, in a short time, become nearly one and the same thing!'[55]

Elsewhere Burke is said to be writing 'a kind of *political elegy*, on the late house of commons; the plan is copied from Grey's Church Yard. There is to be a great quantity of sentiment in it, and such a display of *tropes* and figures, as shall make *old womens* eyes twinkle while they read it. Alas ! poor Edmund!'[56]

John Boyne's caricature study (Plate 58) of Burke as *Ignatius* [Loyola], could well be set in a country churchyard. Resting his book on a rock, the bareheaded Jesuit writes with a serenity that belies the turbulence of the desperate campaign being waged. Maybe it is the robe (more appropriate to a monk than to a Jesuit) but Boyne, not for the first time (*see* Plate 43) gives him a bulk that contrasts with the almost emaciated figure Gillray, for one, imagines (*see* Plates 29 and 38). Indeed, a thinner and decidedly more anxious Burke than Boyne's well-fed Ignatius stares out from another print of March 1784 (Plate 59). 'Oeconomy' is a pressing, and depressing matter for a political leader who must darn his own stocking.

Both sides in the Westminster contest were accused of violence and intimidation. An advertisement complains of 'A great riot and confusion having taken place yesterday at the Hustings, instigated entirely by a banditti of hired seamen' by which Fox's supporters were prevented from voting.[57] Fox for his part was said to have 'a desperate banditti of Irish Chairmen and Pick-pockets', and 'desperadoes with marrow-bones and cleavers'.[58] From sources such as *The History of The Westminster Election,* it appears that London's chairmen were predominantly Irish. An account of 6 April 1784 reports that the sailors (supporters of their admiral, Lord Hood) 'went to

58. John Boyne: *Ignatius*. Published 28 March 1784, by E. Hedges. BM 6472; British Museum.
Burke is named after Ignatius Loyola, the Spanish founder of the Jesuit order.

59. Anon.: *Every Man in His Humour* (detail). Published 'Febʸ 6 March 1784' [*sic*], by B. Walwyn. BM 6439; British Museum.
The heavy cost of purchasing a landed estate at Beaconsfield, coupled with disastrous stock investments, created financial burdens for Burke into old age.

60. Anon.: *Paddy Whacks's First Ride in a Sedan*. Published 28 January 1800, by Laurie & Whittle. Not in BM Cat.; private collection.
Xenophobic sentiments are widespread in English caricature; the Irish (who fared no worse than the Scots and the Welsh) were regarded as domestic foreigners, at one end fortune-hunters; at the other 'bog-trotters' who were resented in London for undercutting labouring wages. Many of the chairmen were Irish and took Fox's side against Admiral Hood's sailors.

61. John Boyne: *Bottom Snout & Quince*. Published 15 April 1784, by J. Wallis. BM 6534; British Museum.
Fox's choice of the Shakespeare tavern as election headquarters offered his detractors theatrical scope: for Boyne Fox is Bottom the Weaver in *A Midsummer Night's Dream*, North is Snout, and Burke Quince. Missing is the Duchess of Devonshire who might have played the spell-bound Titania, queen of the fairies.

PADDY WHACK'S FIRST RIDE IN A SEDAN.

238   *Arrah! my dear Honey - to be sure I'd rather walk, if it wasn't for the Fashion of the thing.*
Published 28 Jan.ᵗ 1800, by LAURIE & WHITTLE, 53 Fleet Street, London.

BOTTOM SNOUT & QUINCE *Vide Shakespeare*
London Published April 15.ᵗ 1784 by J. Wallis N°.14 Ludgate St.

St James's-street, intending to cut the chairs, but on their arrival they met with a very rough welcome from the Paddies'.[59] The foibles of the chairmen are recounted occasionally in social prints, and the fun – more patronising than hostile – is heightened when they take on board an Irish customer (Plate 60).

Burke appears occasionally in prints about the campaign. He is seen with North and Fox as *The Coalition Party Beating up for Recruits*.[60] 'Join the Coalition,' says Burke to a ragged recruit, 'and you shall be Cloathed'. In a print by Dent the heads of North, Fox and Burke adorn *The Political Cerberus*[61] who stands guard at the entrance not to the infernal regions but the Treasury. The collar of Cerberus sports the feathers of the Prince of Wales. Dent's sequel is to put the three heads on spikes at Temple Bar, and Burke's headless body is inscribed 'Hypocrisy'.[62] Having chosen the Shakespeare tavern as his election headquarters, Fox is given a role by Boyne from *A Midsummer Night's Dream* (Plate 61): he is the mock-heroic Bottom, whose ass's head startles his companions Snout and Quince (North and Burke). 'Bless Thee Bottom Bless thee', says Quince, 'thou art Translated'.

Fox's position in the election was initially precarious. Stretched out on a table, he is mourned by Burke in *The Soliloquy of Reynard*[63] and his is the apex of *The Tottering Pyramid* of heads (Plate 62) published on 11 April when he was still trailing badly in third place.[64] He is supported by the Prince of Wales ('If his Highness Wags a Feather I'm down') who thinks it timely to suggest that 'It deserves an Increase of Establishment to be thus Situated'. The Prince's head, in turn rests on those of North and Burke, who grumbles: 'Mine is not an Oeconomical Situation'. A Foxite paper deplores the treatment being meted out to the Prince: 'His follies and imprudences have been blazoned and exaggerated by every art of scandal and sting of malice . . . We are told, that he is addicted to play; that he is attached to women; and that he is

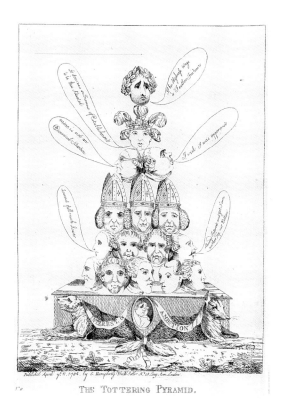

THE TOTTERING PYRAMID.

62. [John Boyne]: *The Tottering Pyramid*. Published 11 April 1784, by G. Humphrey. BM 6518; British Museum.
Although Fox's position is clearly more precarious than anyone else's, North (placed beside Burke in the hierarchy) envies his place at the apex. The three supporting bishops are thought to be the Whigs Hinchcliffe (Peterborough), Shipley (St Asaph) and Watson (Llandaff), who had all opposed the American war.

a friend to the bottle; none however of these can truly be called faults of the heart: they rather perhaps, at an early period of life, are the characteristics of latent generosity and an expanding mind . . .'[65]

No aspect of the Westminster election provoked more comment than the hugely effective canvassing by Georgiana, Duchess of Devonshire on Fox's behalf. In an untitled print portraying Fox and Burke in a debtor's jail as Hudibras and Ralpho,[66] she is Hudibras's lady who visits the pair and releases them. According to his biographer, Fox had started an affair with her in 1782 that seems to have lasted nearly two years. 'The Duchess of Devonshire turned Devonshire House into a gambling den', notes L.G. Mitchell, 'and endlessly deceived her husband, who was a booby'.[67] Linda Colley argues that as an ardent Whig and political hostess in London she served, rather, as the platonic confidante of Fox and the Prince of Wales, and only later had an adulterous affair with Charles Grey.[68] In any event, Horace Walpole reckoned that the Duchess 'certainly procured the greatest part of Mr Fox's votes for him: though the Court Party endeavoured to deter her by the most illiberal and indecent abuse . . .'[69] An example, typical in its coarseness, is provided by *A D[evonshir]e rout or Reynard in his Element* (Plate 63). Boreas, the north wind [Lord North], has lifted the Duchess's dress as she canvasses on the arm of Fox. Burke drops to his hands and knees to peer lewdly under her petticoats: 'Heavens how happily the principels of the Sublime and Butiful are blended'. She smiles archly: 'The Favourable assistance of Bor[e]as is very gratefull when heated by the fatigues of Canvasing'. Some supporters are also enjoying the spectacle; one, a corpulent butcher (mindful of Wray's demand at this stage for an examination of the ballots cast) says 'I thought we were all to avoid a Scrutany if Possible'.

If the caricaturists leered at the delicious young Duchess, they also ridiculed Wray's supporter, the lumpish Mrs Hobart, Rowlandson depicting her as 'Madam Blubber'.[70] While Rowlandson burlesqued Mrs Hobart as a human air balloon[71] offering the novelty of conveying voters to the hustings 'aerostatically' (a pastime that was all the rage in London), the kisses by which her rival was supposed to cajole votes for Fox were the subject of lewd and indecent satire. One advertisement hailed Fox as 'that *in*famous Stallion, called CARLO KHAN got by *Public Defaulter*, out of *Unaccounted Millions*, and now so strained and broke down "He will never be able to *enter* again, unless for the private amusement of all canvassing wives"'.[72] The Duchess was much discomfited, writing to her mother: 'I am unhappy here beyond measure and abus'd for nothing. Yet as it is begun I must go on with it . . . My sister and Lady [name illegible] were both kiss'd, so it's very hard I who was not should have the reputation of it.'[73] Linda Colley points out that while the prints against the Duchess 'have usually attracted attention only for their facile obscenity . . . It was the unnaturalness of female participation in the public sphere that the cartoonists returned to again and again'.[74] One example she cites is a print of 5 May 1784, *The Devonshire Amusement*, which shows a discontented Duke at home changing nappies while, with roles reversed, she enjoys the excitements of the hustings.[75] (Another version of the print was published on 24 June, showing its continuing popularity.)[76]

Reaction to the prints about Georgiana was as divided as the contest itself. On the one side: 'The print shops exhibit in the most striking colours the depravity of the present day, and laudably expose the *temporary familiarity* so very prominent between the great and little vulgar. When titled personages deign to become associates with the lowest publicans, to copy their manners, and meanly solicit their favours, the sarcasm and indecencies to which they expose themselves cannot be too plainly or too

A.D.[evonshire] E. ROUT OR REYNARD IN HIS ELEMENT.

63. Anon.: *A D[evonshir]e rout or Reynard in his Element*. Published 26 April 1784, by F. Clarkson. BM 6555; British Museum.
The Duchess of Devonshire, 'heated by the fatigues of Canvasing' for Fox, is cooled by the draught of the North wind which lifts her skirts for the benefit of a kneeling Burke. Fox may be in his element, but the Duchess would be familiar with more fashionable routs.

publicly held out as the just rewards of their affected humility, and specious condescension'.[77]

On the other side, however, condemnation was scathing. 'The prints exhibited on the late change of politics are in general scurrilous, abusive, destitute of merit, wit and humour, seemingly calculated to draw a gaping and idle multitude together . . . A female character of illustrious rank and beauty, to be exhibited to the vulgar in the most indecent and obscene attitudes and conversations, is a disgrace to the artist, a disgrace to his employer, but more so to the police: at least, our City Magistrates should have taken notice of, and put a stop to so glaring a nuisance, tending to extinguish the remaining spark of morality of the present age'.[78] But it appears that if the magistrates were not prepared to act then others were, for news comes to hand that 'Yesterday afternoon a party of gentlemen waited upon the proprietors of the several print shops in the Strand, and remonstrated with them upon the impropriety of exposing in their windows the several shameful and indecent prints on the most amiable of female characters: the shopkeepers admitted the grossness of such an

THE POLITICAL CLUSTER
in terrorem.

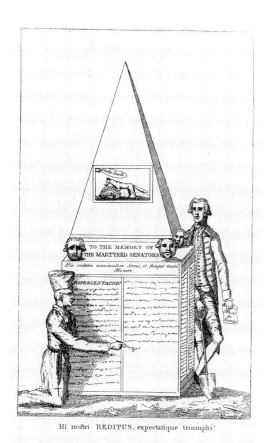

Hi nostri REDITUS, expectatique triumphi!

exhibition, and very handsomely promised to prevent it in future . . . Should any other printseller after this be daring enough to continue a display of these wretched caricatures, there is little doubt but he will be convinced of his error by a more *speedy* and *exemplary* punishment than the law of the land may afford.'[79] Clearly some 'convincing' did take place. A newspaper paragraph lamented that the zeal of some of Fox's supporters 'hurried them into some excesses, such as breaking the windows of several shops where prints and caricatures are exhibited, endeavouring to ridicule the cause . . . It is however not to be wondered at, that the people should not tamely submit to such daily insults as are offered to their feelings by these indecent and scandalous exhibitions'.[80] Yet while outraged that the print shops retailed such wicked scandal about the Duchess, Foxites were no doubt delighted to read that 'Mrs H[obar]t has not *ballooned* a single vote to the Hustings, since she was *caracatured* by the unmerciful Viscount [Townshend] of Hanover-square'.[81] Nor was the Duchess unduly cowed by the experience, for she would be back to run the gauntlet again, canvassing for Fox's candidate Lord John Townshend in Westminster in 1788.

In the event, Fox took the second seat after Samuel Hood, to the excitement of his devoted hackney chairmen whose origins, once more, are subtly alluded to:

> Sir Cecil, be aisy, I wont be unshivil
> Now the Man of the Paple is chose in your stead;
> From swate Covent Garden you're flung to the Divil,
> By Jasus, Sir Cecil, you've bodder'd your head.

There is even a sneaking admiration for Mrs Hobart:

> They says Moder Hobart she loves a shelelagh,
> An Irish shelelagh that's fit for the fair;
> Oh! tunder and ouns! what the Divil could ail her,
> To vote for a baist that creaps up the *Back Stair*?[82]

But Wray's demand for a scrutiny of the ballots was granted, and no return was made for the constituency pending the outcome of the scrutiny, which dragged on for nine months. Fox was worried enough to take an alternative seat for Bridgwater & Orkney but, as L.G. Mitchell puts it, 'the indignity of the Man of the People representing twelve voters from islands to the far north of Scotland was ultimately averted', as the scrutiny confirmed him in his Westminster seat.[83]

Fox may have saved his seat, but the Whigs lost the general election dramatically and decisively, one hundred and sixty of them – dubbed 'Fox's Martyrs' after John Foxe's *Book of Martyrs* – losing their seats. A print in the Guildhall Library, London portrays Fox as *The Political Sampson in Revenge* [who] *sets fire to the Country*,[84] his firebrands including Burke, Sheridan and General Richard Fitzpatrick. In another, Fox, North and Burke (labelled 'Ripe Fruit for Old Nick') are *The Political Cluster in terrorem* (Plate 64) and hang from a vine branch shaped as a gallows. Beneath, Burke's spectacles lie on a document: 'Oeconomy 24,000 Pr. Annum', alluding, says Dorothy George, to 'the meagre results of his Bill of Economical Reform'. Other 'Trophies' on the ground refer to disasters ranging from the American war, the India bill, and coalition to the Westminster election itself. In *Idol of the People* Burke and Georgiana Devonshire mourn the destruction by Pitt of a dragon with the head of Fox.[85] In another print (Plate 65), Burke, a noted composer of mortuary inscriptions,[86] inscribes a long-winded epitaph on a tomb to the fallen ministers while Sheridan, the gravedigger, stands by with a spade. 'To the Memory of the Martyred Senators',

64. William Dent: *The Political Cluster in terrorem.*
Published 24 June 1784, by J. Brown. BM 6627;
collection Andrew Edmunds, London.
The defeated Whigs hang as a bunch of grapes on the
gallows of the public good. Beneath Lord Derby at the
apex is Fox, beside whom Burke (right) is identified by
his long nose. His spectacles, his plan of 'oeconomy',
and the India Bill he drafted for Fox are among the
discarded paraphernalia of the ill-fated coalition.

65. Anon.: *Hi nostri Reditus, expectatique triumphi!*
Published [1784] by J. Whitaker. BM 6657; British
Museum.
A noted epitaph-writer, Burke is shown composing a
long-winded mortuary inscription to the fallen
ministers of the Fox–North administration while
Sheridan the gravedigger looks on. Fox has been
caught in a trap baited by the crown: 'These are our
returns, and our awaited triumphs!'

66. Anon. (perhaps John Boyne): *More Ways than One
or The Patriot turn'd Preacher*. Published 2 November
1784, by E. Todd. BM 6661; British Museum.
Burke, bonneted and kneeling, seems to belong as little
with the fashionable congregation as with those
conducting – and assisting with – the service: an
eloquent Fox, a comfortable North, and an elfish
Sheridan.

writes Burke, *His saltem accumulem donis, et fungar inani Munere*: Let me at least heap
up these gifts and perform this empty service.

A splendid image is of Fox, *The Patriot turn'd Preacher* (Plate 66) whose congregation
includes Sheridan as pew-opener, and Burke as a devout old woman. Their roles are
indicated in verses beneath the design:

> To Comick Richard, ever true
> Be it assign'd the Curs to lash,
> With ready Hand to ope the Pew,
> With ready Hand to take the Cash.
>
> For thee, o beauteous and sublime!
> What Place of Honour wilt thou find?
> To tempt with Money were a Crime;
> Thine are the Riches of the Mind.

GRAND IRISH AIR BALLOON.

> Clad in a Matron's Cap and Robe,
> Thou shalt assist each wither'd Crone;
> And, as the piercing Threat shall probe,
> Be't thine to lead the choral Groan!

One choral groan the satirist might have had in mind was the state of affairs in Ireland. The recently appointed Lord Lieutenant, Charles Manners, fourth Duke of Rutland (who gave magnificent entertainments, and three years later was to die from fever at the vice-regal lodge in Dublin at the age of thirty-three) accused the Foxites of fomenting unrest in Ireland. Writing to Pitt on 16 June 1784, he warned: 'Mr Fox, I am informed, says "He shall make his harvest from Ireland"', and, on 24 July: 'I ask myself . . . whether these factions which the Duke of Portland's administration has planted in this country may not acquire strength by placing the Bishop of Derry at the head of the Papists and all the malcontents who openly, or secretly abet Mr Fox and his adherents here.'[87] On 7 October Dent describes the *Grand Irish Air Balloon* (Plate 67). Dispatched by Portland – in the guise of a devil – and by Hall the apothecary, and filled with 'Patriotic Gaz', it carries aloft a boat ('New Flying Machine from Portland to Derry') containing Fox, Burke and North. It is, we are told, 'constructed on the same principle as the American Air Balloon but containing more inflammible air' and North is to be seen at the tiller, steering with a volume inscribed 'History of the American War'. In the air-balloon, Britannia raises her shield to fend off Hibernia's hoisted sword. 'By Jasus,' says Burke, 'it will be sublime & beautiful to pop down among the Congress.' Frederick Augustus, fourth Earl of Bristol and Bishop of Derry, had been prominent in the Grand Convention of Volunteers in Dublin in November 1783.

Alas, given Burke's profound interest in Irish affairs, we have no more than a handful of caricatures linking him with this subject. What matters to the caricaturists is the immediate, the local, the gossipy, the personal, rather than more fundamental (but less picaresque) polical issues. There was a reference to Ireland in *Razor's Levee*. Another is in *The Whig Club, or the State of the Blue and Buff Council* (by Dent) on 24 December 1784,[88] where Burke, seated with his colleagues in a communal latrine and holding a paper marked 'Oeconomy', proposes mischief to his companions: 'India and Irish affairs will make – a good batch'. The title of the print mockingly recalls Fox's defiant stance during the American war when he attended parliament in the colours of General Washington's army. (The American uniform had been designed by Richard Montgomery of Beaulieu, County Louth (1736–75), friend of Burke, Fox and Barré). In 1785, Pitt's unsuccessful attempts to adjust the commercial relations of Great Britain and Ireland offered scope for the satirists. His propositions aimed at promoting free trade between the two countries and, in return for an anticipated Irish gain from this, an Irish contribution to naval defence.[89] Having underestimated the strength of opposition his proposals would arouse among English manufacturers (led by Josiah Wedgwood) Pitt was forced to make concessions which in turn infuriated members of the Irish Commons.

In May 1785 Burke spoke vigorously against the propositions, and the dangers of exposing British industry to Irish competition.[90] On 21 February, he had spoken of his thankless role as a dutiful parliamentarian. When on previous occasions he had pleaded Ireland's cause 'he had injured his own interest with his constituents in England; and when he saw that matters were likely to be carried too far by the Irish, and he therefore thought it his duty to stand up for England, he found himself ill-treated by Ireland'.[91] Fox and Sheridan, meanwhile, attacked one of the propositions as infringing Irish legislative independence. Dent's interpretation of events is to

67. William Dent: *Grand Irish Air Balloon*. Published 7 October 1784, by J. Brown. BM 6659; British Museum.
The ropes have been cut by a devilish Duke of Portland, and the balloon of Anglo-Irish oratory (heated by the flames of 'Patriotic Gaz') has lifted off to make mischief in Ireland. Between Fox and his cannon of 'Independence', and a short-sighted North active at the tiller of the *History of the American War*, Burke in biretta is, perhaps, the real navigator.

68. William Dent: *Hibernia In The Character Of Charity*. Published '21 March 1784' [thought to be 1785], by J. Brown. BM 6785; British Museum.
Britannia, on her knees, struggles with the burden of supporting Hibernia, who suckles the 'little Innocents' Fox and North, while Burke makes seditious music, plucking an Irish harp (carved with the head of the Earl Bishop of Derry) with the plectrum of 'Faction'.

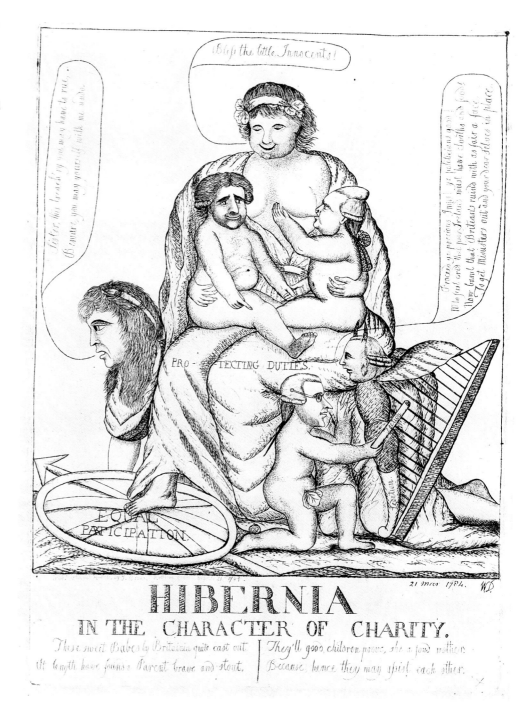

imagine *Hibernia in the Character of Charity* (Plate 68). Murmuring 'Bless the little Innocents!' she suckles Fox and North, while Burke, kneeling at her feet and clutching the staff of 'Faction', plays on an Irish harp with the head of the Earl Bishop of Derry. *The Minister's Bull* (Plate 69), also by Dent, illustrates Pitt's by now impossible task. John Bull, laden with such burdens as *British Manufactories*, and pulled from behind by the opposition of Burke, Fox and North, cannot be whipped over the hill of 'Landed Interest', despite Pitt's cat-o'-nine-tails, the *Irish Propositions*. Fox exhorts: 'Yho ho! – come one effort more, one glorious pull, To Throw young Paddy headlong from the goaded Bull'.

An anonymous print of 26 April 1785 (Plate 70) gives Ireland a role in the story of

69. [William Dent]: *The Minister's Bull.* Published 31 March 1785, by J. Nunn. Not in BM Cat. (but in BM, Dent folder 1785); British Museum.
Under the lash of Pitt's Irish propositions, John Bull tramples under foot petitions from English manufacturers and existing trade laws. But as Pitt attempts to surmount the landed interest he is restrained by Fox and North and (if we can be sure John Bull's tail is long enough) a determined Burke.

THE MINISTER'S BULL
OR A NEW WAY OF MAKING POOR OLD ENGLAND RICH AND HAPPY.
Humbly Inscribed to the Chamber of Commerce.

70. Anon.: [*The House that Jack Built*] (1785). Not in BM Cat. Lewis Walpole Library, Yale University. Depleting the Treasury in this parody of a popular nursery rhyme are (from left): Lord North, America, Fox, Pitt, Ireland, the Marquis of Lansdowne (Shelburne), Charles Jenkinson and Burke.

the house that Jack built, a parody of the nursery rhyme. Burke for once is not the priest, but the cock that crowed in the morn and waked the priest all shaven and shorn (Charles Jenkinson, former minister of war)[92] that married the man all tattered and torn (Shelburne) that kissed the maiden all forlorn (Hibernia, whose harp lies at her feet) that milked the cow with the crumpled horn (Pitt, and referring to his Irish propositions; the cow was a symbol of Britain's commerce)[93] that tossed the dog (Fox) that worried the cat (America, represented by a native Indian) that killed the rat (Lord North, during whose administration America had been lost) that ate the malt that lay in the house that Jack built (John Bull's Treasury). By such follies have Britain's power and wealth been depleted.[94] *Concerto Coalitionale*[95] (Plate 71) is Sayers's contribution to the topic, an ebullient concert given by Fox (in whose pocket can be seen 'Irish Propositions set to music for the White Boys')[96] and other opposition leaders. The ambitious William Eden, who had been Vice-Treasurer of Ireland in 1783 and was one who had stirred up North and Fox on the Propositions, plays contentedly on the Irish harp, inspiring further accompaniment at his feet.[97] Burke blows the trumpet, and the orchestra plays *The Treaty of Commerce*, a song attacking the Propositions and put in the mouth of an Irishman.[98]

Not until 1789, and the regency crisis, would Irish affairs again catch up with Burke in caricature. Meanwhile India, and intense scrutiny of the conduct of Warren Hastings, would dominate his life.

71. James Sayers: *Concerto Coalitionale*. Published 7 June 1785, by Thomas Cornell. BM 6795; private collection.

From the pained expression of the second violin (Thomas Powys, seated on the floor), and the accompaniment, voluntary and otherwise, of various animals, the harmonious nature of the Whigs' concert on the Irish Propositions may be guessed at. Fox, beating time on the torn national anthem, is the leading violin, and carries in his pocket another score: *Irish Propositions set to music for the White Boys*. Behind him, Burke blows his trumpet forcefully, recalling his moment of glory in Plate 39.

CHAPTER FOUR

ASSAILING THE 'SAVIOUR OF INDIA'

The Pursuit of Warren Hastings, 1785–88

One of Warren Hastings's defence counsel, Sir Robert Dallas, wrote of Burke:

> Oft have I wondered why on Irish ground
> No poisonous reptile yet was found
> Reveal'd the secret stands of Nature's work –
> She saved her venom to create a Burke[1]

It is interesting that Burke was sufficiently upset to quote the piece in his closing speech of the trial. It was also quoted by a modern biographer of Pitt (who denounces Burke as being 'as intemperate intellectually as Fox was physically')[2] and underlines the passions still aroused by Burke's crusade. We have already seen how Burke's examination of Indian affairs and the conduct of the East India Company led to his drafting of the ill-fated East India bill of 1783, which, with the King's intervention, foundered in the Lords and brought down the coalition so dramatically. Undeterred, Burke pursued relentlessly the question of the conduct of Warren Hastings. On 30 July 1784 he was reproved by Pitt for his prolixity in bringing forward a motion on the subject: 'if the hon. gentleman went on in that manner, making motions for which there were no parliamentary grounds, there would be no end of it'.[3] Burke is one of those put to flight by Pitt in *The Fall of Achilles,* crying:

> Before thy Arrows Pitt, I fly
> O D[am]n that word prolexity.

The pursuit of Hastings was to occasion some of Burke's finest oratory. But Pitt's charge of prolixity is taken up by Sayers who, in ***** [*Burke*] *on the Sublime & Beautiful* (Plate 72) places Burke, as parliament's chief bore, on the shoulders of two fellow bores, Thomas Powys and John Sawbridge, to issue 'short observations on India Affairs' (a scroll that is anything but short) and other pronouncements. (Sayers had probably been in the House to hear Burke attacking Pitt in a bad-tempered debate, and mocking the notion of Jenkinson, Chancellor of the Exchequer, 'mounted aloft on the shoulders of his right honourable friend . . . *I envy not the statue its pedestal, nor the pedestal its statue'*.)[4] Sawbridge is waiting impatiently to address the House on a favourite topic, his 'Mock Motion for Reform' (he brought forward several times a motion for shorter parliaments) while Powys, equally frustrated, clutches his 'Mem(oran)da of Important Observations Obvious Objections Perpetual Motions Doubts Facts Surmises Queries &cᵃ &cᵃ'. Meanwhile the House is beginning to clear. MPs suffering from Burke's prolixity dubbed him 'the dinner bell', echoing Goldsmith's lines on his fellow Irishman:

> Who, too deep for his hearers, yet went on refining,
> And thought of convincing, while they thought of dining.[5]

And in *The Orators Journey* (Plate 73), Burke is placed in the histrionic company of

... on the *Sublime* & *Beautiful.* —

Sublimi feriam sidera vertice.

72. James Sayers: ***** [*Burke*] *on the Sublime & Beautiful.* Published 6 April 1785, by Thomas Cornell. BM 6788; private collection.
Neither Thomas Powys nor John Sawbridge looks either sublime or beautiful, as they wait impatiently to address the House. But Burke is in no hurry, as he issues 'Invectives', 'Tropes' and 'Short Observations'.

73. [W. Mansell]: *The Orators Journey.* Published 7 February 1785, by S.W. Fores. BM 6776; private collection.
Immortalised by Reynolds as *The Tragic Muse*, in 1784 (in which she is flanked by Pity and Terror) Sarah Siddons is here sandwiched between Fox and Burke. Despite the physical intimacy implicit in this print, Mrs Siddons was, off stage and on, a grand and formidably correct lady: Sheridan once observed that he would as soon make love with the Archbishop of Canterbury.

the actress Sarah Siddons, who has just played Lady Macbeth at Drury Lane. Here Queen Rant (*see* Plate 1) is sandwiched between Fox and Burke, who gallop on horseback from 'Popularity' to 'Perdition'. (Siddons had been 'very ill received' by a hostile theatre audience on 5 October 1784.)[6]

In June 1785 Warren Hastings returned to Britain from India, giving impetus to Burke's dogged drive for an inquiry into his conduct. By the end of the year, Burke had decided that moves against Hastings should be in the form of an impeachment, the ancient (and little used) process entailing a prosecution by the House of Commons, to be tried by the Lords.[7] The issue arose at the recall of parliament in January 1786. Dent foresees it, in *Parliamentary Meeting 1786* (Plate 74) as a tussle for the loaves and fishes, now symbolising not only office – a favourite theme of his – but Indian wealth and patronage as well. Contesting the prize are Pitt, the Attorney General Richard Pepper Arden, and Hastings's agent Major John Scott, MP, on one side, and, on the other, Fox, North and Burke. Burke is coaching his leader and protégé: 'Don't spare, Charley, pay him about the noddle with your Shillany

THE ORATORS JOURNEY.

PARLIAMENTARY MEETING 1786.

IMPEACHMENT.

74. (top) [William Dent]: *Parliamentary Meeting 1786*.
Published 23 January 1786, by William Moore. BM
6915; British Museum.
Pitt, encouraged by the Attorney General Pepper
Arden and Warren Hastings's agent Major Scott, does
battle with Fox for the loaves and fishes, the benefits of
office. Burke, on the extreme right, offers a Hibernian
encouragement: 'Don't spare, Charley, pay him about
the noddle with your Shillany'.

[Shillelagh] – and I'll have a touch with the Little Major – I have a tough bit of
Bamboo, and dam'me I'll Macartney him'. (Lord Macartney, another Irishman, was
Governor and President of Fort St George in Madras. He had been offered the post
of Governor General in succession to Hastings but had declined.)

In February 1786 the *Public Advertiser* drew attention to the parallel between Burke,
in his proposal to prosecute Hastings, and the great Roman orator Marcus Tullius
Cicero, successful prosecutor in AD 70 of the corrupt Gaius Verres, governor of
Sicily.[8] Sayers picks up the analogy (Plate 75) (as Boyne will later, but more
sympathetically, in Plate 87), dressing Burke up as Cicero to threaten a turbaned
Hastings with rolled-up 'Articles of Impeachment'. But even as he accuses Hastings
he shelters beneath his cloak the despairing figure of Powell, that defaulting cashier
whom Burke, when in office, and amid much criticism, had reinstated to the
Paymaster's staff. The verse beneath spells out Sayers's offensive accusation:

Had Hastings been accus'd in Verres' Time,
And Asia's Preservation been his Crime
Tully, 'tis said, with all his Powers of Speech
Had urg'd the Roman Senate – to impeach.
But had that Tully lived in Powell's Day
And known the official "Error of his Way"
He wou'd have drop't the Impeachment and ye Halter
And for his Merits screen'd the good Defaulter.

Two days later, on 19 March 1786, Dent makes a similar accusation (Plate 76) in a
print also called *Impeachment*, blaming Burke's 'false optics' in painting Hastings black
and Powell white. While these conflicting cases catch his eye, his hand moves to pick
from a large bunch of grapes inscribed 'Lack' (rupees) just beyond Burke's hand.[9]
Thus Burke's motive for pursuing Hastings is traduced, while a spurious charge of

75. James Sayers: *The Impeachment*. Published 17 March 1786, by Thomas Cornell. BM 6925; private collection. Cicero's prosecution of the corrupt Gaius Verres is the metaphor Sayers uses to mock Burke's impeachment. Hastings, with an affected gesture of innocence, faces Burke who, while he brandishes the articles of impeachment, shelters with his other arm the disgraced figure of the defaulting cashier Powell.

76. [William Dent]: *Impeachment*. Published 19 March 1786, by J. Brown. BM 6926; British Museum. Burke's spectacles were readily employed in caricature as a sign of shortsightedness or faulty vision. Here the effects of false optics, directed to the 'True Case of [Burke's protégé, the defaulter] Powell' and to the 'True Case of Mr Hastings', do not prevent Burke reaching for the bunch of grapes, labelled 'Lack', or rupees.

double standards is introduced. Ridicule is all the more deadly a weapon of political propaganda when based on a travesty of the facts.

Of course, when the basis is factual — or almost so — the lampooning can reach dizzying heights. One such occasion was the secret marriage (15 December 1785) of the Prince of Wales to Maria Fitzherbert, a Roman Catholic widow. 'Secret' it may have been but speculation about it soon became the talk of the town. On 27 March Gillray rendered a brilliant parody of the affair (Plate 77). He transposes the occasion from Mrs Fitzherbert's London drawing room to the interior of a Roman Catholic church abroad, and the witnesses from her brother and uncle to members of the Prince's set. Who better to give her away than Fox; who better to perform the nuptial ceremony than Burke the Jesuit? North, characteristically, snores to the side of the pulpit; he has been enrolled as coachman, and the Prince's crony George Hanger as best man. Many of Gillray's sly digs are in the detail: here Adam and Eve, pictured on the wall behind the couple, imply that the designing Mrs Fitzherbert has seduced the

Defign'd by Carlo Khan.   WIFE & no WIFE ____ or ____ A trip to the Continent.   Publifh'd by Will. Holland No 50 Oxford Str London March 27 1788

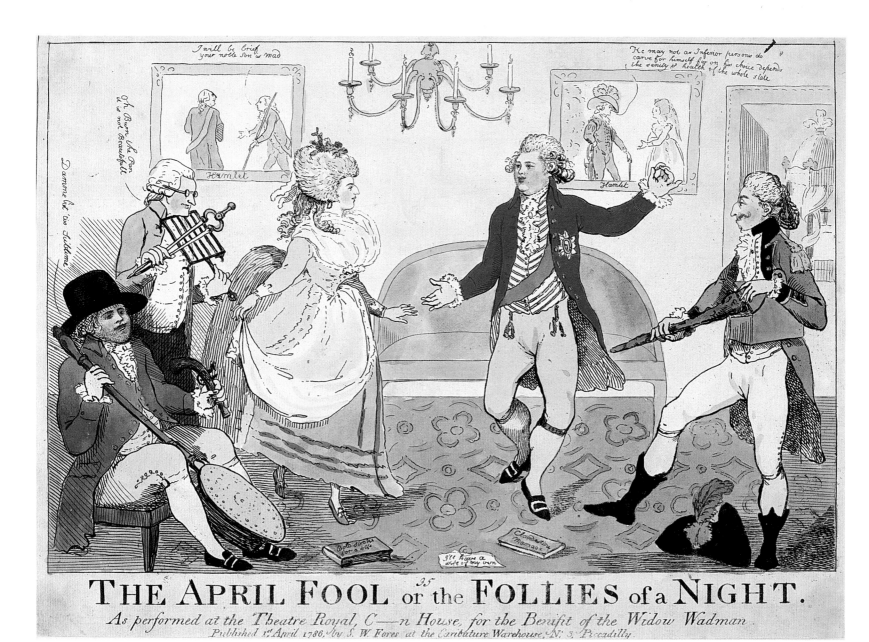

THE APRIL FOOL or the FOLLIES of a NIGHT.

As performed at the Theatre Royal, C—n House, for the Benifit of the Widow Wadman.

Published 1st April 1786, by S. W. Fores at the Caricature Warehouse, N: 3, Piccadilly.

78. [George Towneley Stubbs]: *The April Fool or the Follies of a Night*. Published 1 April 1786, by S.W. Fores. BM 6937A; private collection. Mrs Fitzherbert and the Prince dance to the music of his cook, Weltje (who plays with bedwarmer and pistol), Burke (who bows a gridiron with firetongs) and Hanger (who uses shillalee and salt box). In the room behind Hanger is the matrimonial bed, decorated with crucifix and feathers.

77. (previous page) [James Gillray]: *Wife & No Wife – or A Trip to the Continent*. Published 27 March 1786 (second state, reissued as 27 March 1788), by William Holland. BM 6932; private collection.
The Prince of Wales marries Mrs Fitzherbert, as 'Design'd by Carlo Khan'. The couple have been driven on their 'trip to the Continent' by North who sleeps through the ceremony, which is witnessed by the best man, Fox, and conducted by Father Burke. Between the heads of the Prince and his bride is a picture of Eve tempting Adam.

Prince. Similarly Gillray's readers are invited to make what they will of the juxtaposition of Fox's head and the picture of Judas kissing Christ. The very name of the plate, *Wife & No wife – or – A Trip to the Continent*, conjures up the dubious proprieties, the constitutional and religious undertones of the event.

George Towneley Stubbs (a fresh and lively caricaturist, and son of the famous painter George Stubbs)[10] quickly followed with two prints in which Burke's presence misleadingly emphasises his association with the Prince as a leading Whig advisor. The Prince dances with Mrs Fitzherbert in *The April Fool or the Follies of a Night* (Plate 78), published on 1 April 1786, the night on which a farce of the same name by Leonard MacNally was played at Covent Garden.[11] In the painting behind Burke's head, entitled 'Hamlet', Pitt bows before George III saying 'I will be brief your noble son is mad.' Stubbs then assails *The Royal Society*,[12] a drinking session around the table at Carlton House. The Prince, in flying form, has kicked over and broken a bottle on the table as he urges his companions to drink up. Burke looks on benignly as the Prince steadies himself on the shoulder of one of his closest confidants, Sheridan. An unidentified artist (similar to, but not Stubbs) contemplates *The Introduction of F— to St*

THE INTRODUCTION OF F_____ TO S^T. JAMES'S.

79. Anon.: *The Introduction of F[itzherbert] to St James's*. Published 3 May [1786] (later state, reissued as 3 May 1788), by A. Sherlock. BM 6953; private collection. The Prince of Wales is already somewhat browbeaten as he carries to St James's Palace Mrs Fitzherbert, who clearly knows exactly where – and how – she wishes to go. This is one of many caricatures in which Burke is misleadingly represented as among the Prince's intimate advisors.

James's (Plate 79). 'F–' is, of course, Mrs Fitzherbert, who sits indecently on the Prince's shoulders, thighs and breasts exposed, pointing resolutely towards the gateway to the royal apartments. In attendance, the marching band of George Hanger (beating a drum), Fox (flute), North (French horn) and Burke, who brings up the rear playing the fife, are seen as party to the clandestine marriage.

Fores's print shop at No. 3 Piccadilly forms a backdrop to another Stubbs attack (Plate 80). The Prince is *The Cock of the Walk, Distributing His Favours*; his denuded tail having been plucked to make a number of these favours, each bunch with three feathers. Inscribed to Lady Melbourne, the Duchess of Devonshire and others, they are wheeled before him by the Prince's factotum Louis Weltje and Georgy Hanger. Alas, one bunch, for Mrs Fitzherbert, has fallen to the ground. While adjoining shops – purveyors of geese to his Highness, and of meat – display the Prince of Wales feathers, Fores settles instead for the spiked heads of Burke, Fox and North and proclaims himself purveyor of caricatures to the public. So open a disavowal of the Opposition almost implies that his services are 'by appointment' elsewhere.

In keeping with his way of life, the Prince's debts at this time were outrageous. Pitt

85

80. [George Towneley Stubbs]: *The Cock of the Walk, Distributing His Favours.* Published 31 May 1786, by S.W. Fores. BM 6961; British Museum.
A small wheelbarrow is needed to hold the favours ('To Lady M . . .' and others) being distributed by Weltje and Hanger on behalf of the philandering Prince, a cock whose tail feathers have been embarrassingly depleted. In the background Fores the printseller advertises himself as 'Purveyor of Caricatures to the Public' and, vying with nearby signs, displays the impaled heads of Burke, Fox and North.

THE COCK of the WALK, DISTRIBUTING HIS FAVOURS.

82. Anon., (after James Gillray): *Evening Consolation.* An undated copy (possibly a Dublin piracy) of BM 6791, 25 April 1785. Not in BM Cat.; private collection.
While the impoverished Burke retreats to birch-rod and crucifix, North consoles himself with a buxom young woman and Fox glumly contemplates the empty purse that inhibits his gambling.

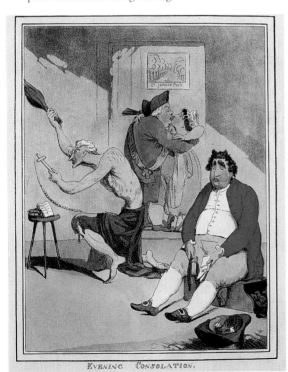

EVENING CONSOLATION.

had shown the King a letter from a correspondent in Brighton warning that 'HRH risks being lost to himself, his family and his country if a total and sudden change does not take place'.[13] When the King refused to pay his debts the Prince, in July 1786, made a great show of sacking staff at Carlton House, and Fox and Sheridan appealed in vain on his behalf. All work at the house stopped, and there was great selling of racehorses and hunters, and even coach horses, at Tattersalls. *A Scene in the School for Scandal* mocks the extravagance of it all by numbering a fashionable cabriolet as Lot 1800.[14] The Prince's excesses could be contrasted with the frugality of his father, whose ordinary beverage at table, sniffed Wraxall, 'was only composed of a sort of lemonade, which he dignified with the name of *cup*; though a monk of La Trappe might have drunk it without any infraction of his monastic vow'.[15] The Prince's companions, too, were in financial straits, and they are pictured by Dent as *The Jovial Crew or Merry Beggars. A Comic Opera as performed at Brighton by the Carleton Company.*[16] Each inspires a verse. Burke looks upwards, his hands clasped in prayer:

I was a Jesuitical preacher
I turn'd up my eyes when I pray'd
But my hearers half-starv'd their teacher,
For they believ'd not one word that I said.

In November 1786 Boyne links their 'bankruptcy' with news that the government proposed to establish a convict settlement in Australia, depicting them in a Stygian scene as *Non Commission Officers Embarking for Botany Bay* (Plate 81),[17] who just manage to evade the clutches of their creditors.[18] Burke has acquired a bishop's mitre and with a thin smile consoles the shore party with his benediction. Burke's financially straitened personal circumstances are repeatedly referred to by the caricaturists; in April 1785 Gillray had captured him, emaciated, mending his own breeches. In a companion print (Plate 82), Gillray shows Burke flagellating himself

NON COMMISSION Officers EMBARKING for BOTANY BAY

81. [John Boyne]: *Non Commission Officers Embarking for Botany Bay*. Published 1 November 1786, by H. Humphreys [*sic*]. BM 6990; British Museum. The Prince of Wales and his friends push off from Execution Dock for the new convict settlement in Australia, escaping in the process money-lenders and a distraught Perdita Robinson. From the left are: Sheridan, Captain Charles Morris, Erskine, George Hanger, the Prince, Fox, Portland, North and Burke, whose episcopal blessing is unlikely to be appreciated by their creditors. Burke's mocking gesture reflects an anti-Jewish sentiment common in caricature, while traducing his own position.

with religious fervour before a book inscribed 'Reform'.[19] Perhaps Gillray recalls a heading to one of the sections in the *Sublime and Beautiful*: 'How Pain Can be a Cause of Delight'. His companion North has found his own cause of delight in a buxom young woman.

In *A Convention of Not-Ables*,[20] Henry Kingsbury (a caricaturist working *c*.1775–98) plagiarises Gillray to portray an emaciated Burke as one of the Prince of Wales's group seeking to address their financial difficulties by besieging the Treasury.[21] Kingsbury takes his title from the convention of notables, an assembly that met in Paris on 22 February 1787. In another print, in May 1787,[22] Rowlandson casts Fox, Burke and Sheridan in a debtor's prison marked 'Bastile', which (as Dorothy George points out) was a noteworthy emblem of tyranny before July 1789.[23]

But help is on the way for the Prince of Wales. Gillray contrasts his changing fortunes in two curious little prints. In the first, Pitt and others pull scaffolding away from Carlton House, the Prince's debts having forced a halt to his extravagant

DIDO FORSAKEN. Sic transit gloria Regina.

83. [James Gillray]: *Dido Forsaken*. Published 21 May 1787, by S.W. Fores. BM 7165; collection Andrew Edmunds, London.
Mrs Fitzherbert, her crown blown away by Dundas and Pitt, is Dido, Queen of Carthage, abandoned to her funeral pyre by Aeneas, who sails off to fresh adventures in the barque 'Honor' with Fox at the tiller and Burke trimming the torn sail.

spending.[24] The Prince, consoled by Fox, Burke and Sheridan, cannot bear to look. In the second, his debts are being paid and his income increased by Treasury secretaries George Rose and Thomas Steele, who, with Pitt and others, are appropriately obsequious. The scaffolding has been reinstated and the Duke of Richmond is lending a hand with the refurbishments.[25] Alas, the price for all this has been the apparent abandonment of Mrs Fitzherbert. Gillray pictures her as *Dido Forsaken* (Plate 83), her girdle of 'chastity' broken, her crown upset, as the Prince sails away. He swears: 'I never saw her in my Life' and Fox replies, 'No, never in all his Life, Damme'. Burke echoes 'Never' as he trims the torn sail of the barque *Honor*. Again Gillray amuses his audience by parodying an epic painting, this time by Reynolds, *The Death of Dido*, exhibited at the Royal Academy in 1781, and recalling an episode from Virgil's *Aeneid*, in which the Queen of Carthage, deserted by her new husband Aeneas, constructs her funeral pyre and stabs herself before the people, as his ship sails off to fresh adventures.

In Gillray's version the Prince is not just abandoning his wife (and in the process destroying her prospects of being Queen) but fleeing from her attendant emblems of popery, which attest to the illegality of their marriage, from rosary, scourge and crucifix to the harrow at her side inscribed 'For the conversion of Heretics'. But while the Prince may not choose to be converted, he has not shaken off all the dreaded emblems, for Burke still wears his Jesuit's headgear as he disavows Maria's existence. It is typical of Gillray that a minor detail (which at first glance merely identifies Burke by his trademark biretta) prompts reflection on the continuing dangers posed to the heir to the throne by the Catholic 'entryism' of advisors like Burke, for whom lying and dissimulation were assumed to be the necessary means by which they stealthily attained their subversive goals. Nor did it trouble Gillray that neither Burke nor North had taken any part in the debate about the Prince's debts and marriage ceremony.

Despite the picture painted in caricature, Burke, in fact, remained at a distance from the Carlton House circle and later in a Commons speech in December 1788 would say he 'knew as little of the inside of Carlton House as he did of Buckingham House'.[26] Fox's denial of the clandestine marriage bitterly upset Mrs Fitzherbert and her refusal to see the Prince induced a royal illness. Gillray is again on hand to portray *The Sick Prince*.[27] Fox, Burke, North and perhaps Sheridan join Liberty in her prayers for his life, while behind a curtain lurk Pitt and Thurlow (with daggers) and the Duke of Richmond. The contretemps ended and Mrs Fitzherbert lived with the Prince of Wales until 1794 and, after a period of separation, from 1800 to 1803. The separation arose initially from the Prince's liaison with Lady Jersey, which was cruelly celebrated (26 August 1794) by Isaac Cruikshank in *My Grandmother, Alias The Jersey Jig Alias the Rival Widows*.[28] The obese Prince sings as he fondles the breast of an old crone:

I've kissed & I've prattled with fifty Grand dames
And changed them as oft do ye see
But of all the Grand Mammys that dance on the Steine
The widow of Jersey give me.

While Cruikshank was engraving this ditty the King was writing excitedly to Pitt: 'I have this morning seen the Prince of Wales, who has acquainted me with his having broken off all connection with Mrs Fitzherbert, and his desire of entering into a more creditable line of life by marrying; expressing at the same time that my niece, the Princess of Brunswick, may be the person.'[29] Enter that 'more creditable line of life' he did, with the princess in question, Caroline of Brunswick. Their mismatch would provoke in due course the greatest outpouring of satirical prints of the age.

Meanwhile, moves to impeach Warren Hastings had continued apace, evidenced by a wagon-load of documents (Plate 84), drawn on *The Common Stage Wagging from Brooke's Inn St. James Street (Papers Moved on ye Shortest Notice),* and pulled by four asses with the heads of Sheridan, Burke, North and Fox. A poster advises that 'For a Few Days will be performd a Comedy called Impeachment by a Ragged Company (late) His Majestys Servants'. Pessimistic about the outcome, Burke had moved carefully, and succeeded in outlining the case against an overconfident Hastings by a series of motions asking that the House receive evidence in the form of papers laid before it.[30] From these, individual articles of charge were prepared and debated. Dent imagines the scene in the workshops of Vulcan, legendary god of fire and the working of metals, where, until he was hurled from heaven, the cyclops helped him to forge thunderbolts for Jove. Dent's version (Plate 85) has *Poor Vulcan and his Cyclops Preparing Impeachment Proof*. From the twisted metal available to him, Burke is beating

84. (following page) Anon.: *The Common Stage Wagging from Brooke's Inn*. Published 1 April 1786, by Alexander McKenzie. BM 6939; British Museum.
A grotesque wagon-load of evidence against Warren Hastings, amassed at Brooks's club, is now moved to parliament for the performance of 'A Comedy called Impeachment by a Ragged Company (late) His Majestys Servants . . .'

85. (following page) [William Dent]: *Poor Vulcan and his Cyclops Preparing Impeachment Proof*. Published 29 April 1786, by J. Brown. BM 6948; collection Andrew Edmunds, London.
The convoluted 'Accusation' against Hastings has been assembled and hangs on its nail. Now Burke must hammer out the proof (with the covert assistance of Philip Francis). As cyclops to Fox's Vulcan they use an anvil which shows Burke twice in relief, as brooding hen and (beneath) as mutilated victim of 'The Force of Envy'. North, as stoker, has wind enough to dispense with the usual bellows.

The POLITICAL-BANDITTI assailing the SAVIOUR of INDIA.

86. [James Gillray]: *The Political-Banditti Assailing the Saviour of India*. Published 11 May 1786 (second state, reissued in 1788), by William Holland; BM 6955; private collection.
Hastings, gorgeously mounted and attired and displaying as triumphs 'Territories acquired . . .', 'Eastern Gems for the British Crown', is unperturbed behind his 'Shield of Honor', provided by the Crown. Gillray's motley bandits are inspired by the work of the caricaturist John Hamilton Mortimer: in front of a histrionic Fox, a corpulent North forgets his blunt weapon, battered in the American débâcle, as he reaches for Hastings's rupees. In armour but barefoot, Burke is depicted as impractical, excitable and ineffective.

into shape his 'proof' with another smith (his head concealed), who is probably Sir Philip Francis. Pictures of brooding and envy adorn their anvil.

But it was Gillray, with one of his most brilliant and cruel attacks, who set the scene for the impeachment battle in the manner most calculated to damage Burke's prospects. *The Political – Banditti Assailing the Saviour of India* (Plate 86) are led, appropriately, not by Fox but by Burke, who discharges his blunderbuss at the 'Shield of Honor' of Hastings, mounted in splendour on a camel. Fox is dramatically poised to plunge a dagger into Hastings's back, while North (from whose broken scabbard, 'American Subjugation', emerges the battered tip of his sword) contents himself with removing a sack of 'Lacks Rupees added to the Revenue'. Other symbols of Hastings's triumphs are as ambiguous as the title Gillray gives him: a bag is inscribed 'saved to the Company', another contains 'Eastern Gems for the British Crown', and a rolled map shows 'Territories acquired by W. Hastings'. All in all, a far cry from North's 'American Subjugation' of painful memory.

The King's speech at the opening of parliament in January 1787 was depicted in

The time is come, Fathers, when that which has long been wished for, towards allaying the envy, your House has been subject to, & removing the imputations against trials, is (not by human contrivance, but superior direction) effectually put in our power. An opinion has long prevailed, not only here at home, but likewise in foreign countries, both dangerous to you, and pernicious to the state, viz. that in prosecutions, men of wealth are always safe, however clearly convicted. There is now to be brought upon his trial before you, to the confusion, I hope of the propagators of this slanderous imputation, one, whose life and actions condemn him in the opinion of all impartial persons; but who, according to his own reckoning, and declared dependance upon his riches, is already acquitted; I mean W——H——. I have undertaken this prosecution, Fathers, at the general desire, and with the great expectation of the British People, ——— with the direct design of clearing your justice and impartiality before the world. For I have brought upon his trial, one, whose conduct has been such, that, in passing a just sentence upon him, you will have an opportunity of re-establishing the credit of such trials; of recovering whatever may be lost of the favour of the British People; and of satisfying foreign states and kingdoms in alliance with us, or tributary to us. I demand justice of you, Fathers, upon the robber of the public treasury, the oppressor of Asia, and the invader of the rights & privileges of Britons, the scourge and curse of Indostan. If that sentence is passed upon him which his crimes deserve, your authority, Fathers, will be venerable & sacred in the eyes of the public. But if his great riches should bias you in his favour, I shall still gain one point, viz. To make it apparent to all the world, that what was wanting in this case was not a criminal, nor a prosecutor, but justice, & adequate punishment.

London Pub.d by Boyne & Walker N° 11 Great Turnstile Lincolns Inn Fields. Feb.r 7th 1787.

Edmund Burke.

Farmer George Deliver'd of a most Grevous S[peec]h, as a newborn child, the object of a tug of war between Pitt and the Foxites while the King is being revived by smelling salts.[31] 'That's my Diamond Darken his Daylights' says Burke with a thin smile. The caricaturist thus advances an insinuation doing the rounds that the gift of a diamond, forwarded to the King by Hastings the previous June, was a bribe.[32] Pitt, grasping the infant's arms, cries 'Save Oh Save my Baby'. Hastings was not the only subject on the agenda: there was an unpopular shop tax that Fox would move to repeal, a budget and a treaty of commerce to oppose.[33] Another caricaturist (possibly John Boyne) sees the opening of parliament as *The Meeting of the Legion Club*[34]: Pitt, riding out on an ass followed by his supporters, encounters Fox, Burke, North and others mounted on a great phallic cannon, which discharges at the Prime Minister the 'voice of the people'.

Fox and Pitt trade fisticuffs in *The Political Contest*[35] over Fox's concerns, 'Rights and Liberties of the People' and 'Repeal of the Shop Tax', while other pairs are also scrapping, Sheridan with Lord Thurlow, North with John Wilkes, and Burke with Hastings. Burke's papers indicate the plan of his attack: 'Princesses of Oude; Charges; 50,000 lost to the I. Company; Charges; Tyranny & Oppression; A list of Murders Committed in the East; Indians, 80,000 Butchered'. Boyne, for once supportive, casts Burke (Plate 87) as the noble *Cicero against Verres*, as Sayers, in less sympathetic vein, had done earlier (Plate 75). Clad in a toga and with lofty features, he makes a speech that is, in fact, the start of Cicero's oration against Verres (with words such as 'Rome', 'The Republic' being altered to 'British People', W[arren] H[astings]'. In the distance, Britannia comforts a woman, intended for India, who gazes up at the orator while Fox and North, who has his back to Burke, are seated behind him. The irony of the situation is not lost on them: Fox and Burke had often threatened North with impeachment. (*See* Plate 101.)

It had looked, for a while, as if Hastings would escape prosecution. Burke had lost the vote on the first charge, debated in the House at the beginning of June 1786, but two weeks later Pitt, who had been silent earlier, spoke and voted against Hastings on another charge, having decided that the balance of merit lay with the prosecution.[36] Other charges also succeeded, most famously that urged by Richard Brinsley Sheridan. Meanwhile Burke's relentless advocacy and the pun offered by the word 'hastings' – the name given to a kind of early pea sold in the London markets[37] – inspired John Boyne (Plate 88) to give him *Employment During Recess,* as a penurious street vendor of salt fish, crying his wares. Semi-naked, with a coat worn back to front (perhaps a gesture to his Irishness),[38] he trudges along Pall Mall past playbills alluding to the impeachment. One acknowledges Sheridan's accompanying role: 'Much-Ado about Nothing / Principle Performer Mr. B[urk]e/ with The Fathless Irishman'.

Sheridan's celebrated speech on 7 February, 1787 (in which he sought Hastings's impeachment on the issue of the treatment of the begums of Oudh) is the occasion for Dent's *Battle of Hastings* (Plate 89), where the British Battalion, the 'Ayes' led by Burke, are on the offensive in the Commons against the Bengal Battalion, the 'Noes'. It is a scene packed with incident. 'To be, or not to be, Impeachment is the Question', pronounces the Speaker as Hastings stands astride the table. In the foreground, wearing a helmet inscribed 'Sublime and Beautiful Sherry' (to indicate he is the mouthpiece of Burke) Sheridan, 'Chief Combatant for the begums', raises the bellows of 'Argument' against the Indian spear of Hastings's agent Major Scott. Bolts of lightning, 'truth', 'conviction' and 'Justice' issue from Sheridan's mouth, while tucked in his belt ('Humanity') he carries another bellows, of 'Wit'. Burke's expression, as he beats his battle drum of Impeachment, shows he is content with

87. John Boyne: *Cicero Against Verres*. Published 7 February 1787, by Boyne & Walker. BM 7138; private collection.
Sayers, in Plate 75, casts Burke as Cicero compromised by his support of Powell. Here Boyne gives a loftier image as Burke echoes the gesture of the seated Britannia. Fox looks on but North, not unmindful of Burke's earlier threats to impeach him, pointedly turns his back.

88. [John Boyne]: *Employment During Recess* (detail).
Published 15 November 1786, by H. Humphreys [*sic*].
BM 6994; British Museum.
Burke as a beggarly street vendor cries his wares.
Posters on the wall behind bill him as 'Principle
Performer' in *Much Ado about Nothing* and promote the
'Impeachment of Warren Hastings a Farce, as
performed by the Tools of Faction St Stephens
Chaple'.

89. [William Dent]: *The Battle of Hastings*. Published 9
February 1787, by E. Macklew. BM 7139; collection
Andrew Edmunds, London.
The scene is the House of Commons; on the left, the
Bengal Battalion, grouped around Pitt, vote against
impeachment and are rewarded with streams of booty
issuing from the nabob Hastings. Pitt himself, however,
prods sharply with the spear of 'refined Candour'. On
the right, drummed up by Burke, the British Battalion
vote to impeach. On their behalf, Sheridan in front
wields the bellows of argument against Hastings's
agent, Scott.

90. James Sayers: *A puerile Attack upon an old Servant*.
Published 17 March 1787, by Thomas Cornell. BM
7151; private collection.
Burke, applauded by Sir Philip Francis (author of the
Letters of 'Junius'), manipulates Sir James Erskine in his
attack on Hastings, during a debate on the articles of
impeachment.

Sheridan's performance. Burke's opposite number is Henry Dundas, in Scottish attire, fingering a set of war-pipes filled with coins or precious stones and labelled 'Music hath charms to sooth &c'. (Treasurer of the Navy, Dundas was also, through his position as virtual head of the Board of Control for India, a powerful controller of Indian patronage. A popular theme in the prints is of his distribution of patronage to fellow Scots.)[39] From Hastings's mouth and his right hand (marked 'Peculation') and from his wounded side, flow great streams of booty seized upon by a 'Foraging Party' of MPs. But, while most on the government side are content to call 'no', Pitt has stabbed Hastings with the spear of 'Refined Candour' to make the gaping wound. Court connections must have been dismayed.

On 15 March 1787 it was the turn of Sir James Erskine (1762–1837, MP and later

Pub.d as the Act directs for the Proprietor by E. Machlew 109 Haymarket Feb.y 26, 1788

The BATTLE of HASTINGS.

Bella, horrida, bella!

A puerile Attack upon an Old Servant.

General) to contribute to the debate. Dressed as a small girl, he is accused by Sayers of *A puerile Attack upon an Old Servant* (Plate 90) as he goes to beat the family dog, Hastings, though the child's harness shows he is being controlled in this by Burke. Burke's abettor Sir Philip Francis applauds: they themselves have thrown stones at Hastings, marked 'Malice', 'Eloquence' and 'Calumny'. The wig attached to Erskine's lash indicates he is, ironically, the nephew of Lord Loughborough (Alexander Wedderburn, 1733–1805), who had defended Lord Clive in 1773, when as Governor of Bengal he underwent a parliamentary inquiry. Burke had been sympathetic to Clive, and critical of the proceedings.[40]

Pitt having cast his vote against the former Governor General, a committee of the Commons chaired by Burke became the 'committee of managers' to prosecute the trial. In an undated print of about this time,[41] Sayers, ever hostile to Burke, depicts the managers filing in behind the Speaker, Charles Cornwall, below which he cites 'Acts of the Apostles Cap xxiv': 'And after five Days the High Priest descended with the Elders and a certain Orator named Tertellus who informed the Governor against Paul. And when he was called forth Tertellus began to accuse him saying &c.' Sir Philip Francis, source of much crucial information against Hastings, and an MP since 1784,

THE GRAND PITCH BATTLE.

Between those celebrated Prize fighters, the *Irish Buffer* and the *Bengal Bruiser* — Fought this day at *West——r*, on a commodious stage, erected for the purpose at a great expence; where, (from the long time the Combatants have been in training, and from the various shiftings and evasive fallings, expected to be excercised by the party supported by *Law*, and from the other finding *Justice* in the *Wit, Cuning* and scientific Skill of his Bottle Holder and Second; & it being agreed that should neither side obtain a master blow before the evening the Battle to be drawn till and resumed in the morning the Amateurs of the Art are in high expectation of its being the longest & sharpest contest hitherto known, and doubt not the number of rounds they will be able to stand to will afford several days excellent sport — especially as all the great fighting-men; from Big Ben to Little Mendoza, will be present, & bye Battles allowed —— the odds at one time 6 to 4 in favor of the Buffer — then 4 to 1 on Buffer — at present the Betting even —. some say the Bruiser will be quite done over—. others declare, from the judgements he has shown in chusing *Law* for his Second, he'll appear as clear as a white sheet of paper—But the knowing Ones think at the end of the contest he'll give in with trifling Damage. —

---

91. [William Dent]: *The Grand Pitch Battle*. Published 13 February 1788, by W. Moore, and by W. Dickie. BM 7269; collection Andrew Edmunds, London. Dent enjoys the metaphor of the prize fight: later he will have Fox and Burke confront each other in *The Battle of Whigs* (Plate 157). Here Hastings 'the Bengal Bruiser', having laid his turban aside, squares up to Burke 'the Irish Buffer', whose glasses and wig lie on the ground. On the extreme left, the Lord Chancellor and Speaker act as umpires.

is shown as one of the managers; when to the fury of Burke the House voted to exclude him on 5 December 1787 he was then asked by the managers to assist them.

The trial began on 13 February 1788, and lasted intermittently for over seven years. In a print published that day, *The Grand Pitch Battle* (Plate 91) Dent anticipates a long drawn out encounter between 'those celebrated Prize fighters, the Irish Buffer and the Bengal Bruiser'. Parodying an engraving of the celebrated contest between the pugilists Humphries and Mendoza (on 9 January), Burke and Hastings square up to each other, urged on by their seconds and watched by the 'Umpires' Lord Chancellor Thurlow and the Speaker, positioned behind Hastings. In a description beneath the design, Dent hints – with a pun – that 'in chusing Law for his Second' (Edward Law KC, later Baron Ellenborough, was one of his counsel) Hastings will benefit from Thurlow's decisive influence. The pomp and panoply of the trial is captured in a contemporary print[42] (Plate 92), not a caricature though the diminutive figures of Burke and Fox have been distinctly rendered, seated at the committee table in the foreground. In the centre of Westminster Hall, flanked by a bevy of judges, the Lord Chancellor is well placed to preside, midway along the axis from prisoner to throne.

92. [?T.] Prattent: *A View of the Court sitting on the trial of Warren Hastings Esq' in Westminster Hall.* Published 1 May 1788, by G. Robinson & Co. The Pierpont Morgan Library, New York. Peel Collection No. 81. The scene in Westminster Hall, arranged for the trial of Hastings (P) who sits, centre stage, with his back to the viewer.

Burke opened the first charge, followed by Fox. In *Sublime Oratory – A Display of It* (Plate 93)[43] they are seen by the Hanoverian artist, Johann Ramberg, a protégé of George III,[44] as ruffians throwing mud and filth scooped from the gutter at Hastings, an elegant Eastern prince who reaches for his sword. Thus diverted, poor Hastings has his purse snatched by a pair of barristers, probably his own counsel.[45] Burke, dressed as a Jesuit, is urged on by a satyr, who dances with glee as he clutches the orator's

Prattent

A VIEW of the COURT
sitting on the trial of
Warren Hastings Esq'
in Westminster Hall.

A | Honble House of Commons
B | Foreign Ministers
C | Duke of Newcastles Gallery
D | Councell for the Prosecution
E | Councell for the Prisoner
F | Dukes &c   G. Peeresses
Z | Board of Works &c

I | The Throne
K | Recess for his Majesty
L | Recess for the Royal Family
M | Judges
N | Lord High Chancellor
O | Viscounts & Barons
P | Warren Hastings Esq' Prisoner
Q | Committee of the Commons

Pub^d. May 1st. 1788, according to Act of Parliament by G. Robinson, & Co. Pater Noster Row.

SUBLIME ORATORY ———————— A DISPLAY OF IT.

Published by T. Harmar Engraver & Printseller Nº 16 Piccadilly March 5, 1788

93. Johann Heinrich Ramberg: *Sublime Oratory – a Display of it*. Published 5 March 1788, by T. Harmar. BM 7270; private collection. The sublimity of Burke's oratory is jeered as deriving from the street filth which, like Fox to his right, he hurls at Hastings.

94. [William Dent]: *Thunder, Lightning and Smoke*. Published 22 April 1788, by W. Moore, and by W. Dickie. Not in BM Cat.; Lewis Walpole Library, Yale. Burke and Fox, as capricious as the wind, having once threatened North with impeachment, shift their attention to India and Hastings, a more formidable opponent than poor North who, with 'America Lost', contemplates *The Blessing of Poverty*.

95. James Sayers: [*Philip Francis*]. Published 31 March 1788, by C. Bretherton. BM 7292; collection Andrew Edmunds, London.
Sayers's study of Francis was used by Dent to provide the central figure in Plate 94.

robe. A ragged urchin joins in the fun. Burke's powerful indictment did overheat in places: as to the crime, 'we charge this offender with no crimes that have not arisen from passions which it is criminal to harbor, – with no offences that have not their root in avarice, rapacity, pride, insolence, ferocity, treachery, cruelty, malignity of temper, – in short, in nothing that does not argue a total extinction of all moral principle, that does not manifest an inveterate blackness of heart, dyed in grain with malice, vitiated, corrupted, gangrened to the very core'. Here is the passion and over-emphasis that made him a fit associate of Queen Rant (Plate 73), and the prolixity that was mocked by Sayers (Plate 72). On Hastings, Burke continues 'we have not chosen to bring before you a poor, puny, trembling delinquent, misled, perhaps, by those who ought to have taught him better, but who have afterwards oppressed him by their power, as they had first corrupted him by their example . . . no, my Lords, we have brought before you the first man of India, in rank, authority, and station. We have brought before you the chief of the tribe, the head of the whole body of Eastern

98

THUNDER, LIGHTNING and SMOKE,
or, the WIND shifted from the NORTH to the EAST.

offenders, a captain – general of iniquity, under whom all the fraud, all the peculation, all the tyranny in India are embodied, disciplined, arrayed, and paid'.[46]

Overheated rhetoric becomes, for Dent, *Thunder, Lightning and Smoke*[47] (Plate 94) as Burke and Fox, perched as weather vanes on the head of Philip Francis, shower Hastings with their grandiloquence. Francis (the author of the Junius letters) is labelled the source of all the mischief; reaching for his dagger of envy he looks bitterly at his inveterate enemy Hastings. Dent has ' borrowed' Francis's pose from (and has been reminded of his spleen by) Sayers's caricature study[48] (Plate 95) published a few weeks earlier, on 31 March 1788. And Dent is harping on another old issue, for the weather vanes have turned their attention from the beggarly figure of their coalition partner, the sleeping Lord North, and his flag proclaiming that America has been lost on his watch.[49] Billowing out behind Burke and Fox is the smoke of their rhetoric, once employed against North (*see* Plate 33): 'He has utterly ruined his Country! – I Hold the Man infamous that associates with him! Consider the Man curst that ever goes over the threshold with him – We will not suffer him to escape – We pledge ourselves to bring him to the Scaffold!!! – We will not rest till we have brought him to the Block !!!'

In another plate, Dent parodies the trial as *The Raree Show*[50] (Plate 96) with Burke,

THE RAREE SHOW

Executed for the Benefit of Mr Somebody at the expence of John Bull.

96. [William Dent]: *The Raree Show*. Published 25 February 1788, by W. Moore, and by W. Dickie . BM 7273; collection Andrew Edmunds, London. Standing beside Sheridan and Fox beneath a banner that displays his capacity to 'drown the stage with tears' – 'the Power of the pathetic over the beautiful' – Burke, with his trumpet, is characteristically the publicist of the troupe. *See* Plates 39 and 89.

97. Admission ticket for the trial of Warren Hastings, seventh day. Issued by Peter Burrell, Deputy Great Chamberlain [February 1788]. Collection Andrew Edmunds, London.

98. James Sayers: *For the Trial of Warren Ha[stings]*. [February 1788]. BM 7276; collection Andrew Edmunds, London.
The arms of the deputy Great Chamberlain are adapted: the rams' heads become those of Burke, Fox and Philip Francis; the embowed arm no longer holds an olive branch, but wields the scourge 'Lex Parliamenti omnipotens' and assails the Common Law and Justice. Burke (bottom left), grim-faced and poised to prompt is at Fox's side in Westminster Hall as he berates Hastings (centre).

99. 'J.S.' [James Gillray, parodying James Sayers]: *Impeachment Ticket*. (*c*. February 1788). BM 7277; British Museum.
In Gillray's parody, the escutcheon is supported by a victim of Indian misrule who kneels in supplication, and by the Lord Chancellor seated on a close-stool, while in the scene below, Hastings prostrates himself before the all-powerful Thurlow.

Sheridan and Fox as clowns and zanies. One tableau in the show depicts Burke reducing his susceptible audience to, literally, a flood of tears – 'the Power of the pathetic over the beautiful'. As for Sheridan's speech on the charges relating to Hastings's treatment of the begums of Oudh, its reception by a thronged audience inspired the following doggerel:

> The gallery folk, who, misled by the sport
> Conceived 'twas a playhouse, instead of a court,
> And thinking the actor uncommonly good,
> They clapp'd and cry'd "Bravo!" as loud as they could,
> Then Edmund gave Sherry a hearty embrace
> And cry'd, as he spluttered all over his face,
> "At Supper this night thou shalt have the First Place!"[51]

Such was the demand for tickets to Westminster Hall where the impeachment was taking place that the tickets themselves, bearing the name and arms of the Deputy Great Chamberlain, became the subject of parody. The three rams' heads of Sir Peter Burrell's coat of arms (Plate 97) are replaced by the battering rams of Burke, Fox and Francis in a print by Sayers (Plate 98). Sayers in turn is parodied by Gillray (Plate 99) – even to the point of counterfeiting, not for the first time, his signature. Again the battering rams are Burke, Fox and Francis, but in the background (instead of Fox making a violent speech) Hastings kneels before Thurlow – an unflattering allusion to the Lord Chancellor's crucial proposal, accepted by the Lords, that the rules of evidence used in the ordinary courts be followed in the hearing of evidence rather than the *lex parliamenti* earlier used in the impeachment of the Earl of Strafford and others, as urged by the managers.

A print in a distinctive hand, perhaps that of J. Doughty, makes no bones about it. The artist sees *The Struggle, for a Bengal Butcher and a Imp-Pie* (Plate 100) as a fight

The STRUGGLE, for a BENGAL BUTCHER and an IMP–PIE.

100. Anon. (perhaps J. Doughty): *The Struggle, for a Bengal Butcher and an Imp-Pie*. Published 18 March 1788, by J. Doughty & Co. BM 7285; British Museum.

Lord Chancellor Thurlow, with satanic assistance, seems to be winning the tussle for Hastings and his Imp-pie. An unsuccessful attempt had been made to impeach Sir Elijah Impey for his conduct as Chief Justice of Bengal. Tugging against Thurlow are Burke, Fox, Sheridan and (probably) Burke's friend William Windham MP. In front of Burke is Sir Gilbert Elliot MP, who led the case against Impey and was later Governor General of India.

between the managers and Thurlow for the pie that Hastings is about to cut, and out of which imps are emerging. They represent Sir Elijah Impey, whom, for his conduct while Chief Justice in Bengal, the opposition also attempted to impeach. Burke says: 'For the sake of Injured Millions, I and my worthy Friends and Colleagues demand these Wretches as Victims to Publick Justice', to which Thurlow (with cloven hoof, and accompanied by the Devil) retorts: 'And – for the sake of Consigned Millions, I – with the assistance of my old Friend and Colleague here am resolved to protect these worthy Gentlemen'.

Having dealt with injured millions and consigned millions, the same artist has harsh things to say about the other side as well. In *Such things may be. A Tale for future times* (Plate 101) a cart, led by North and pushed by Sheridan, has brought a dejected Hastings to the gallows, where Fox prepares the rope around his neck. Burke, dressed as a parson with gown and bands, thinks it 'a poor atonement . . . for Millions &c', provoking Fox's rejoinder: 'A *Poor* Atonement do you call it Ned! Egad it would have been a devil of a Job for me if my F[athe]r had made *such* an *Atonement* for – *Unaccounted* Millions . . .' (His father, Lord Holland, it will be recalled, had been denounced in a city address to the King as 'the Public Defaulter of unaccounted millions' (*see* p. 31). As L.G. Mitchell has noted, 'London enjoyed the joke that the money Henry Fox was suspected of embezzling from public funds while Paymaster-General during the Seven Years War should come back into circulation as payment for his son's debts.')[52] North, too, feels a certain *frisson*: 'Don't you remember Sheri – that my *now* Rt. Hon[ble] Friend [Burke] often threat'ned to bring *me* to *this* or the *Block*.' (A direct hit, this, for among Burke's papers in Sheffield City Library may be found his draft of a proposed impeachment.)[53] 'Psha Fred – ' replies Sheridan, 'you know that was only to frighten you from your Station &c. but drive on, or our friend Edmund will stand preaching here all day.' Hastings, forlorn, recalls that 'Walpole said every Man had his Price but Alass! I never could find out any of your Prices . . .'

101. Anon. (perhaps J. Doughty): *Such things may be. A Tale for future times.* Published 1 March 1788, by J. Doughty & Co. BM 7279; private collection. Burke as parson attends Hastings, about to be hanged. North, ready to draw the cart away, reminds Sheridan (on the right) that he himself had been threatened with a similar fate. Fox, too, confesses unease, admitting that his own father, Lord Holland, had been spared making such an atonement for 'Unaccounted Millions'.

Such things may be. A Tale for future times.

Pub. March y 1. 1788. for J. Doughty & Co. No. 19 Holborn LONDON.

Price 2s 6d. Plain or Coloured.

A SLOW AND SURE DELIVERANCE, *An Anticipation Sketch*

102. [William Dent]: *A Slow And Sure Deliverance*.
Published 2 April 1788, by W. Dickie, and by J.
Brown. BM 7297; collection Andrew Edmunds,
London.
Hastings, in his chair, protected by a royal umbrella
from Burke's fulminations, is carried over the heads of
the Lords, attended by a contented lawyer, and a Lord
Chancellor who grasps a money bag labelled 'Treatise
on Friendship'. Meanwhile, toiling uphill towards the
fickle weathercock of 'Evidence' Fox and Sheridan
carry a witness with another full purse, berated by Fox
for not swearing in court 'what you asserted
elsewhere'.

103. Anon.: *An Indian Prince on a visit to a Friendly
Court*. Published 10 April 1788, by J. Berry. BM 7299;
private collection.
A splendidly accoutred Hastings can rely on the Lord
Chancellor, Thurlow, to attend and shelter him on his
way to Westminster Hall. Burke and Fox look on,
with slim chances of effecting Burke's threat to 'bring
the Culprit to Justice'.

An Indian Prince on a visit to a Friendly Court

Given the constant theme of the impecunity of Burke, Sheridan and Fox, this is a powerful endorsement of their probity.

By contrast, an undated caricature of about this time recalls the incident in 1786, when Hastings presented the King with a diamond sent by the Nizam of the Deccan and Sheridan had insinuated bribery on the part of the Governor General.[54] The story is now enlivened by relating it to the contemporary fairground performances of a celebrated stone-eater. *A purging Draught for Extracting Diamonds From the Rich Mine of Bengall*[55] has enabled Thurlow to pull a rope of jewels from the mouth of Hastings. George III, enthroned behind Thurlow, swallows another rope, saying, 'These is provision for a K[in]g poor soul I'll take care he shan't be hurt'. Similar jewels are being pulled from Hastings's rump by Fox and Burke.

One of the most cynical representations of the trial came from Dent. *A Slow and Sure Deliverance, An Anticipation Sketch* (Plate 102) is a good example of the extraordinary licence afforded at the time to the authors and publishers of graphic satire. In it the King and Lord Chancellor are accused of the corrupt screening of Hastings, the peers of culpable neglect of their duty, and a witness of denying his former testimony. Hastings is conveyed by his counsel in a fancy sedan, preceeded by their leader, Edward Law KC who proudly flourishes a fat purse marked 'Fee'. At the side of Hastings strides Thurlow, clutching an equally fat purse inscribed 'Treatise on Friendship'. His sword of 'Justice' has become part of an umbrella – the centrepiece of which is the Crown – which shields Hastings from Burke's cloudburst. The group stride purposefully towards St James's Palace across the coronets and mitres of the sleeping peers, a route designated 'Honor'. (Of the 160 peers before whom the trial opened only 29 ultimately gave their verdicts.) In contrast a humble sedan struggles up the hill of 'Evidence' conveyed by Fox and Sheridan. Fox turns in exasperation to his smug, tight-lipped passenger, asking 'Why not Swear here what you asserted elsewhere?' The answer, unspoken, is to be inferred from the witness's fat money-bag, labelled 'Treatise on the Yellow Jaundice'. He is probably the managers' witness Fox Calcroft whose evidence pointedly favoured Hastings.

Dent's theme is taken up in a print published a few days later by J. Berry: *An Indian Prince on a visit to a Friendly Court* (Plate 103) is the turbaned Hastings. As he strolls towards 'New Palace Yard', cane in hand, the bowl of his hookah (from which bubble 'Articles of Impeachment') is borne before him by an Englishman in court dress, who is probably Major Scott (though he looks suspiciously like Pitt). Thurlow holds aloft a great umbrella, saying, 'My Magnimity will cover a Multitude of thy Crimes and Misdemeanors.' Two dogs at the side of the road, Fox and Burke, sit beneath a gibbet 'for the Governor'. 'Brother Edmund', says Fox, 'I'll finish the Law' and a scrawny Burke replies, 'I'll bring the Culprit to Justice'. The oriental smoking pipe also features in *The First Charge – Exit in Fumo*,[56] parodying Burke's charge that the Rajah of Benares, Chait Singh, had been insulted by the confiscation of his hookah after his arrest. In the print Chait Singh cries out, 'Gadzooker he has taken my Hooker' while Burke proclaims, 'Guilty of not suffering him to smoke for the space of two Days'.

Sayers's brief, it seems, is to trivialise or distort Burke's charges. He satirises Burke's speech on 22 April 1788, on the veneration due by the Islamic religion to 'the parental character', quoting a treatise by one Demetrius Cantemir.[57] Lampooned is a passage in which, though young virgins were sent as presents to the Sultan, 'yet he touches none of them but what is brought by his mama'. Sayers pictures Burke, therefore, in reverie as Prince Demetrius; in his dream a Turk sitting beneath the Koran greedily receives a mortified young girl from his grinning mother, who says: 'I

104. James Sayers: *Galante Show*. Published 6 May 1788, by Thomas Cornell. BM 7313; collection Andrew Edmunds, London.
Burke's magic lantern has magnified the charges against Hastings out of all proportion, so that a flea becomes an elephant, a wart becomes Mount Ossa heaped on Pelion and Olympus (as when the giants tried to scale heaven), and the tears of Indian victims, the begums, form an ocean in which an ouzle, or weasel, swims as a whale.

105. 'J.S.' [James Gillray, parodying James Sayers]: *Camera-Obscura*. Published 9 May 1788, by S.W. Fores. BM 7314; collection Andrew Edmunds, London.
Gillray's response to Plate 104 is to give Hastings a lantern capable of reducing the scale of the charges against him. Now a rampaging elephant becomes a flea, Mount Ossa shrinks to a wart, a scene of murder and plunder (labelled 'Begums in Tears') turns out to be 'skin'd mice', and a whale dwindles to an ouzle. 'Charmingly diminished' nods the cynical Lord Thurlow.

have procured another Lamb for my Lord'. As to the charge against Hastings relating to the begums of Oudh, Sayers places the head of Sir Philip Francis under the Bow Begum's seat, confessing 'I am at the Bottom of it',[58] and elsewhere Sayers shrewdly taunts *The Managers in Distress*[59] as they tumble into the water from a collapsing bridge, Burke clutching his 'Impeachment' papers. 'D[am]n the Piers', says Fox, 'they won't support us'. In all this Sayers, as expected, takes the Court line (and, attorney that he is, he will in due course be rewarded by Pitt with a sinecure at the Court of Exchequer). In another attack on Burke he sets the scene of a *Galante Show* (Plate 104), with Burke as a grim projectionist whose magic lantern distorts its images in parody of Burke's supposed exaggerations. ('What shadows we are', Burke had exclaimed at Bristol in 1780, 'and what shadows we pursue'.)[60]

But Sayers's style and the initials J.S. were occasionally hijacked by Gillray to cause mischief. So the *Galante Show* is itself beautifully parodied a few days later by *Camera-Obscura* (Plate 105). Hastings is now the showman, his magic lantern diminishes rather than exaggerates, and gratifies King, Queen and Lord Chancellor. The King and Thurlow are implicated by Gillray in the protection of Hastings in *The Westminster Hunt*.[61] The King is an ass on whose back Thurlow rides to whip in a pack of hounds (led by Sheridan) who chase Hastings; North, Burke and Fox are being crushed and kicked under the ass's heels. And Gillray has no doubt about the attitude of the peers: they are cattle in the pens of Smithfield on *Market Day*[62] under the guard of Thurlow, whose heavy purse indicates he has made a good sale. Some of them attack a watchman's box to dislodge Fox, Burke and Sheridan. Maybe Thurlow's sale has been to Hastings, for he has made a purchase and rides off with a calf – the King – thrown across his horse.

106

Again pretending to be Sayers, Gillray has Pitt, Hastings and Thurlow as *State-Jugglers* (Plate 106) performing outside St James's Palace. Above them, and part of the troupe, the King and Queen in oriental costume perform a balancing act on a precarious see-saw. Hastings is producing a stream of coins from his mouth which a crowd tries to catch. Meanwhile, Fox, on the shoulders of Burke, is furtively trying to fill his hat with booty without being spotted by the fire-eating Thurlow. (The flames issuing from Thurlow's mouth are a nice dig at his habitual strong language.) With Gillray even the smallest detail may contain a sly hit: the Queen on her see-saw

106. 'J.S.' [James Gillray, parodying James Sayers]: *State-Jugglers*. Published 16 May, 1788, by S.W. Fores. BM 7320; British Museum.
The King and Queen's balancing act forms part of a circus performance involving Pitt, Hastings and Thurlow. In the crowd that presses forward to catch Hastings's coins, Dundas (with long, pointed nose) is well placed, as is Lansdowne beside him. Fox, on Burke's shoulders, proffers an empty hat with little prospect of success, while the audience on the left clamour for the honours and ribands which Pitt is effortlessly, if miraculously, producing.

107

Pub.ᵈ May 22ᵗʰ 1788 by S.W. Fores N.3 Piccadilly.
Gillray

O Liberty! O Virtue! O my Country!

OPPOSITION

FATHER PAUL & THE LAY PORTER,
Or the particular State of particular EXPENCES:
Published according to Act of Parliament. —

admires a silver snuff box she has been given. She had set tongues wagging by showing favour to her fellow German, the rich and rapacious Mrs Hastings, a divorcee, and is charged in these prints with being duly rewarded. In an audacious print, again by Gillray, she rides on the roof of a coach, hugging a basket of golden eggs and a hissing goose, while the King mounts guard on the boot at the back of the coach and Hastings and his bejewelled wife enjoy the comforts of the journey within.[63] Lines below the design provide further proof of the caricaturist's latitude:

> The very stones look up to see,
> Such very gorgeous Harlotry;
> Shaming an honest Nation.

A companion plate tells a different story as a furious Burke (Plate 107), lashing his team (and alarming his guard Fox), is driving the managers' coach with its coat of arms, 'Pro Bono Publico', into increasingly deep water.

There continues to be intermittent comment on Burke's finances. In April 1788 F.G. Byron shows him as an emaciated parson declaiming from the pulpit: 'And behold he lived upon the fat of the land and was fed with good things!' – an ironic contrast with his antagonist, Hastings.[64] Part of the managers' problem relates to the expenses of Hastings's trial. In *Father Paul & the Lay Porter*[65] (Plate 108) Burke, a cadaverous figure clad in the frugal clothing and sandals of a monk, approaches the Lord Chancellor on the subject: 'We ask no more than is needfull, and so little have

THE LONG-WINDED SPEECH,
Or the oratorical organ harmonized with sublime and beautiful inflation.
Sold by W. Dickie, Strand & W. Moore, Bond Street, June 4, 1788.

Mr S------N's SPEECH,
Or, the triumph of Genius over Injustice.
With an Illustration of a Nabob's Defence.
Sold by W. Dickie, opposite Exeter change, Strand & W. Moore N° Kelly...

107. [James Gillray]: *Opposition* — . Published 20 May 1788, by S.W. Fores. BM 7323; British Museum.
In his relentless pursuit of Hastings, Burke drives furiously towards the 'Slough of Despond' (the deep bog to be crossed in Bunyan's *Pilgrim's Progress*) to the alarm of his passengers.

108. William Dent: *Father Paul & the Lay Porter.* Published 25 (?26) May 1788, by W. Dent. BM 7326; collection Andrew Edmunds, London.
With the costs of Hastings's trial mounting, a cadaverous Burke vainly seeks help from the corpulent Lord Chancellor who holds a great wine goblet aloft as he responds: 'It's false; you feast and gormandize, whilst we are wasting'.

we had, that we are almost starved'. He proffers a paper, 'Account of expences attending the Trial . . . Esqr'. Thurlow, in contrast, is excessively fat and holds a great goblet inscribed 'Pleasure'. 'It's false,' he retorts, 'you feast and gormandize, whilst we are wasting'. These are just the sort of details that enrich Gillray's great plates. Across four sheets he has designed *The Installation – Supper. As given at the Pantheon, by the Knights of the Bath on the 26th of May 1788.*[66] In the midst of this grand spectacle Burke is to be seen, his empty dish held out to Hastings, who sits across the table from him, guarding a whole ham.

In June 1788, Sheridan made a long and famous speech relating to the begums of Oudh. In two separate prints, Dent takes contrary views. In *The Long-Winded Speech, or the oratorical organ harmonized with sublime and beautiful inflation,* Sheridan, as Burke's mouthpiece, displays his prolixity (Plate 109). The inflation in question is administered by Fox who pumps a bellows (with the head of Burke) to his posteriors, causing Sheridan's words to tumble out: 'Jaghire Elephant Oude Bamboo Cages begums begums begums Plundered Princesses Sacrificed begums Filial duty wantonly destroyed Shackled Eunuchs Sustenance forbid Strangled Ministers Treaties violated Rebellion Nominal Cruelties confirmed Incontrovertible Evidence Natives Annihilated. Witnesses Biased Defence Denied.' In the second print *Mr S[herida]n's Speech* (Plate 110) is seen as *the triumph of Genius over Injustice,* and Sheridan as an Irish

109. (previous page) William Dent: *The Long-Winded Speech*. Published 4 June 1788, by W. Dent. BM Cat. VI, p. 499; British Museum. Fox applies the bellows of prolixity – Burke – to create Sheridan's second great oration on Hastings's conduct towards the princesses of Oudh. Some biographers have suggested that Sheridan's initial reluctance about an impeachment was overcome by Burke's flattering appeal to his gifts of oratory: 'I know that his mind is seldom unemployed but then, like all such great and vigorous minds, it takes an eagle flight by itself and we can hardly bring it to rustle along the ground, with us birds of meaner wing, in coveys'.

110. (previous page) William Dent: *Mr S[herida]n's Speech*. Published 9 June 1788, by W. Dent. BM 7331; private collection. Sheridan, attended by trumpeters Burke and Fox, is a Hibernian Apollo, whose oratory has toppled Hastings.

111. 'J.S.' (anon., in parody of James Sayers): [*Richard Brinsley Sheridan*]. Published 29 June 1789, by W. Fores. Not in BM Cat.; private collection. This anonymous caricature, showing R.B. Sheridan, and fathered on James Sayers with the faked monogram J.S., is an unsympathetic portrait suggesting slyness, pugnacity and (in the colouring) inebriety.

112. John Nixon: *The Examination of S[i]r Elijah Impey at the Tryal of Mr Hastings*. [May 1788]. BM 7316; British Museum. The evidence of the former Chief Justice of Bengal is not being well received by Burke (left) and his colleagues in the managers' box.

Apollo, with harp instead of lyre. 'Hence vile Author', he exclaims as Hastings and his 'Oriental Tragedies' tumble from the summit of Mount Parnassus, to the trumpet blasts of Burke and Fox. A sequence of designs in the corners of the print shows the embarrassing consequences of Hastings's defence having been cobbled together quickly by many hands, with vulnerable passages subsequently withdrawn.[67]

A less flattering view of Sheridan the impeachment orator is offered (Plate 111) by another of those artists who teases Sayers by borrowing the initials 'J.S.'[68] By 1788 prints had begun to show Sheridan's face as blotched with drink (*see* Plate 114), and he would be labelled as *Poor Sherry*. Now to the overheated nose and flushed cheek of an imbiber is added an expression, wily and furtive, that signals a propensity for intrigue. In reality, the conduct of the impeachment was rather less than Apollonian. Nixon's etching of *The Examination of S[i]r Elijah Impey* (Plate 112) gives a flavour of more mundane proceedings, its immediacy suggesting a sketch being hurried out to a waiting audience rather than satirical mischief making. Even so, Fox's pained expression reflects the discomfiture felt by the managers as Impey, Chief Justice of Bengal, defended his conduct successfully. From the opening of the trial in February 1788 until its adjournment at the close of the parliamentary session that summer, Indian affairs dominate the political satires. But the interest of the audience, so passionate at the outset, was to prove shortlived. Frequently interrupted, the trial wore on interminably, and the public (and with them the caricaturists, purveyors of what their customers wanted to gossip about) turned their attention to matters less complex and more local, more topical, than the legal interpretation of a colonial judge's conduct (in sentencing Hastings's accuser, the Indian Nandakumar to death) thirteen years previously in Bengal.

Three years later Dent would still be forecasting *No Abatement*[69] of Hastings's continuing nightmare (Plate 113). Looming before him is the demonic Burke, bearing zealously a great crucifix of 'charges'. Pointing to the macabre apparition of victims he has conjured up, he invokes 'my good Spirits Black, White, Blue and Grey' to torment Hastings with a choice of death. Surrounding the Governor's bed, demons – one of which is Pitt and another appears to be Fox – offer him a poisoned chalice, a gallows rope, a dagger and a pistol. 'Let him not rest night nor day', continues Burke, 'whilst I raise up those Shades. . .' Philip Francis is invoked as source of the

The Examination of S.r Elijah Impey at the Tryal of Mr Hastings

113. William Dent: *No Abatement*. Published 31 May 1791, by W. Dent. Not in BM Cat.; The Pierpont Morgan Library, New York. Peel Collection No. 236. Burke conjures up a vision of Hastings's crimes and urges him to choose death in one of the forms offered by his attendants, poison, rope, dagger, pistol. Sir Philip Francis (extreme left), 'my chief spirit . . . source of the charges', is instructed to hold Burke's spectacles in front of Hastings that he may view the vision as Burke does, and confess.

charges and 'Imp of Envy' and holds Burke's Spectacles to Hastings's eyes, 'that he may see as I do, confess, die and be dam'd for hoarding his Riches'. How long will it all last? A picture in the background indicates 'Trial's End. Doomsday', but the 'Blue & Buff Poor Box' near Burke hints at an alternative. On it the labels 'Pray let our emptiness be filled' and 'End of the Trial' are juxtaposed suggestively. Even by November 1788, Sheridan, for all the renewed celebrity it had brought him, was already bored by the grinding process of the impeachment and wished that 'Hastings would run away and Burke after him'.[70]

In the meantime what could be more diverting than another contest in the Westminster constituency? Samuel Hood and Fox had won the two seats in the memorable contest of 1784. Now on Hood's appointment as a Lord of the Admiralty he was obliged to seek re-election under the Place Act of 1707, having accepted a place of profit under the Crown. The Whigs dashed what should have been a formality with the decision to fight the by-election, and in 14 July 1788 put forward Lord John Townshend in a contest that was hugely expensive and unexpectedly successful.

We know that Gillray's services were enlisted on Hood's side: an account

The BUBBLES of OPPOSITION.

Pub.d July 26.th 1788. by H. Humphrey New Bond Street.
Gillray   G.Hanger

Fox   Burke   Sheridan   26 July. 1788

BLOOD & Co. setting Fire to the Tower, & stealing the Crown.

114. [James Gillray]: *Bubbles of Opposition.* Published 19 July 1788 [name erased]. BM 7342; British Museum. Fox's attempt to float his Westminster candidate, Lord John Townshend, another 'bubble of opposition', seems unlikely to fizzle out. Created from 'Devonshire Sope' (generously provided by the Duke) Townshend's progress is watched anxiously by others: floating highest are Windham, Burke, the Prince of Wales and Sheridan, beneath them Stormont, Portland, Norfolk and Hanger.

115. [James Gillray]: *Blood & Co. setting Fire to the Tower.* Published 26 July 1788, by H. Humphrey. BM 7354; British Museum.
A bizarre incident in the previous Westminster contest (1784) may have partly inspired this extravagant image: thieves stole the Great Seal of England from the house of Lord Chancellor Thurlow on the night of 23–24 March 1784, the eve of the dissolution of parliament. It delayed the dissolution by a day, and caricaturists at the time enjoyed pointing the finger at Fox and his companions.

submitted to the Treasury from 17 July to 9 August included £20 for 'Mr Gilwray',[71] and he produced seven trenchant election plates against the Opposition. As far as Gillray is concerned, Townshend is the latest in a series of *Bubbles of Opposition* (Plate 114) made in the 'Coalition Washing Tub' and drifting up from Fox's pipe. Already floating above are Burke, Sheridan, the Duke of Norfolk, Lord Stormont and others, notably the Prince of Wales. The tub stands on a base of 'Portland stone' and so too does the wherewithal: golden guineas in a wrapper marked 'Devonshire Sope'.

The cost of running the campaign was central to another Gillray satire, where Fox is *Mason, the Duke's Confectioner, Disposing of the Trinkets.*[72] Mason, it appears, was an associate of Captain Blood who had attempted to steal the crown jewels from the Tower of London in 1671[73] and Fox's spoils, as he approaches the hustings, will provide the 'Ways & Means'. Townshend and his supporters are on the platform, Burke in attendance, as Fox slips through a door marked 'Liberty & Property Secured'. It is insinuated that misappropriations are funding the election,[74] but Fox is being accused of more, of attempting to purloin the prerogatives of the Crown, and it is a theme Gillray returns to in *Blood & Co. setting Fire to the Tower & Stealing the Crown* (Plate 115) where the culprits are Burke, clutching the sceptre, Sheridan the orb, and Fox, the crown itself.

As in 1784, the butchers and chairmen (the latter often characterised in these prints

113

The BUTCHERS of FREEDOM.

OPPOSITION MUSIC or FREEDOM of ELECTION

as Irish) formed mobs in support of the Whig candidate, while sailors supported Admiral Hood. In a notable example of the excesses perpetrated with seeming impunity in caricature – perhaps it helped to be in the pay of the administration! – Gillray depicts Fox and his followers as *The Butchers of Freedom* (Plate 116) causing mayhem as they swing their cleavers in a vicious riot. Burke and Sheridan, side by side, are in the thick of it and are about to strike a defenceless mother and child whose hands are raised in desperate supplication. A supporter waves a flag for 'Townsend and Liberty'. Only Townshend, the candidate (trampling on a flag of the Royal Navy), is putting cleaver and marrow-bone to their intended use as improvised musical instrument, rather than weapons. Its rarity as a print today points to the possibility that copies may have been bought up or suppressed in some way by the Whigs. Whether or not this happened, the vicious theme of the print is crudely copied (Plate 117), and the notion of cleavers and marrow-bones making *Opposition Music* is hawked, perhaps, to a wider audience than can afford Gillray's elaborate aquatint. Gillray

Gillray   Sheridan.   Townsend   Burke
When Sampson as Justice ——ty Soldiers defended,
——bent to quell wicked Whigs who've mild peace oft offended,
Bold Brindsley seiz'd on him, & swore he'd well shake him,
Crying, Justice ne'er did, nor e'er should overtake him.
                    Sir Sampson Wright.   Bow way road

Pub. July 1788 by H. Humphrey New Bond Street
            Fox
                    C. Hanger
The BATTLE
of
BOW-STREET.

Sampson down on his knees like a Saint at devotion,
Drops his Jaw Bone,—while F——x seconds Brindsley's motion;
The Guards do their duty—prick Charles—he beseeches,
And alarm'd then lets fly—thro' his sad satten Breeches.

116. [James Gillray]: *The Butchers of Freedom*. Published July 1788, by H. Humphrey. BM 7352; private collection.
Sheridan, in butcher's apron, and Burke beside him swing murderously at a defenceless woman and her infant. Behind Sheridan, Lord Derby is assailing a veteran with a wooden leg and (to the right) George Hanger launches a deadly attack, his foot astride an earlier victim. But it is Fox's assault on 'The King's Head' itself that is most calculated to damage his candidate's prospects.

117. Anon.: *Opposition Music or Freedom of Election*. (*c*. July 1788) BM 7362; British Museum.
As in 1784, not only were riots sparked off by the Westminster election but also it is possible that Gillray's elaborate aquatint (Plate 116) was suppressed, or bought up. This cheap copy may have been intended to replace it or bring it to a wider audience.

parodies another episode as *The Battle of Bow-Street* (Plate 118): Fox – who has come to complain about an incident involving the over-zealous deployment of the military – jumps with pain as his rump is pierced by a soldier's bayonet at the office of the Chief Magistrate Sir Sampson Wright, who in turn is being assaulted by Sheridan. Burke and the candidate raise their hands in horror. Of Sheridan's role in the mêlée (and Gillray's print), his younger sister Betsy Sheridan noted in her journal:

> He said that he desired Sir Sampson to make the Soldiers draw back on which the Justice sneek'd behind a Grenadier crying drive them off, that being provoked a *little* he did take the Fellow by the Collar and having dragg'd him forward gave him a shaking. I hear they have made a Print of the Scene but did not see it. Mrs Sheridan told me she had just given ten guineas (a collection she made) to the poor Black who at the risk of his life had step'd forward and received a cut on the head that was intended for Charles Fox.[75]

The beautiful Duchess of Devonshire is back in the fray, coaxing votes on behalf

115

Election-Troops, bringing in their accounts, to the Pay-Table..

118. (previous page) [James Gillray]: *The Battle of Bow-Street*. Published July 1788, by H. Humphrey. BM 7353; British Museum. The Westminster candidate Lord John Townshend and Burke hold up their hands in horror as Fox is bayoneted and Sheridan assaults an equally horrified Chief Magistrate, Sir Sampson Wright. One of Gillray's election plates as a government propagandist; he revels in small details such as the brandy bottle and dice (one and two are unlikely to be a winning throw) which decorate 'Valiant' Townshend's flag.

of Fox's candidate Lord John Townshend from the androgynous *Harry Jenkins, the Masculine & Feminine Bellows Mender*[76] with the assistance of 'Mother' Windsor the notorious brothel keeper and some of her 'nuns'. The title continues: [Jenkins] 'having declared his intention not to remain Neuter in the Westminster Contest, is canvassed by the Duchess of D[evonshire] & coaxed by Mother Windsor, & absolutely poll'd for Lord John, on Monday July 28th, altho' he never had any Habitation except a Cow-house, a Privy, a Pig Stye or a Watch House'. In other words, egged on by Duchess and by procuress, and piled high with her ladyship's guineas, Jenkins is being led to the hustings to take 'the bribery oath' before the poll clerks, that as a rate-paying householder he is a qualified elector of Westminster. Burke is made party to the event, depicted at the candidate's shoulder as Townshend welcomes the perjuring voter. We must suppose that Burke was by now well inured to the stream of invective poured out daily by the caricaturists but, whatever his feelings about the present bit-part he has been given by Gillray, we can guess that his sense of gallantry must have been affronted by the treatment meted out to a lady of

119. James Gillray: *Election-Troops, bringing in their accounts, to the Pay-Table*. Published 14 August 1788, by H. Humphrey. BM 7369; collection Andrew Edmunds, London.
Edward Topham, proprietor of the *World* and writer of puffs and squibs, heads a queue of ministerial propagandists and ruffians demanding to be paid for their part in the Westminster election. Even the soldier who has assaulted Fox in Plate 118 queues up, his bayonet still dripping with blood.

rank, whatever her indiscretions. As for Fox, the most caricatured figure of his time, he seemed quite impervious to their abusive etchings and collected prints to amuse his visitors.[77]

These, then, are but a handful of the prints alleging bribery, impersonation and chicanery in the conduct of the election, which closed on 4 August 1788 with victory to Townshend. Gillray must have had difficulty in collecting his fee as a government propagandist for, having taken Hood's side during the contest, he was quick to mobilise the *Election-Troops bringing in their accounts to the Pay-Table* (Plate 119), highlighting not just the demands of Hood's supporters for payment of their expenses, but the variety of ways in which those expenses were incurred: 'For Puffs & Squibs and for abusing opposition'; 'For changing Sides; for hiring of Ballad Singers & Grub Street Writers . . .'; 'For the attack in Bow Street'; 'For Voting 3 times'. An embarrassed Pitt stands behind the locked gate of the Treasury: 'I know nothing of you my Friends, Lord H[oo]d pays all the expences himself – Hush! Hush! go to the back-Door in Great George Street under the Rose!' (George Rose was a secretary to the Treasury). This was the first plate to which Gillray put his signature and his annoyance did not stop there; he followed it with another (published, most unusually, by himself) that attacked Hood savagely for lying to the electorate.[78]

But the nation's second distraction from the trial of Hastings was about to occur, and, occasioned by the behaviour of the King, would be a great deal more alarming.

CHAPTER FIVE

FIGHTING FOR A CROWN

The Regency Crisis and its Aftermath, 1788–90

Following the King's conduct at a levée on 24 October 1788, rumours abounded as to his mental state, and his derangement was announced to ministers on 6 November. Suffering (as doctors have now diagnosed) from porphyria, a rare metabolic disorder,[1] he had the previous day violently attacked the Prince of Wales and, exhausted by delirium, collapsed in a coma. For a few days he hovered near death.[2]

The government's position seemed more than precarious: the King was too unwell to rule; the Prince being heir to the throne, would as regent assume the conduct of royal business. The caricaturists immediately exploited the political implications of so dramatic a development. For the Prince conspicuously supported, not Pitt and the government, but the opposition, and had been caricatured doing so since 1780 (*see* Plate 17). As recently as 30 October 1788 that support had been alluded to by Dent in an audacious print (Plate 120). The Whig leaders are *Revolutionists*, urged on by a fanatical Burke, who scale a mountain-top to assault the King, whose throne is perched on the peak of the 'Constitution'. Only a fortificatory ditch, the 'Pitt of Circu[m]vention' remains to be breached by Fox (his axe ominously inscribed 'Cromwell') and his Whig companions. Among them is George Hanger, whose shillelagh, or cudgel, bears the colours of the Prince of Wales, with their ironic motto 'Ich Dien'.

Earlier in the summer of 1788, the wayward Prince had again been in the news, this time for a drunken prank at Newmarket, when he had pushed one of the brothers of the Duc d'Orléans (either the Abbé de Saint-Far or the Abbé de Saint-Albin) into an ornamental pond. Thereupon, according to the *Morning Chronicle* of 10 July, Orléans chased the Prince with a whip until he found refuge in a nearby pavilion. An artist imagines the scene in *The Newmarket Humane Society!* (Plate 121), as a solicitous Burke attends to the unfortunate abbé, and the irate Orléans is restrained from renewing his attack on the chastened heir to the throne.[3]

On 5 November,[4] the day before ministers learn of the King's derangement, the etcher of *A Canterbury Tale* (Plate 122) again laments the folly of the Prince's association with the opposition. He portrays Fox, Hanger (one of those who had restrained Orléans), the Prince, and Burke as a gang who, pressed for funds, appear to have raided Lambeth Palace. The first three are about to cast off in a rowing boat and Burke, leaning over a parapet with a sack of swag, exclaims 'Damme Charly dont leave me in the Lurch'. Fox, however, is pushing off, saying 'Self preservation is the First Law in Nature'. Responding, however, to the extraordinary developments, the caricaturist rushes out an altered state of the print (Plate 123) which reflects the sudden transformation in the political fortunes of those he has lampooned. He reworks the plate, adding a mitre to Fox's head, and inscribing Burke's bag as 'Robes'. 'Here take the Robes my Lord', says Burke to Fox, who responds: 'I should make an Excellent Bishop'. The Prince (from whose coat the artist – or perhaps the publisher – now thinks it discreet to erase the star of the Garter) duly obliges: 'By the Grace of God

120. William Dent: *Revolutionists*. Published 30 October 1788, by W. Dent. Not in BM Cat.; private collection.
Each assailant of the King brings his own mode of attack: Fox, for instance, wields the axe of 'Cromwell'. To his right, George Hanger (later Baron Coleraine) pins to his shillelagh, or bludgeon, the colours of his friend the Prince of Wales, with their ironic motto, 'I serve'. Apothecary Hall's artillery is mortar and pestle, with pen and quill. Burke, predictably, is cast as fanatical crusader; above him, to his left, Sheridan is armed with his pistol of 'wit'.

REVOLUTIONISTS.

121. Anon. [attributed to Frederick George Byron]: *The Newmarket Humane Society!* Published 1 September 1788, by William Holland. Not in BM Cat.; Lewis Walpole Library, Yale University.
Ducked in an ornamental pond at Newmarket by a boisterous Prince of Wales, the victim, a brother of the Duc d'Orléans is revived by Burke (centre) as Orléans threatens to horsewhip the culprit. The title of the print derives from the Humane Society founded in 1774 for the rescue of drowning persons.

The Newmarket Humane Society!

122. Anon. [*A Canterbury Tale.*] [Published 5 November 1788, by S.W. Fores] BM 7375; private collection. Title and publication line to this and to the BM impression have been added by hand.
Self-preservation governs the decision of Fox and, behind him, Hanger and the Prince of Wales, to abandon Burke and the proceeds of what appears to have been a raid on Lambeth Palace.

123. Anon.: *A Canterbury Tale.* Published 5 November 1788 by S.W. Fores. BM 7375A; British Museum.
With news that the Prince is likely to become regent, Plate 122 has been altered to indicate that not merely booty but offices and sinecures will be available for the asking.

Arch-Bishop Charles'. The booty being stolen in the first state of the print now gives way to the capturing of office itself.

Fox was in Italy with his mistress Mrs Armistead when the crisis broke. The scene of *Charley's Return From Over The Water* (Plate 124) is enacted by Dent on 26 November. He steps from the *Prince of Wales Cutter* at 'Pickled Herring Stairs' to be received by his grateful and vociferous supporters. Burke's greeting explains their enthusiasm: 'O Blessed Return! hadst thou been lost it would have been all Dicky with us'. Dicky was Sheridan, who in Fox's absence, and to their great resentment,

A CANTERBURY TALE.

A CANTERBURY TALE

CHARLEY'S RETURN FROM OVER THE WATER.

O Blessed Return! hadst thou been lost it would have been all Dicky with us—

Over the water, over the lee,
And over the water went Charley,
Charley loves his Box and Dice,
And Charley loves good Brandy,
And Charley loves his pretty Wench
As sweet as sugar Candy.

Over the Water, over the lee,
And over the water with Charley,
Ar—d tuckt her Petticoats up,
For she loves Gin and Brandy
And Ar—d loves her Charley Boy
As sweet as sugar Candy.

Over the water, over the lee,
And over the water to Charley,
Charley loves Rare News, as well
As she loves Gin and Brandy,
So Charley returns to his P——
As sweet as sugar Candy.

124. William Dent: *Charley's Return From Over The Water*. Published 26 November 1788, by W. Dent. BM 7279: collection Andrew Edmunds, London. Dent conjures up a Jacobite scene as Fox comes home to a hero's welcome, a crown and sceptre proffered by Edward Hall symbolising the Whigs' new prospects. Mrs Armistead (Elizabeth Bridget Cane, 1750–1842), caricatured for her affairs over the years, married Fox secretly in 1795, a matter he revealed to his family and friends in 1802.

had already seized his opportunity as one of the Prince's chief advisers to intrigue with the Lord Chancellor, Thurlow. (Sheridan's face may be spotted between the kneeling figures of Burke, in his Jesuit's soutane, and the plumper Edward Hall, apothecary and Foxite supporter, also wearing spectacles. In the circumstances he is keeping a low profile.) Over the years Sheridan and the Prince had become intimate companions and were genuinely fond of each other, though, as one commentator has put it, 'simple snobbery no doubt exercised its insidious allure on the actor's son from Dublin'.[5] Ambitious, and to Burke's mind an unprincipled careerist, Sheridan had been prepared to act as cat's paw in many an awkward or unsavoury situation and (where Fox had incurred her wrath) had earned Mrs Fitzherbert's particular affection for defending her honour before a cynical House of Commons, with what Lord Holland called 'unintelligible sentimental trash'.[6]

Burke's biographer, James Prior, writing in 1824, allowed that 'the witty and ingenious Mr. Sheridan' had exceptional talents, as poet, comic dramatist, politician and orator. But 'power, fortune, and distinction, all the inducements which usually work on the minds of men, threw out their lures in vain to detach him from pleasure,

125. [James Gillray]: *Bandelures*. Published 28 February 1791, by S.W. Fores. BM 7829; British Museum.
In a scene of intimate domestic dalliance reminiscent of Fragonard, *Bandelures* shows Mrs Fitzherbert – with crucifix around her neck – keeping Sheridan and the Prince happy simultaneously. On the mantelpiece, beside the Prince's dice and a figure of Bacchus, stands a bust of Claudius, perhaps to warn the Prince of the infidelities of imperial consorts.

127. Anon.: *Frogs Chusing a King*. [1789]. Not in BM Cat.; Lewis Walpole Library, Yale University. Burke, bespectacled, Fox and North (with his ribbon of the Garter) bring destruction on themselves by supporting the regency of the Prince of Wales.

to which alone he was a constant votary'.[7] And pleasuring Mrs Fitzherbert is Sheridan's aim in a later Gillray print of 1791 (Plate 125), for this is how the artist interprets her particular affection: reclining on a settee against Mrs Fitzherbert, the drowsy Prince is playing a fashionable toy, the bandelure (what we today would call a yo-yo). Her right hand rests playfully on his stomach but the other reaches up to stroke Sheridan's chin while he presses amorously against her cheek, his hand groping in her *décolletage*. To complete the *ménage à trois* the Prince's elbow leans suggestively on her thigh. 'Thus sits the Dupe content!' says Gillray.

Fox's hasty return from Bologna had brought on dysentery. In a crucial debate on 10 December, acutely ill, he overplayed his hand, asserting the automatic and indefeasible right of the Prince to assume the reins of office. Pitt, charged by a furious Burke with being 'one of the Prince's competitors',[8] proposed that the declaration of a regency should await a search among historical precedents, and a decision of both Houses. Wrongfooted, the opposition found itself upholding hereditary right while Pitt was asserting the principle of parliamentary authority. Playing for time, and an

126. William Dent: *The Monstrous Hydra or Virtue Invulnerable*. Published 11 January 1789, by W. Dent. Not in BM Cat.; Library of Congress.
The plumes of the Prince of Wales decorate the hydra rising from Pandemonium to ensnare Pitt and his restrictive Regency Bill. Above Pitt's head Burke (right) is poised to strike.

FROGS CHUSING A KING.

opportunity for the King to recover, Pitt set about the task of framing proposals for a regency in which the powers of the Prince would be restricted. These he did 'on the supposition that his Majesty's illness is only temporary and may be of no long duration'.[9] He proposed, therefore, stringent restrictions, vesting the care of the King's person and the running of the household in the Queen, and preventing the Prince from granting any part of the King's real or personal estate, or granting any pension or office other than at his Majesty's pleasure. Nor, to all intents, was the Prince to bestow peerages.[10] These were bound to dismay the Prince, and with Burke's help he protested in what has been described as 'one of the ablest state-papers composed in English'.[11]

The regency struggle unleashed a propaganda battle of epic proportions. From November 1788 to mid-May 1789, each of the eighty or so political prints recorded in the British Museum is related to the gripping crisis.[12] Great licence was also taken in the press, and scurrilous accounts that got into the public domain were ideal to travel further in caricature. Fanny Burney, the Queen's companion, recorded in her diary the Queen's distress on one particular occasion: 'She had been greatly offended with some anecdote in a newspaper – the *Morning Herald* – relative to the King's indisposition. She declared the printer should be called to account. She bid me burn the paper, and ruminated upon who could be employed to represent to the editor that he must answer at his peril such treasonable paragraphs'.[13]

To symbolise the Prince's prospects, the 'rising sun' is much in evidence. In a print by Dent,[14] North, Sheridan and Burke kneel before it, while the confident Fox invokes a full moon to aid his plans, which project from his pocket as 'Arrangements New Ministry'. For Pitt, the sun to invoke is 'Public good' and this he does when ensnared by *The Monstrous Hydra*[15] (Plate 126). It is one of the twelve labours of Hercules to kill the many-headed snake; cast in this role by Dent, and surrounded by the serpentine necks and heads of opposition leaders, Pitt arms himself with his 'Regency Limitations & Restrictions'. Burke, wearing spectacles and a wig with a queue, is particularly menacing, a barb darting from his mouth. One neck lacks a head but is surmounted by the feathers of the Prince of Wales, though the Prince himself may be seen at the base of the design, emerging as part of Hydra from the flames of 'Pandemonium'. The rising sun again forms the background to *The Battle of St Stephen's*.[16] Wounded by Fox's blunderbuss of *Indefeasible Right*, (while his own, *Precedent*, has probably fired and missed) Pitt falls back and is caught by his companion Edward Topham, the playwright, ministerial propagandist and newspaper proprietor lampooned by Gillray during the Westminster contest (*see* Plate 119). Topham offers him a phial of *Puff Drops* and urges him to 'Retire Dear Sir with this best consolation: the post of Honor is a private Station'. In the background, Burke is helping to give Sheridan a leg up to the window of the Treasury, a venture intended to reflect Sheridan's prominence in the negotiations as well as his own financial difficulties. There he is confronted by the Duke of Richmond and an agitated Lord Hawkesbury. 'Make haste in, my dear Sherry', says Burke, 'and turn out Uncle Toby[17] and that Fool of Power Hawk[esbur]y'. '& Pray secure something good for me', adds Lord Derby.

Elsewhere (Plate 127), the Prince lounges in reverie on a grassy slope, dreaming of an encounter in which Justice tells Britannia that 'the Son shall arise in Due time'. Reclining beneath the Prince, but alert, the imperial lion guards sceptre and crown. Its suspicions have been aroused by the croaking of frogs in a nearby pond, among which Fox, for whom Britannia has lowered a noose, and Burke (identified by his spectacles) are prominent. They are *Frogs Chusing a King*.[18] (In one of Aesop's Fables

128. Anon.: *The Free Regency*. Published January 1789, by J. Bradshaw. BM 7487; private collection.
In a regency free of the limitations which Pitt had sought to put in place, the new courtiers would include Sheridan at the Prince's right hand and Fox and Burke. With a backward glance – appealing, perhaps, to Justice – Pitt is hurried out of the throne room by the Queen and the Duke of Richmond as an audience is given to England's enemies, France and Spain.

The FREE REGENCY

the frogs call upon Jupiter to give them a king and, for their pains, get a crocodile which devours them;[19] in another, the lion cries out as he crushes the frog: 'Fancy such a little thing as you making such a big noise'. Or perhaps an earlier print by Rowlandson is being recalled, where a huge toad (Fox) whispers in the ear of the Prince of Wales as he sleeps on a grassy bank: 'Abjure thy Country and thy parents And I will give thee dominion over Many powers'.)[20]

The implications of *The Free Regency* (Plate 128), unimpeded by the limitations Pitt sought to impose on the Prince, are foreseen in an anonymous aquatint published in January by J Bradshaw. An elegant Prince of Wales reclines on the throne, surrounded by his confidants – prominent being Fox and Burke but, in place of honour at his right hand side, the opportunistic Sheridan – as the Regent graciously receives supplicants from England's enemies, France and Spain. Poor Pitt, still glancing back at this distressing scene, is led from the throne room by the Queen and Richmond.

In the many satires on Pitt, much was made of his own ambitious schemes in seeking to impose restrictions on the Prince. *The Prospect Before Us* (Plate 129) published on 20 December 1788, and accusing Pitt of manoeuvring the Queen (with the connivance of the very large and much lampooned Mrs Schwellenberg, keeper of the robes) in order to control the regency, is engraved from a delightful pen and ink drawing with brown wash (Plate 130).[21] Pitt holds, as a leash, drapery attached to the Queen's gown while she explains that she follows Billy's advice. The political message is noticeably beefed up for publication from Rowlandson's draft, which has Pitt say, 'I have long humbug'd the nation and by this last grand effort shall secure my situation and command the Treasury at the next general Election'. In print this becomes: 'Behind this petticoat battery with the assistance of Uncle Toby [Richmond, Fox's uncle and Master of the Ordnance] I shall beat down the legal fortifications of this Isle, and secure the Treasury at the next general Election'. In response to which, Rowlandson himself may have thought to add another onlooker who mocks Pitt's

129. [Thomas Rowlandson]: *The Prospect Before Us*.
Published 20 December 1788, by Tom Brown. BM
7383; British Museum.
The Queen, treading on the prospects of the Prince of
Wales, is seen to share the regency crown with the
manipulative Pitt, while the ambitious Mrs
Schwellenberg, keeper of the robes, holds the bag of
the Great Seal and hopes 'to preside at the council'.

130. Thomas Rowlandson: sketch for *The Prospect
Before Us*. Brown and black pen and ink and wash over
graphite (*c.* December 1788). Yale Center for British
Art, Paul Mellon Collection.
With rapid, flowing lines Rowlandson (1756–1827)
creates the theatrical procession of the Queen and her
allies in the regency crisis. Hastings, the diminutive
figure to Pitt's right, rejoices that 'my diamonds will
now befriend me'. Rowlandson's comic genius was
more suited to social than political satire.

125

131. [Thomas Rowlandson]: *Suitable Restrictions*. Published 28 January 1789, by S.W. Fores. BM 7497; private collection.

The principal players, in the game of marbles for the Crown, are Fox and Sheridan: Burke ('My turn next Sher[r]y') has to fight for his place. The infantile Prince, keen to join them, is restrained by Pitt.

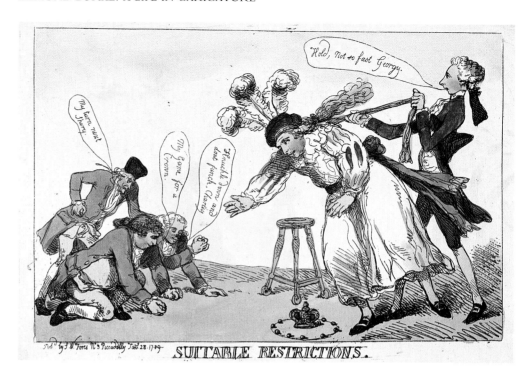

supposed sexual orientation: 'he never meddled with a Petticoat *before*'.

In *St Stephen's Mad-House; or, The Inauguration of King William The Fourth*,[22] Pitt, the William in question, is accused of usurping the crown. He and his followers are the mad inmates of parliament. 'Nelly Rogers shall be Queen!' cries Pitt, causing Burke to observe that 'Benevento's Devils were nothing to this'. *Suitable Restrictions* (Plate 131) shows Rowlandson on this occasion to be more sympathetic than others: 'Hold, not so fast Georgy', says Pitt as he restrains the Prince. The latter, dressed like

132. 'J.S.' [Thomas Rowlandson, parodying James Sayers]: *Neddy's Black Box*. Published 30 January 1789, by S. Fores. BM 7499; private collection.

Burke, encouraged by Sheridan, offers the Prince the head of Charles I, saying 'My Liege I told them in the House no day so proper to settle the Regency as Charles's Martyrdom'.

126

a toddler and wearing a 'pudding' or cushioned cap, is trying to join Fox, Sheridan and Burke in a game of marbles for the crown. An interesting exchange takes place between the players:

'My Game for a Crown', says Fox, preparing to aim.
'Knuckle down and dont funck, Charley', replies Sheridan.

To funk is to advance the hand unfairly in playing marbles,[23] but from Dr Johnson's dictionary we see it has other meanings: 'to stink through fear', 'to poison with an offensive smell'. ('A low word', says Johnson). Burke agitates from behind: 'My turn next She[r]ry'. How much of the vulgar fun do we miss, two hundred years later, as we put this material under our worthy political and art-historical microscopes? Some of the vulgarity is, however, only too apparent: a coarse print typical of the period is Rowlandson's *Loose Principles*[24] which acknowledges Sheridan's new-found political influence as the Prince's confidant. As the 'Principal Promoter of loose Principles' he applies a syringe, 'R[egen]t's Clyster', to Fox's posterior. Burke gropes disgustingly in the close-stool, whose lid is suitably inscribed 'Not searching from Precedents but consequences'. He calls 'To Ordure – Ordure', a pun on his being so often called to order for his speeches on the regency.

Some of Burke's speeches during the crisis were, indeed, intemperate: on 5 February 1789 he spoke of the King having been 'hurled by Providence from the throne'[25] a phrase that would come back to haunt him, and Rowlandson was quick to lampoon him for an overheated speech on 27 January. He had found it offensive that Pitt had not observed the formality of using a treasury box, or black box, when writing to the Prince, and saw this as discourteous. He was upset that the House would not sit on 30 January, the anniversary of Charles I's execution ('of all days the most fitting for taking that step which was to annihilate the constitution'). And he disparaged the Lords of the Household, who stuck 'by the King's loaf' while protesting that they 'did not value the money three skips of a louse'.[26] Rowlandson was another who – like Gillray – teased Sayers (and, no doubt, confused his followers) by adding the initials 'J.S.' to a print.[27] This he does in *Neddy's Black Box containing what he does not value three Skipps of a Louse* (Plate 132). Neddy is Burke, who, encouraged by an eager Sheridan, kneels to hand the receptive Prince a 'Treasury Box' containing the head of Charles I. 'My Liege', he says, 'I told them in the House no day so proper to settle the Regency as Charles's Martyrdom'.

And so it was not surprising that a wag should post an additional bulletin in Whitehall in the manner of the medical reports on the King: 'The Right Hon. Edmund Burke had last night three hours sleep; he is calm this morning, but tending towards unquietness'.[28]

The sun is not always depicted as representing the Prince's hopes. In *House-Breaking, before Sun-Set*[29] (Plate 133) it symbolises the monarchy 'obscured, not lost' as Pitt valiantly defends the Treasury from assault. Fox, who has broken the pickaxe of 'Presumptive Right', aided by the masked Sheridan with his crowbar of 'Begum Sophistry' and Burke, picking the royal lock with his 'Tropes', are about to be apprehended by the loyal watchman Thurlow, an irony given his intriguing with Sheridan early in the crisis.[30]

The title suggests that although the attack has been mounted with indecent haste, it is only a matter of time before the Foxites prevail. In labelling the sun as 'obscured' the artist points delicately to the nature of the King's illness. But shortly thereafter, in *The Eclipse at an End*,[31] Rowlandson develops more boldly the visual pun of lunacy as the King emerges from his blackness to shine light on the political jousting below.

133. Anon. (perhaps Samuel Collings): *House-Breaking, before Sun-Set*. Published 6 January 1789. Not in BM Cat.; The Pierpont Morgan Library, New York. Peel Collection No. 206.
Pitt, from an upper window, defends the Treasury with the blunderbuss of the Constitution, from the assaults on it of Fox, Burke and a masked Sheridan. Burke is given the more subtle tools: instead of Fox's pickaxe of 'Presumptive Right' and Sheridan's crowbar of 'Begum Sophistry', he applies the tropes of debate to pick the lock.

HOUSE - BREAKING, before SUN-SET

1. Sawbridge. 2. Wilson Bp Bristol 3. Warren Bp Bangor. 4. Lᵈ Sandwich. 5. Watson Bp Llandaff. 6. Lᵈ Derby. 7. Marq. Lothian. 8. Burke. 9. D. Norfolk. 10 Lᵈ Derby. 11. Mʳ Powis. 12. D. Queensbury. 13. Lᵈ Stormont. 14. Lᵈ North. 15. Lᵈ Loughborough. 16. D. Portland. 17. Fox. 18. Sheridan.

134. James Sayers: *The Comet*. Published 18 February 1789, by Thomas Cornell. BM 7508; British Museum. The princely comet falls to earth. Foremost in its tail is a devastated Sheridan; Burke, with spectacles, scowls further back.

Pitt, with a poor hand, had played his cards shrewdly, dragging out the debate on the regency bill for so long that the King began to recover, something Fox had not reckoned with. There was spontaneous rejoicing throughout London. The 'rising sun' quickly became a falling star in *The Comet* (Plate 134), a Sayers print of 18 February 1789. Sheridan, whose hopes were cruelly dashed, is the first of the Comet's tail, and an angry Burke is to be found near the end. ('Sheridan,' laments Wraxall in his *Memoirs,* 'may rather be considered as a dazzling and seductive meteor, setting ultimately in darkness, than as a steady luminary dispensing an equal light'.)[32] And in *The Regency Twelfth Cake not cut up*, also by Sayers,[33] Weltje drops the knife with which he is about to cut the cake of spoils, transfixed by a ray of light and a scroll proclaiming that the King shall enjoy his own again. 'Den by Got' blurts Weltje, 'we sall heb no Cake'. Sheridan, whose hand is poised over those tantalising portions of the cake marked *1st Comm[issioner] Board [of] Control* – the patronage of India – and *Treas[urer] Navy* exclaims: 'Now our Ruin is complete'. Fox's hands are thrust in his (empty) pockets. Burke, arms folded in disgust, glowers at the scene.

The Whigs had been outwitted by Pitt. Had they accepted his bill, restrictions and

'DOCTOR LASTS EXAMINATION'.

135. [Thomas Rowlandson]: *Doctor Lasts Examination.*
Published 7 February 1789, by W. Holland. Not in
BM Cat.; The Pierpont Morgan Library, New York.
Peel Collection No. 209.
Dr Willis, standing on a stool, and coached by Pitt
who urges him not to 'hesitate to serve the Cause', is
examined by the House of Commons on the King's
medical condition. Burke's question ('How do you
cure insanity') seems to indicate a more personal
anxiety than concern for the King.

all, allowing the Prince to become regent, they might well have been able, in the
ensuing change of government, to manage the crucial medical bulletins to different
effect. Pitt was alert to this threat and had drafted the restrictions to preclude the
Prince's control of the Household. Notwithstanding this, the inducement for the
physicians to switch loyalties would be powerful. Burke, too, was alert to the crucial
role of the doctors, denouncing Pitt's bill as 'putting into the hands of Dr Willis and
his keepers the whole power of changing the government . . . The whole business is
a scheme, under the pretence of pronouncing his majesty recovered, to bring back an
insane king'.[34] And, indeed, medical opinion was deeply divided as to whether the
illness was that of 'a compleat lunatick', the view of the Duke of York in a letter to
Prince Augustus,[35] or the result of some physical ailment such as the 'flying gout'. Dr
Richard Warren, the Prince's physician, had seen no likelihood of the King's
recovery. (The leading society doctor, he was said when examining his own tongue
in the mirror to transfer a guinea piece from one pocket to another.)[36] The Reverend
Francis Willis, a clergyman with a medical degree who had studied insanity and had
kept a private asylum for thirty years, ingeniously distinguished between 'delirium'

136. [Thomas Rowlandson]: *A Sweating for Opposition by Dr W[i]llis Dominisweaty and Co.* Published 6 March 1789, by S. Fores. BM 7514; British Museum.
Dr Willis and the fashionable quack Dominicetti apply their therapy for insanity to the Prince, in the middle tub, and his followers (from left): Mrs Fitzherbert, Weltje, the Irish actress Dorothea Jordan (mistress of the Duke of Clarence), Sheridan, Fox and Burke.

and 'insanity'. While other physicians dismissed him as little more than a quack, he had been given charge of the case by insisting that a cure could be effected under his treatment. 'His majesty's life', thundered Burke, 'was not safe in such hands'.[37] Rowlandson captures the drama in *Doctor Lasts Examination* (Plate 135)[38] as Dr Willis gives evidence to a committee of the House of Commons, coached by Pitt. 'Don't hesitate to serve the Cause', urges the Prime Minister, 'that W[a]rr[e]n is too honest we must kick him out'. Rising to question Willis is an agitated Burke who (as if to elicit an answer to his own condition) asks 'How do you cure Insanity'. Perched on a stool, the eccentric consultant replies: 'I does it all by my Eye'.[39] Willis's therapy involved a regimen of coercion and intimidation that would have finished off many a patient healthier than the King. Rowlandson gives the Prince and his followers a taste of this treatment in *A Sweating for Opposition by Dr W[i]llis Dominisweaty and Co.* (Plate 136). Willis and a fashionable quack of the day, Dominicetti, are stoking the fires of a row of hot tubs from which Burke and the other patients emerge in obvious discomfort. For Rowlandson, alas, this is pot-boiling in more senses than one. Master of so many exquisite compositions where beauty and the grotesque meet in elegant landscapes teeming with supple movement and comic detail, Rowlandson here produces another cheap and cheerful commission, hackwork dashed off to pay the

137. James Sayers: *Barataria*. Published 11 March 1789, by Thomas Cornell. BM 7517; private collection.
A scene from *Don Quixote*, Sancho Panza's installation dinner as Governor of Barataria, is parodied as the Duke of Leinster offers the regency of Ireland to the Prince of Wales as a dish of potatoes. As with the roast beef – the British regency – Thurlow intervenes to have the dish taken back. Leinster is wearing the Order of St Patrick with the motto *Quis Separabit*, who shall separate us?

pressing bills and (like nearly all his political prints) no measure of his brilliance.

In the midst of the excitement at the King's recovery, an Irish parliamentary delegation offering the Prince the unrestricted regency of Ireland arrived, with farcical mistiming, 'just soon enough to be too late', (as Dent gibed in *The Irish Audience* of 2 March).[40] In one of many satires on the delegation (Plate 137), the Prince is Sancho Panza, Don Quixote's squire, whose inauguration as governor of *Barataria* is marked by a feast. (Barataria had been a soubriquet for Ireland since letters in the style of 'Junius' appeared in the *Freeman's Journal*, in 1771.)[41] Seated at a bare table in a great dining hall, he is offered a dish of potatoes by the Duke of Leinster, while Sheridan,

131

The Funeral Procession of MISS REGENCY.

138. [James Gillray]: *The Funeral Procession of Miss Regency*. Published 29 April 1789, by S.W. Fores. BM 7526; private collection.

With the return to health of the King (Burke reads an 'Ode upon his Majesty['s] Recovery'), the Regency is dead: the coffin, with its furniture of feathers, empty purse and dice, is carried to the grave by six 'Irish Bulls', representing the Irish delegation who arrived in London with farcical mistiming to invite the Prince to become Regent of the Kingdom of Ireland.

ever resourceful, tries unsuccessfully to make off with a joint of roast beef. But, as in Cervantes' story, the table is presided over by a doctor – here Thurlow – who causes every dish to be taken away uneaten. In vain the Prince pleads that if he cannot have the roast beef (the English regency) he should be allowed the Irish potatoes for which he had paid. Burke and Fox, two hungry and disconsolate dogs chained together in front of the table, strain in different directions.

It only remains for Gillray to record, on 29 April, *The Funeral Procession of Miss Regency* (Plate 138), an idea derived from a pamphlet doing the rounds.[42] Burke, officiating priest, walks before the coffin, reading from an ode upon his Majesty's recovery. The coffin in borne by six lamenting bulls (representing the Irish delegation led by the Duke of Leinster); on it rests a crown with the Prince's feathers, dice and an empty purse. A weeping Sheridan is quarrelling with Fox. Derived from the same pamphlet is a similar print (Plate 139), in three sections, also published on 29 April by J. Aitken.[43] As the *Funeral Procession of Mrs Regency* makes its way, Burke walks beside Mother Windsor, the noted procuress. Her *décolletage* has slipped and she clutches a

139. Anon.: *The Funeral Procession of Mrs Regency* (detail). Published 29 [April] 1789, by J. Aitken. Not in BM Cat.; The Huntington Library, San Marino, California.

Few of the mourners of Mrs Regency escape lightly: the Irish peers who had hoped the Prince would become Regent of Ireland are shown half-naked and wearing their coats back to front (*see* Plate 88), the tipsy Prince is represented as Folly, and Burke – beside the brothel keeper Mother Windsor – is in a straitjacket and is dubbed 'the Mad Jesuit'.

140. [James Gillray]: *Cooling the Brain*. Published 8 May 1789, by J. Aitken. BM 7529; British Museum. According to Gillray it is now Burke who suffers from the King's malady: as Major Scott shaves his head, Burke, chained to the ground by the 'Censure of the Commons' and the 'Contempt of the Lords' cries out his accusations to a vision of Hastings. But the dangerous Gillray has more targets than one; laden with wealth (to suggest a corrupt relationship) the Governor receives a royal welcome at St James's Palace.

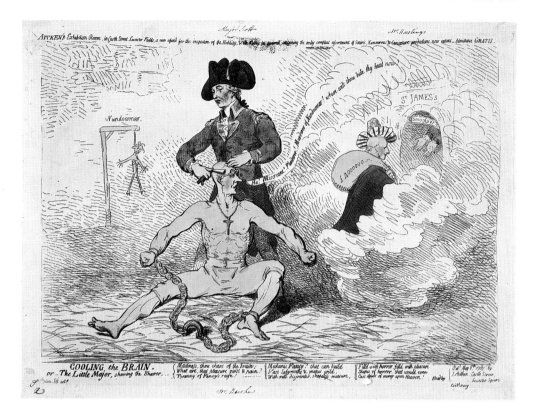

bottle of spirits, inviting 'Neddy' to drink a dram to the repose of her soul. The unfortunate Burke, characterised beneath as 'Edmund the Mad Jesuit', is bareheaded and naked apart from a straitjacket from which hangs a rosary. 'I am feeble & sore broken' he says, '& I have roared, by reason of the disquietude of my mind'.

Perhaps some personal scores are settled by the artist as he adds to the cortège two mourners described as 'Mutes/ Ridg[wa]y: the Pettyfogging Bookseller & Aust[i]n, the Caricaturist'. At the rear, a group of 'Impertenent Tradsmen' wave in despair their unpaid bills. Sheridan (again accused of plagiarising the works of William Congreve) comes in for special mention as one sums up for them all the loss of their regency prospects:

> Our bills now rest in fruitless hope
> Lets give our sorrows their full scope
> Ah sprightly witty *Congreve Dick*
> Who's prob'd our pockets to the Quick
> think what we feel – this Regent Dart
> has touch'd thy trad[e]smen to the *heart*.

Given the drama of the King's infirmity it is not surprising that the caricaturists took up the theme of madness and cruelly ascribed to this ailment Burke's impeachment crusade against Hastings. His trial, interrupted by the illness, was resumed on 21 April 1789, and a vote censuring Burke was carried in the House on 4 May for his accusation that Hastings had murdered the Maharajah Nandakumar 'by the hands of Sir Elijah Impey', Chief Justice in Bengal (*see* Plates 100 and 112). A petition from Hastings has been furnished in the Commons by his agent, Major John Scott, that this was extraneous matter not included in the charges of the House. In *Cooling the Brain, or The Little Major shaving the Shaver* (Plate 140), Gillray depicts Burke as a lunatic, his head being shaved by Scott as he sits in chains shackled by 'The

FRITH the MADMAN HURLING TREASON at the KING.

141. [Isaac Cruikshank]: *Frith the Madman Hurling
Treason at the King*. Published 31 January 1790, by
S.W. Fores. BM 7624; British Museum.
On 21 January 1790, a deranged subject, John Frith,
had thrown a large stone at the passing royal coach.
Cruikshank now recreates the scene: Burke, a
simpleton with a hatful of stones, is restrained by a
Bow Street constable while Fox, an old woman, looks
back poignantly and Sheridan, her sailor companion,
turns away, muttering: 'Damn'd unlucky'.

Censure of the Commons' and 'The Contempt of the Lords'. 'Ha! Miscreant!', he
rages, 'Plunderer! Murderer of Nundocomar! Where wilt thou hide thy head now?'
But Gillray rarely gives undiluted enjoyment to his victim's detractors: Hastings is
seen about to enter St James's Palace with a sack of '£4,000,000' over his shoulder.

Some months later, on 31 January 1790, Isaac Cruikshank sees Burke as *Frith the
Madman Hurling Treason at the King* (Plate 141), a ragged simpleton trying to fling a
stone at the monarch as he passes in the royal coach (as one John Frith had done ten
days earlier)[44] and being restrained by a Bow Street officer and the Prince of Wales.
Fox, an old woman carrying a basket, looks back poignantly at Burke, while her sailor
companion, Sheridan, turns away saying 'Dam'd unlucky' – reflecting more his own
sense of misfortune than sorrow at Burke's affliction. On casual reading Isaac
Cruikshank's print is an amusing run of the mill dig at Burke. Cruikshank may lack
the draughtsmanship of a Gillray or a Rowlandson but he is politically astute and well
informed. The son of a Scottish customs officer he has come to London around 1784
and, though his work is variable, is emerging to rank next to Gillray in political satire.

134

In the next generation his elder son Isaac Robert will be a competent journeyman, while the talent of his second son George will make the family name synonymous with humorous illustration. Cruikshank, like his colleagues, uses the technique that is still today a tried and trusted formula in creating cartoons: he marries two or three separate stories that have excited public feeling. Here, the petty assault of a deranged subject; the popularity of the King since his recovery (yet the ambivalence inherent in his having been deranged); Burke's long standing run-in with the crown; his tendency to over-heat in debate and, specifically, the wild words used against the King during the regency crisis; disappointment and deteriorating relations between the Whigs caused by the crisis and its outcome, especially resentment of Sheridan's intriguing; the impact of such strains on mentor and protégé – these are the components with which Cruikshank skilfully assembles a print that, as well as being funny, or because it is funny, adds damagingly to Burke's public profile.

Burke, in fact, was very shortly to commit himself passionately to another great cause, one that would lead to an irreparable breach with his colleagues (starting with Sheridan), but would bring him immeasurably closer to the King. In a parliamentary speech on 9 February 1790, he declared his uncompromising and comprehensive hostility to the French Revolution and remonstrated with Fox for his apparent endorsement of it. Fox, acknowledging his immense intellectual indebtedness to Burke, sought to assure him that 'never would he lend himself to support any cabal or scheme formed in order to introduce any dangerous innovation into our excellent constitution'.[45] Sheridan, however, intervened to declare 'that he differed decidedly from his right hon. friend in almost every word that he uttered respecting the French Revolution', provoking Burke's response that 'henceforth his hon. friend [Sheridan] and himself were separated in politics'.

This rupture in friendship and politics marked a watershed in Burke's career, and left him open to a range of accusation and satire which provided new material to the caricaturists and, one suspects, new kinds of suffering for Burke at their hands.

CHAPTER SIX

THE KNIGHT OF THE WOEFUL COUNTENANCE

Opposition to the French Revolution, 1789–93

It was predictable that Burke's breach with the Whigs would be represented as indicating inconstancy, and it was predictable, too, that such inconstancy should be represented as arising from self-interest. We have seen images of Burke up to this point helping to oust George III from his 'tavern'; wielding the sceptre himself in the company of Captain Blood (Plate 115); as ally of *Cromwell ye 2ⁿᵈ* (Plate 48); as firebrand and, indeed, as one of the *Revolutionists* (Plate 120). But sometime before May 1789, before his parliamentary attack on the French Revolution, there was published a prescient image of a conscientiously bifurcated Burke. This was in a verse satire celebrating 'a Contest between two old Ladies in the Service of a celebrated Orator' (Plate 142). According to legend the wise King Minos of Crete became, after his death, supreme and impartial judge in the infernal regions, before whom the dead pleaded their causes. Such a trial is illustrated in the untitled frontispiece, where two old women, both of them Burke, confront each other. One is classically draped, 'Sublime & Beautiful', the other an old Irish peasant woman whose character may be judged from the papers she carries on the 'Pres[en]t Disconte[nts]'. The first addresses Minos, who resembles Lord Camden (and is assisted by two other judges, possibly Pepper Arden, by now Master of the Rolls, and Thurlow):

> To One Master, my Lord we two Women belong
> Whom I strive to lead right, and she strives to lead wrong,
> Edmund Burke's Moral Conscience, my lord is my Name,
> His Political Conscience, is she to her shame.

The double, or bisected, portrait is a device which will be called on soon again, by Gillray (Plate 171) and Dent (Plate 178).

The rift with his allies, and the accusation of political apostasy, were immediately taken up by Dent who represents Burke and Sheridan as *Peachum and Lockit* (Plate 143), the thieves who fall out in the *Beggar's Opera*.[1] Sheridan has snatched Burke's wig from his head, revealing the word 'Tory' inscribed on his pate. Sheridan is Lockit, in Gay's ballad opera the warder of Newgate Gaol. Despite having to discard two broken keys labelled 'Regency disappointment' and lying across each other to mock a frustrated papal connection, he still carries in his pocket another, to the 'Prince's Closet'. Burke is cast as Peachum, receiver of stolen goods and informer against his clients. 'Brother, brother', he says, 'we are both in the wrong.' His pocket contains a paper marked 'Secrets'. Behind him an open book describes the nature of the quarrel: 'To day Argue for Republicism' and 'To-morrow Argue for Monarchy'. Above hangs a picture entitled 'The Sublime and Beautiful Janus' in which Burke (in the manner of the two-faced Roman god) 'speaking on English Affairs', turns to the left

142. [John Boyne]: [*Burke's Two Consciences*]. Frontispiece to *Gynomachia; or, a Contest between two old Ladies, in the Service of a celebrated Orator*. Published (1789), Walter, Piccadilly. BM 7527; British Library. The owl of mock wisdom is attentive as the supposedly irreconcilable contradictions in Burke's character are put before the court of King Minos (enacted, perhaps, by Lord Camden) in the infernal regions. On the left is Burke's 'Moral Conscience', elderly, voluble and needing a crutch. On the right, trusting for the moment to her naturally impaired vision, is his more belligerent 'Political Conscience'.

The words in the image: "Brother, brother, we are both in the wrong."

"The Sublime & Beautiful JANUS."

"Hurled by Providence from the Throne" / "Speaking on ENGLISH Affairs" / "Kings should be held Sacred" / "Speaking on FRENCH Affairs."

"Almanack FULL MOON" / "To Day argue for REPUBLICISM" / "Tomorrow argue for MONARCHY"

PEACHUM and LOCKIT,

Or the fall out and make up, a Scene in the Beggar's Opera, as Acted, at the Great Theatre, by two distinguished Characters.

143. William Dent: *Peachum and Lockit*. Published 15 February 1790, by W. Dent. BM 7627; private collection.
Burke is Peachum, the receiver and informer in Gay's *Beggar's Opera*, here unmasked by his erstwhile accomplice Lockit (Sheridan) who snatches off Burke's wig to reveal the word 'Tory' underneath. Charges against Burke of inconsistency abound: behind, he is 'The Sublime & Beautiful [but two-faced] Janus', while the Almanac on the table proclaims it to be the time of the full moon.

crying, 'Hurled by Providence from the Throne' (*see* page 127) while, 'speaking on French Affairs', he turns to the right declaiming that 'Kings should be held Sacred'. (The charge that Burke is two-faced will be peddled for years to come – for example *see* Plate 189).

It is commonplace in caricatures of Burke to include a cross representing his Catholic sympathies; here Dent uses it to augment his charge of inconsistency – one piece of the cross is inscribed 'Revolution', the other 'Toleration', and he rubs in the notion of Burke's instability by propping the book against two papers: the first – 'At present fully satisfied with my conduct respecting my Persecution of Mr H[astings]' – implies he will come to regret it bitterly; the second simply announces 'Almanack Full Moon'.

An attempt by the Duke of Portland to patch up the quarrel between Burke and Sheridan was recorded by Isaac Cruikshank in *Different Sensations* (Plate 144) on 26 February 1790. The design is in two compartments, the first depicting Burke and Sheridan biting at each end of their bone of contention, Revolution, until it snaps.

137

BONE of CONTENTION.

DIFFERENT SENSATIONS.

PORTLAND INVENTION

Pub.d Feb 26. 1790 by S.W. Fores at his Museum N.3 Piccadilly. Where may be seen the compleatest Collection of Caricatures, in the Kingdom Admit.

144. [Isaac Cruikshank]: *Different Sensations*. Published 26 February 1790, by S.W. Fores. BM 7631; British Museum.

The bone of contention between Burke and Sheridan snaps, causing Burke to say 'Seperated for EVER'. Portland's attempts at reconciliation prove unsuccessful, his soup too hot for Burke's taste.

145. Anon.: *Sedition and Atheism Defeated* (detail) Published 18 March 1790, by S.W. Fores. BM 7635; British Museum.

Burke's supposed Catholicism is again attacked: having set the future King and Queen (presumably the Prince of Wales and Mrs Fitzherbert) at their Roman Catholic devotions, the monk Burke retires contentedly, reciting the Nunc Dimittis, his task accomplished.

'Separated for EVER' exclaims Burke. The second reveals the Duke serving a bowl of 'Portland Soup' to the antagonists. While Sheridan dips in his ladle, Burke blows furiously at his, saying 'C'est trop chaude'. Sir Gilbert Elliot later reminisced: 'Sheridan is universally allowed to have been wrong originally, and the Duke of Portland says Burke was afterwards wrong in not favouring a reconciliation'.[2] Lady Jersey wrote to the Duchess of Devonshire on 12 February 1790: 'The D. will tell you of Burke & Sheridan's reconciliation which was perfectly irish for they are now upon worse terms then ever.'[3]

When parliament came to vote on the repeal of the Test and Corporation Acts (which excluded Dissenters from state and municipal office), a proposal moved by Fox on 2 March 1790, Burke's position was wrongly anticipated by some caricaturists. In an undated print, of about February, he is one of a series of isolated figures in a strip design, declaiming in gown and Jesuit's biretta: 'My Brethren let Brotherly love continue, it is a Just Cause you must believe your Pastors we'll make them repeal the Test Act',[4] and as late as 18 March a print hostile to repeal includes an attack on Burke's supposed Catholicism. *Sedition and Atheism Defeated* (Plate 145) contains within it a design depicting 'A Future K[in]g & Q[uee]n at their Devotion' (probably the Prince and Mrs Fitzherbert) before an altar with its crucifix and papal portrait. Burke in the cowl and garb of a monk rejoices: 'Lord now lettest thou thy Servant depart in peace . . . for mine Eyes have seen thy Salvation', the familiar text of the Nunc Dimittis having been used in a radical sermon published by the Dissenter Dr Richard Price.

Though Burke had all his life supported the cause of toleration for both Protestant and Catholic dissent he was troubled by the writings of Price and other leading Dissenters such as Samuel Palmer, John Robinson, and Joseph Priestley, who showed 'a warm, animated, and acrimonious hostility against the Church establishment'. He stated that he would therefore withhold his support until they came to consider the Church of England as 'a jealous friend to be reconciled, and not an adversary that must be vanquished'.[5] But he did propose as a solution (and in doing so anticipated the eventual repeal of the Act in 1828) that Dissenters take, instead of the sacramental test, an oath renouncing any attack on the Established Church.

Other caricaturists may have got it wrong, but Dent makes no mistake. He imagines *The Host of Dissenters and St Charles their Black Convert routed by the Church Canon*,[6] (Plate 146) as Fox, Price and his colleagues mount an assault on the dome of St Paul's Cathedral. They are crudely repulsed by the bombardments of Burke, on the pinnacle, squatting on the cross of 'Orthodoxy' and of Pitt and 'St Stephen's Disciples', looking down from the lantern ballustrade from where they defend the flag of the 'Thirty Nine Articles'. Burke has removed his breeches and holds a copy of *Sublime and Beautiful* against his backside to effect his unsavoury offensive. Tumbling over with Fox are his dice and dice box ('Creed') and playing-cards ('Belief'), and with the preachers their burning bushes[7] of 'Presbyterianism', 'Deism', 'Arianism', and 'Unitarianism'. The dove of peace arrives to say the struggle is over, a paper in her beak announcing a government majority of 189.

It was Price's sermon, preached on 4 November 1789[8] and published in a pamphlet of the Revolution Society (named after the English Revolution of 1688) that provoked Burke to write the great tract *Reflections on the Revolution in France And* [to give it its full title] *On the Proceedings In Certain Societies in London Relative to that event In a Letter Intended to have been sent to a Gentleman In Paris*. While the period February 1790–April 1791 may be seen as one of parliamentary truce between Burke and most of the Whigs, publication of the tract on 1 November 1790 was an event which greatly increased their hostility towards him.[9] It was, too, an event keenly seized upon by the caricaturists. The first, published next day,[10] (Plate 147) picks out the famous passage beginning 'It is now sixteen years since I saw the Queen of France' and reproduces it below, ending: 'I thought ten thousand swords must have leaped from their scabbards to avenge even a look that threatened her with insult – But the age of Chivalry is gone'. An enraptured Burke kneels before his vision of Marie Antoinette, his brain inflamed by the torch of a cherub. But gone are the biretta and Jesuit's gown; instead he wears a wig with a simple queue and court dress.

In February 1790 Burke had sent an early draft to Philip Francis. His reply, on 19 February, deeply hurt Burke:

> Remember that this is one of the most singular, that it may be the most distinguished and ought to be one of the most deliberate acts of your life. Your writings have hitherto been the delight and instruction of your own Country. You now undertake to correct and instruct another Nation, and your appeal in effect is to all Europe. Allowing you the liberty to do so in an extreme case, you cannot deny that it ought to be done with special deliberation in the choice of the topics, and with no less care and circumspection in the use you make of them. Have you thoroughly considered whether it be worthy of Mr Burke, of a Privy Councillor, of a man so high and considerable in the house of commons as you are, and holding the station you have obtained in the opinion of the world to enter into a war of Pamphlets with Doctor Price? . . . Let everything you say be grave, direct and serious. In a case so interesting as the errors of a great nation, and the calamities of great individuals, and feeling them so deeply as you profess to do, all manner of insinuation is improper, all jibe and nickname prohibited. In my opinion all that you say of the Queen is pure foppery. If she be a perfect female character you ought to take your ground upon her virtues. If she be the reverse it is ridiculous in any but a Lover, to place her personal charms in opposition to her crimes.[11]

Burke was stung to reply that:

> the recollection of the manner in which I saw the Queen of France in the year 1774 and the contrast between that brilliancy, Splendour, and beauty, with the prostrate Homage of a Nation to her, compared with the abominable Scene of 1789 which I was describing did draw Tears from me and wetted my Paper. These Tears came again into my Eyes almost as often as I looked at the description. They may again. You do not believe this fact, or that these are my real feelings, but that the whole is affected, or as you express it, "downright Foppery". My friend, I tell you it is truth – and that it is true, and will be true, when you and I are no more, and will exist as long as men – with their Natural feelings exist. I shall say no more on this Foppery of mine.[12]

Tactless and negative as Francis appeared to Burke, his worldly advice, to one he admired, anticipated just the sort of cynical response the *Reflections* inspired in the caricaturists. In *The Knight of the Wo[e]ful Countenance Going to Extirpate the National Assembly* (Plate 148) Burke, on the back of an ass (with the head of Pope Pius VI), emerges as Don Quixote from the premises of his publisher James Dodsley. Clad in armour, with the skull and crossbones of the Prussian Death's Head Hussars pinned to his biretta, an owl perched aloft, and around his neck a medallion of Marie Antoinette, he carries a spear and 'the shield of Aristocracy and despotism'. Below the design, Burke is quoted against himself, asserting that those who are habitually

London Pub.d Novem.r the 2. 1790. by Will.m F. Colland N.o 54, of m.d. F.n in. whose rooms may be seen the largest Collection in Europe of Caricatures. admit 1sh

FRONTISPIECE to REFLECTIONS on the FRENCH REVOLUTION.

It is now sixteen or seventeen years since I saw the Queen of France, then the Dauphiness, at Versailles: and surely never lighted on this orb, which she hardly seemed to touch, a more delightful vision. I saw her just above the horizon, decorating and cheering the elevated sphere she just began to move in, — glittering like the morning star, full of life, and splendor, and joy. Oh! what a revolution! and what an heart must I have, to contemplate without emotion that elevation and that fall! Little did I dream that, when she added titles of veneration to those of enthusiastic, distant, respectful love, that she should ever be obliged to carry the sharp antidote against disgrace concealed in that bosom; little did I dream that I should have lived to see such disasters fallen upon her in a nation of gallant men, in a nation of men of honour: and of cavaliers. I thought ten thousand swords must have leaped from their scabbards to avenge even a look that threatened her with insult. — But the age of chivalry is gone.

London Pub.d Nov.r 15. 1790. by W.m Holland N.o 50 Oxford Street.

It is undoubtedly true, though it may seem paradoxical; but in general, those who are habitually employed in finding and displaying faults, are unqualified for the work of reformation: because their minds are not only unfurnished with patterns of the fair and good but by habit they come to take no delight in the contemplation of those things. By hating vices too much, they come to love men too little. It is therefore not wonderful, that they should be indisposed and unable to serve them. From hence arises the complexional disposition of some of your guides to pull every thing in pieces. — Burke on the French Revolution. Page 250.

In Holland's Exhibition Rooms may be seen the largest collection in Europe of Caricatures admittance one shilling.

DON DISMALLO, AFTER AN ABSENCE OF SIXTEEN YEARS, EMBRACING HIS BEAUTIFUL VISION!

148. [Attributed to Frederick George Byron]: *The Knight of the Wo[e]ful Countenance.* Published 15 November 1790, by William Holland. BM 7678; private collection. Edmund Burke rides out from his publishers to tilt at the French Revolution with a spear fashioned from his gigantic pen.

149. Anon.: sketch for *The Knight of the Wo[e]ful Countenance.* (1790) The Pierpont Morgan Library, New York. Peel Collection No. 233.

150. [Attributed to Frederick George Byron]: *Don Dismallo, After An Absence of Sixteen Years, Embracing His Beautiful Vision!* Published 18 November 1790, by William Holland. BM 7679; British Museum. While Burke, turning away from his wife, wonders 'what's her bacon and eggs to the delicious Dairy of this celestial Vision!!!', Marie Antoinette lapses into a Burkean parody, enlivened with *double entendre.*

employed in finding fault are unqualified for the work of reformation: 'By hating vices too much, they come to love men too little'. (A preliminary sketch still in existence[13] (Plate 149) serves as a reminder that the printing process reversed the image, posing difficulties in lettering that must have contributed to spelling errors. 'Woful' in the title to this print is, possibly, an example.) F.G. Byron produced a companion plate (Plate 150), of *Don Dismallo, After an Absence of Sixteen Years, Embracing his Beautiful Vision!* Welcoming to her arms this Adonis of cavaliers, this god of chivalry, Marie Antoinette proposes a more intimate, if less chivalrous, encounter. An elderly Mrs Burke weeps to hear her husband's ecstatic response to this Dulcinea: 'Christ Jasus, what an ass I have been a number of years; to have doated on an old woman – Heavens! what's her bacon and eggs to the delicious Dairy of this celestial Vision'. The owl perched on his biretta goes 'Whoo oo oo oo! The first man in the house of commons ! the first man every where!' More was to follow. *Don Dismallo Running the Literary Gantlet* (Plate 151) sees him stripped to the waist and flogged by

DON DISMALLO RUNNING THE LITERARY GANTLET.

151. [Attributed to Frederick George Byron]: *Don Dismallo running the Literary Gantlet*. Published 1 December 1790, by William Holland. BM 7685; British Museum. Burke, dressed as a clown, suffers under the lash of supporters of the French revolution (from left): Helen Maria Williams, Dr Richard Price, Anna Letitia Barbauld, Sheridan and, to the right, Horne Tooke and Catherine Macaulay Graham. Beside Sheridan, Justice prods Burke with her sword; to her right Liberty assists a ragged old man thought to be the Bastille prisoner J.F.X. Whyte, born in Dublin and known as Count Whyte de Melville.

152. [James Gillray]: *Smelling out a Rat*. Published 3 December 1790, by H. Humphrey. BM 7686; collection Andrew Edmunds, London.
As Dr Price composes a tract *On the Benifits of Anarchy Regicide Atheism* (below a painting of the 'Death of Charles 1st, or the glory of Great Britain'), he is confronted by a grotesque image of Burke, upholder of church and crown. Thus Gillray aims a deadly blow at the reputation of the dissenting preacher while ridiculing Burke for his supposed apostasy.

153. William Dent: *Sublime and Beautiful Reflections on the French Revolutioh* [*sic*]. [Published 14 December 1790, by W. Dent]. Publication line in manuscript. BM 7689; collection Andrew Edmunds. Burke's ideas fluctuate, claims Dent, like the phases of the moon.

his pamphleting opponents. Dr Price is urging Anna Letitia Barbauld[14] to 'cut the Jesuitical Monster in pieces'. Waiting her turn at the other end is Catherine Macaulay Graham (1731–91), 'our Republican virago' as Burke described her, and anonymous author of *Observations on the Reflections*.[15] She is determined to 'tickle to some tune' with her scourge and grumbles that the hypocrisy of Cromwell was nothing to Burke's, to which John Horne Tooke rejoins: 'Cromwell, madam, was a Saint, when compared with this Literary Lucifer'. Burke's quarrel with Sheridan, another with a scourge, is recalled as he pleads in vain for mercy.[16]

If Gillray is occasionally for hire he is a dangerous man to choose: his political acumen, brilliant draughtsmanship, comic inventiveness, and sly ambiguity, mark him out as the greatest, and the least manageable, caricaturist in this golden age of graphic satire. With unerring instinct he focuses on Richard Price's role and his vulnerability, as a dissenting preacher, in being associated with what Burke has stressed as the atheism of the French Revolution. *Smelling out a Rat; – or – The Atheistical-Revolutionist disturbed in his Midnight Calculations* (Plate 152) catches Dr Price at his writing desk, working 'On the Benifits of Anarchy Regicide Atheism', when he is startled by the vision of Burke's enormous bespectacled nose. Yet as Draper Hill observes, 'with typical ambiguity, the content of the engraving is critical of Price but the form ridicules Burke'.[17]

Meanwhile, William Holland's customers are clearly enjoying the Don Quixote analogy and Burke makes another appearance as *Don Dismallo among the Grasshoppers in France*, being insulted and dragged to a gibbet by a hostile crowd.[18] Dent is not to be left out of the fun. *Sublime and Beautiful Reflections on the French Revolutioh* [*sic*] or

144

Smelling out a Rat;——or The Atheistical-Revolutionist disturbed in his Midnight Calculations.

the Man in the Moon at Large (Plate 153) emphasises (as the title implies) the alleged fluctuation of Burke's principles. Burke sits behind his desk in a crescent moon, manacles to each arm broken or untied, writing his pamphlet. 'By Vision Celestial and Fury Infernal', he says, 'I'll give them a Crown Touch'. An inscription in each corner of the design reflects the moon's changes.

> NEW MOON. The People have no Right to new form of a Constitution – they should look up with awe to Kings . . .
> FIRST QUARTER. The influence of the Crown ought to be diminished . . .
> FULL MOON. <u>Hurled</u> by Providence from the Throne . . .
> LAST QUARTER. Kings and Crowns should be held Sacred!!! . . .[19]

The postscript sums it up: 'N.B. The Man, as well as the Moon may be expected to continue his changes till fixt by a Total Eclipse.'

Dent continues his attack in *The Tell Tale in High Credit With the State Gossips* (Plate 154). Burke, in Court dress, is entertained to tea by the King and Queen. Madame Schwellenberg, keeper of the Queen's robes, is in attendance and watches him so intently as he gesticulates that she pours tea onto the tray. Burke, holding a copy of

THE TELL TALE IN HIGH CREDIT WITH THE STATE GOSSIPS.

154. William Dent: *The Tell Tale In High Credit With The State Gossips*. Published 8 January 1791, by W. Dent. Not in BM Cat.; collection Andrew Edmunds, London.
At tea with the King (who is reading Thomas Paine's *Rights of Man*) and Queen, and Mrs Schwellenberg, keeper of the robes, a garrulous Burke praises his own *Reflections* ('This precious Book'). As he protests 'my political Life is on the close – what's a Title or a Ribbon to me', he raises his left arm, perhaps to shield from view the coronet which Pitt discreetly slips to him.

his *Reflections*, rants at some length. 'This precious Book', he says, 'is the best Book ever written – for this glorious Book first brought to light the designs of my Associates . . . I am an honest Man – not the less so for not making known what Company I kept till provoked by having my Book grinned at . . . That Book in your hand', (the King holds a copy of Paine's *Rights of Man*) 'which in reading I have felt *Pain* is of a piece with the Faction – but I know him, and know them all, and you shall know all about them . . . my Book, therefore is worth a Hundred Thousand Crowns, and whoever says to the contrary is a Jack Cade, Wat Tyler an infernal and the Devil himself knows what and I'll tell you, these fellows I apprehend, mean to, to, to I'll tell you – what they Mean – .' Behind Burke stands Pitt, who muses: 'How the Fellow has abused us – but we must hold the candle to the Devil sometimes'. Ignoring (or unaware of) Burke's profession 'what's a Title or a Ribbon to me – my thoughts are fixt on *better things*', Pitt slips him a coronet. The Queen says nothing but stares coolly across.

Burke is again Don Quixote – this time Isaac Cruikshank's version – in *The Aristocratic Crusade, or Chivalry revived by Don Quixote de St Omer & his Friend Sancho*

146

155. Isaac Cruikshank: *The Aristocratic Crusade* (detail). Published 31 January 1791, by S. Fores. BM 7824; private collection.

Burke has travelled a long way since *The Tombs of the Worthies* of 1784 (Plate 56), which include Wat Tyler, leader of the Peasants' Revolt of 1381 and *The Butchers of Freedom* of 1788 (Plate 116). He now leads *The Aristocratic Crusade*, trampling underfoot the 'base born Plebeians'.

(Plate 155). In his knightly armour, from which a bare buttock emerges, Burke stands on the back of a monster, sword in one hand and the shield of his *Reflections* in the other. A five-headed version of the 'beast of Rome',[20] the monster tramples under foot 'base born Plebeians' (a reference to the swinish multitude; *see* p. 173). A Latin tag above Burke's head sets the scene: *Horridum Monstrum! Procerum potentium Saeva Potestas!!!* (The savage power of mighty people is a frightening monster). Burke's crusade of mighty people, the reactionary forces of Anglican bishops, robed peers and corrupt borough-mongers, are marching to confront a French procession bearing placards on the rights of man. Caught up in this is the royal carriage of Louis XVI and Marie Antoinette to whom Burke calls out: 'angel just above the Horizon like the morning Star glittering! alas ! the age of Chivalry is gone & the glory of Europe lost for Ever'. Those in the procession he decries as 'a set of low bred illiterate Traders Lawyers & Country Clowns'. As for their English sympathisers, the Revolution Society, an eight man band led by Dr Price and Lord Stanhope, he damns their 'Babylonian pulpite Pisgay Perorations!'

Burke is again accused of apostasy and desire for office in *Ecce Homo versatilis! alias Edmund the Apostate* (Plate 156), published on 7 March 1791 and frontispiece to 'The Wonderful Flights of Edmund the Rhapsodist, into the sublime and beautiful regions of Fancy, Fiction, Extravagance and Absurdity . . .' It is a pamphlet ridiculing Burke's overheated imagination on a series of issues: America, economical reform, Hastings, the regency and now his response to the French Revolution. The print conjures up an awesome scene in the underworld from where Burke is setting off on one of his periodic flights of fancy, borne aloft on a broomstick in a cloud of smoke. Donkey's ears suggest he is emulating Pegasus, the winged horse.

Years later (1795) Burke would refer to the *Reflections* as 'that unfortunate book of mine, which is put in the *Index Expurgatorius* of the modern Whigs'.[21] While most Whigs disapproved of the *Reflections,* Burke for some months continued − at least nominally − to be a member of the parliamentary group. But in a Commons debate

Ecce Homo versatilis! alias Edmund the Apostate. Burke.

The Pyramids in the back ground contain millions of slaughtered victims to the divine rights of kings or the sanguinary principles of the Priesthood of all ages. The characters are explained in the pamphlet.

1791

156. Anon.: *Ecce Homo versatilis! alias Edmund the Apostate*. Published 7 March 1791, by H.D. Symonds. BM 7833; British Museum.
With the flimsiest aerodynamic apparatus, Burke the apostate takes off from the underworld on yet another flight of fancy. Donkey's ears mock his emulation of Pegasus the winged horse, who looks on in some surprise.

on 15 April 1791 Fox triggered their painful breach by stating 'that he for one admired the new constitution of France, taken together, as the most stupendous and glorious edifice of liberty, which had been erected on the foundation of human integrity in any time or country.'[22] Burke's first opportunity to respond came on 21 April during discussion on the Quebec bill, and their bitter quarrel came to a head when the debate resumed on 6 May. Burke denounced the new French constitution as disastrous to the French West Indies: 'Blacks rose against whites, whites against blacks, and each against one another in murderous hostility; subordination was destroyed, the bonds of society torn asunder, and every man seemed to thirst for the blood of his neighbour.'

> Black spirits and white
> Blue spirits and grey
> Mingle, mingle, mingle

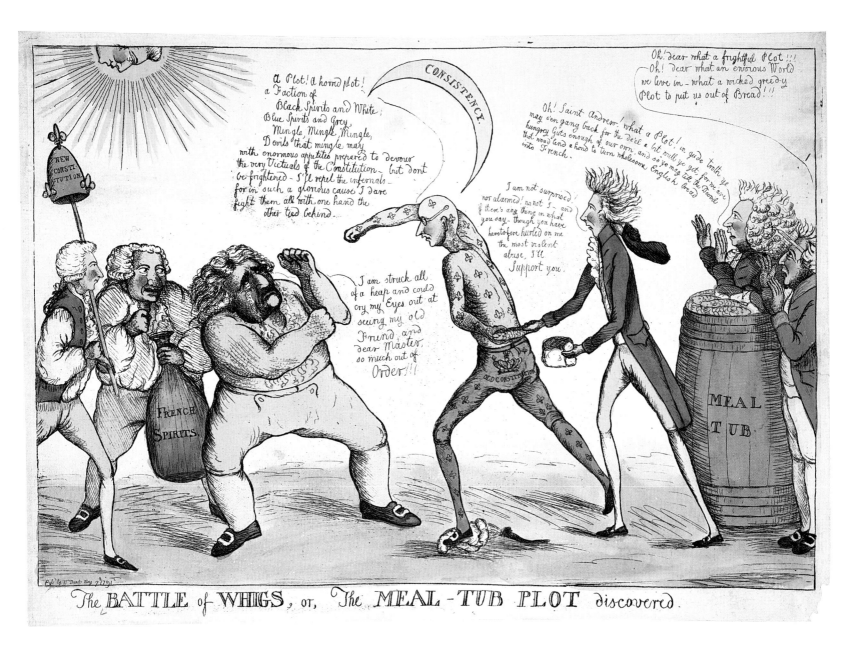

The BATTLE of WHIGS, or, The MEAL-TUB PLOT discovered.

157. William Dent: *The Battle of Whigs, or, the Meal-Tub Plot discovered*. Published 7 May 1791, by W. Dent. BM 7854; private collection.

Dent records the painful breach between Fox and Burke as a prize fight in which the Whig leader, supported by Sheridan and Charles Grey, holding aloft the cap of liberty, withstands Burke's attack. In a pose reminiscent of that in Plate 154 Burke, tatooed with fleurs-de-lis, covertly accepts from Pitt the loaves and fishes of government reward, amid the protestations of Dundas and Rose.

All was toil and trouble, discord and blood, from the moment that this doctrine was promulgated among them; and he verily believed that where the rights of men were preached, such ever had been and ever would be the consequences.[23] Fox, repeating that he thought the French Revolution 'one of the most glorious events in the history of mankind', implied that Burke was out of order and his supporters began to shout down Burke's reply. Burke, incensed, announced that 'their friendship was at an end'. The *Parliamentary History* continues: 'Mr *Fox* rose to reply: but his mind was so much agitated, and his heart so much affected by what had fallen from Mr Burke, that it was some minutes before he could proceed. Tears trickled down his cheeks, and he strove in vain to give utterance to feelings that dignified and exalted his nature. The sensibility of every member of the House appeared uncommonly excited upon the occasion.'[24]

These details of the quarrel provide background to the spate of caricatures inspired by the event. Quickest to respond was Dent, whose satire next day, *The Battle of Whigs, or, the Meal-Tub Plot discovered* (Plate 157) pictures the combatants as prize-fighters, stripped to the waist. The burly Fox, tears coursing down his cheeks, claims to be struck all of a heap at seeing his 'old Friend and dear Master' so much out of

149

order. He strikes, nonetheless, a pugilistic pose and is urged on by his seconds, Sheridan (a bottle-holder wielding an enormous decanter of 'French Spirits') and Charles Grey. Writing of the event, Conor Cruise O'Brien observes that Fox, despite his old affection and veneration for Burke, resented Burke's intellectual and moral ascendancy over him and was now in revolt against that ascendancy, and probably egged on by Sheridan.[25]

Burke is covered, torso and head, with emblems of the *fleur-de-lis* and his breeches are decorated with a crown and the words 'Old Constitution'. While he lunges his right fist at Fox, he holds his left hand behind his back to receive a symbolic loaf and fish from Pitt. He had taken Burke's side on the question of being in order, and now promises his support despite Burke's violent abuse heretofore. Above Burke's head, a crescent moon inscribed 'consistency' denotes, of course, the opposite (*see* Plate 153) as he rails against infernal devils preparing 'to devour the very Victuals of the Constitution'.

The loaf and fish which Burke receives from Pitt, favourite symbols of Dent (and analogous to the Irish taunt nowadays of 'Mercs and Perks') come from a great 'Meal Tub' to the consternation of its guardians Dundas and George Rose. Because it is Dundas, Dent favours us with a Scottish equivalent of 'Arrah by Jasus': 'Oh ! Saint Andrew ! what a Plot,' he exclaims, 'in gude troth ye may e'en gang back for the de'el a bit wull ye get, for we ave hungrey Guts enough of our own'. The Treasury Secretary translates: ' Oh dear . . . what a wicked greedy Plot to put us out of Bread!!!'

The implication of the print (which ties in with a false rumour circulating at the time) is that Burke was acting in concert with Pitt to denounce Fox as a republican, and would be rewarded with a place in Pitt's administration.[26] But a print of 10 May 1791 (etched by John Nixon) perhaps reflects more truly Pitt's feelings at the turn of events. In *The Wrangling Friends or Opposition in Disorder* (Plate 158) he watches the quarrel being played out, with the words 'If they'd cut each others Throats I should be Relieved from these Troublesome Fellows'. Fox, weeping copiously (a river of tears is gathered into a bucket by a boy at his feet), laments: 'Ah well a day my poor heart will allmost Break, 25 years Friendship & use me thus Oh – Oh – Edmund!!!' A small demon is successfully applying a bellows to Burke's heated brain: 'by Lucifer', he says, 'it Boils bravely', as steam rises from Burke's wig. Burke, armed with papers on France, treason and conspiracy, is declaiming incoherently. An angry Sheridan, with blotched face, calls to order 'the man that betrays his friend'.

Unusually, the original sketch for this print[27] has been preserved (Plate 159). It is interesting to see how it has been worked up, losing in the process some of the chaotic immediacy captured in pen and ink. In the course of moving to Burke's side, Pitt's expression of resigned tedium has shifted to one more akin to petulance.

The dispute has other implications too, signalled in a print of 11 May 1791 (Plate 160). With Burke and Fox so preoccupied, and their row fascinating the House of Commons, members' attention is distracted from Pitt and his taxation measures. Delighted with this opportunity to press on quietly with unpopular business, he is 'Little Bill Horner', sitting in his corner with a pocketful of budget proposals, while *The Quarrel between the Political Builders* holds centre-stage. Recalling an architectural analogy he had used in the debate,[28] Burke deplores the French system as 'a Building of untempered mortar built by Goths & vandals'. A tearful Fox hates to quarrel about a paltry building, but still holds it to be 'a stupendous fabric of human wisdom'. Unsigned, the print is 'Done by one in the Shop at the time of the Quarrel!', and M.D. George tentatively attributes the design to George Townshend, by this stage a Marquis.[29]

The WRANGLING FRIENDS or Opposition in DISORDER

I think myself justified in saying this, because I do know that there are People in this Country avowedly endeavouring Disorder
its Constitution & Government & that in a very Bold manner — Vide Burks Speech —— Publ May 10 1791 by SW Fores No 3 Piccadilly,

158. 'J.N.' (probably by John Nixon, after another
artist): *The Wrangling Friends or Opposition in Disorder.*
Published 10 May 1791, by S.W. Fores. BM 7855;
private collection. The hand is similar to, but not that
of, Isaac Cruikshank.
Only Pitt remains calm in a disorderly House of
Commons, Burke's brain nicely addled by a demon,
Fox in tears at his rejection by his old friend. Pitt is
inclined to hope these two 'Troublesome Fellows'
might cut each others throats.

159. Anon.: sketch for *The Wrangling Friends or
Opposition in Disorder.* [May 1791]. Collection House
of Commons.
The preliminary sketch for Plate 158 neatly catches,
amid the chaos of the bitter quarrel, Pitt's expression of
resigned tedium.

160. Anon. (possibly after George, Marquis Townshend, 1724–1807): *The Quarrel between the Political Builders*. Published 11 May 1791, by W. Maynard. BM 7856; British Museum.

The rupture of relations – here cast in architectural terms – is represented as between a sentimental Fox and Burke driven, as so often, by a demon. The attention of the House thus diverted, Pitt (left) will quietly advance unpopular financial measures.

161. James Sayers: *Mr Burke's Pair of Spectacles for short sighted Politicians*. Published 12 May 1791, by Thomas Cornell. BM 7858; British Museum.

Much use was made of Burke's spectacles in caricature; they identified him quickly, they implied faulty vision, he could discard them, as in Plate 142, to avoid seeing what he did not wish to see. And here, as in Plate 113, they could be used, in the hands of others, to show the world as Burke saw it. In this feverish vision Fox – to Portland's horror – attacks the great oak of the constitution to make way for the plant newly propagated in France.

Next day (12 May 1791) comes James Sayers's contribution. Beyond – or should it be through? – *Mr. Burke's Pair of Spectacles for short sighted Politicians* (Plate 161), the ovals of which portray Fox and Sheridan, is Burke's feverish vision of this revolutionary pair. A demon, whose *bonnet rouge* is surmounted by the Prince of Wales's feathers, holds out 'A Plan of the new Constitution of France' (a small potted tree of 'Atheists', 'Demagogues' and 'The Mob'), thus encouraging Fox to strike at the great oak of the English constitution. Dressed as Cromwell, yet wearing a French tricorn, Fox wields an axe marked 'Rights of Man', while his fellow-conspirator Sheridan reaches to extinguish an irradiated Star of the Garter in the midst of the emblem-laden foliage. A string indicates that Fox leads Portland by the nose. Horrified by what he sees, Portland (who – as Sayers anticipates – will also split with the Foxites on the question of 'French Principles') sits astride a section of pillar labelled 'Part of the Subscription Whig Pillar of Portland Stone intended to have been erected in Runnimede', a painful reminder that only a few years previously the Whigs had proposed to erect a memorial commemorating the centenary of William III's landing in 1688. Riding on a winged demon above, Joseph Priestley tilts at bible, mitre and chalice while, below, the skeleton of a grinning Dr Richard Price (who had died three weeks earlier) waves from his burial plot with the text, Nunc Dimittis, from his famous sermon: 'Lord now lettest thou thy Servant – Depart in peace [for] mine Eyes [have s]een thy Salva[tion]'.

Gillray produces two prints on the falling-out. In *The Impeachment, – or – "The Father of the Gang, turned Kings Evidence"* (Plate 162), Burke seizes his two prisoners, Sheridan and Fox, as the abettors of revolutions, the authors of plots and conspiracies, who are aiming to overthrow the British Constitution. Sheridan curses that they have been found out, while Fox sobs to think 'that the Man who has been my dearest Friend, and my Chum in all infamy, for Twenty five years, should now turn Snitch at last!' In Gillray's second print (Plate 163), Fox is *Guy Vaux Discovered in his Attempt*

Mr Burke's Pair of Spectacles for short sighted Politicians

nought shall make us rue
If England to itself do rest but true.
Shakespeare.

Publ. by Thos Cornell, Bruton Street
12 May 1791

162. [James Gillray]: *The Impeachment, – or – "The Father of the Gang, turn'd Kings Evidence".* Published May 1791, by S.W. Fores. BM 7861; British Museum.
Burke is represented as the 'Father of the Gang' who is prepared to 'turn snitch' against his former accomplices, Fox and Sheridan. While Sheridan laments that 'we're all found out!', Fox characteristically weeps for the loss of 'my dearest Friend, and my Chum in all infamy'.

163. [James Gillray]: *Guy Vaux Discovered in his Attempt . . .* Published 14 May 1791, by H. Humphrey. BM 7862; private collection.
Burke comes upon Fox (alias Vaux, or Fawkes) and Sheridan about to apply a flaming *Rights of Man* to a keg of gunpowder, and with his rattle raises the alarm. It was Lord Thurlow in *House-Breaking, before Sun-Set* two years earlier (Plate 133) whose rattle warned government of the subversions of Burke himself and these former comrades.

154

164. [Attributed to Frederick George Byron]: *The Volcano of Opposition.* Published 16 May 1791, by W. Holland. BM 7863; collection Andrew Edmunds, London.

In 1785 Sayers had shown Burke driving members from the House of Commons with his prolixity (Plate 72). Six years later they rush out calling for Doctor Monro, expert in lunacy, to attend to this 'Volcano of Opposition'.

to Destroy the King & the House of Lords – his Companions Attempting to Escape, as he tries to set off gunpowder barrels with a lighted copy of Thomas Paine's *Rights of Man (see* p. 00). A grim Burke arrests the miscreant 'in the name of the British Constitution which thou art undermining'. Circumstances have changed since Burke was caricatured helping *Guy Vaux* to blow up Pitt's India Bill or Captain Blood to set fire to the Tower (Plate 115): all references to his Jesuit clothing and accoutrements are gone; he wears a hat above his wig and a long jacket bearing a badge of the crown as befits a loyal watchman. Sheridan slopes off, with the consoling thought that if Fox goes down 'there's the more room for me!'

For the artist thought to be F.G. Byron, the quarrel on the floor of the House is a *Volcano of Opposition* (Plate 164) that erupts from Burke's mouth and threatens to engulf a weeping Fox: 'Black as ten furies! Jacobite Miscreants, the very dregs of infamy, Terrible as Hell, Infernal Spawn, Damnation, Jacobite renegades, Friends of

THE VOLCANO OF OPPOSITION.

Hell, Pimps Panders Parasites Devils'. As always, prolixity is one of Burke's attributes. Fox strikes a dignified pose, weeping into his handkerchief. He is consoled by Sheridan, who puts his arm around his shoulder soothingly: 'Be comforted, my dear Charles, let not the effusions of a Demoniac afflict you so severely. Live to be a comfort to your poor Sherry'. But Fox is inconsolable: 'Talk not to me of comfort. the derision of the world thrown on my poor old master will break my heart'. As the Speaker, Henry Addington, and other members flee from the House in horror; one calls 'Monro! Monro!', for Dr John Monro, the expert in lunacy.[30]

The same artist continues to ridicule Burke in three further prints published within a week. His supposed Catholicism is mocked in *The Ghosts of Mirabeau and Dr Price Appearing to Old Loyola*)[31] Their spectres appear (Mirabeau had died on 4 April 1791, Dr Price on 19 April) each holding a copy of *Reflections* to a kneeling Burke who holds up a crucifix and rosary in defence, while an old woman (intended perhaps, for Mrs Burke) sprinkles his head with the contents of a chamber pot, saying: 'This Holy Water, my dear master, shall wash you pure from every stain in the world . . .' Burke responds: 'Thus fortified I don't fear the Devil nor any of his Imps! No, nor the whole Host of Opposition'. The caricaturist next moves to traduce Burke's motives for quarrelling with the Whigs. In *Political Playthings for Prostitute Patriots* (Plate 165) he sits in splendour to receive from Pitt an earl's coronet. 'This', says Pitt, 'is for thy long and secret services'. Burke answers: 'Thanks, my noble Master – all the Weird sister of Beaconsfield prophesied is now fulfill'd', an allusion to Burke's country seat and to

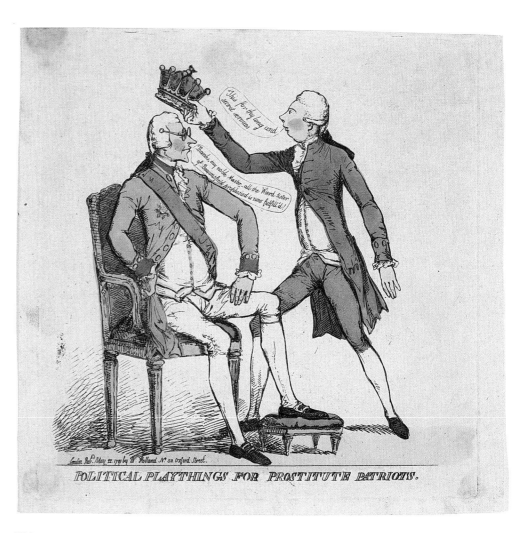

165. [Attributed to Frederick George Byron]: *Political Playthings For Prostitute Patriots*. Published 22 May 1791, by W. Holland. BM 7865; private collection. Where Dent had imputed to Burke a sense of unease in being slipped a coronet by Pitt (Plate 154), this attack on Burke is more savage: Pitt acknowledges 'long and secret services', and the pose of the 'Prostitute Patriot' is assertive.

166. William Dent: *The Disappointment, or, The King's Evidence*. Published 28 May 1791, by W. Dent. BM 7868; private collection.
Burke has made a bonfire of his earlier Whiggish principles and prays for admission to royal favour ('I'll do any thing for a Crown'). But the King keeps his door closed, and tells the disappointed apostate to 'depart in Peace'.

167. [Attributed to Frederick George Byron]: *Contrasted Opinions of Paine's Pamphlet* (detail). Published 26 May 1791, by William Holland. Not in BM Cat.; private collection. Burke reacts with predictable displeasure to a passage from Thomas Paine's *Rights of Man*.

the witches' song in *Macbeth*, 'Black spirits and white . . .' To complete the accusation of apostasy, the artist casts Fox and Burke in the roles of *Launce and his Dog Crab*[32] from Shakespeare's *The Two Gentlemen of Verona*, 'Nay twill be this hour ere I have done weeping' says Launce (Act II, Scene 3) '. . . I think Crab my dog to be the sowrest-natur'd dog that lives . . .' Crab, with Burke's head and spectacles, says: 'I'm now Mr Pitt's in Downing Street / and I'll bark at all the Whigs I meet'.

Dent, too, is withering. *The Disappointment, or, The King's Evidence Treated with the Caution he Deserves*[33] (Plate 166) shows Burke kneeling in supplication before the King's door, 'Open to the Honest and Honorable'. 'Pray admit me!' he begs of George III, who is at an open window. 'I'll do anything for a Crown'. 'I pity you' replies the King, 'but hence and depart in Peace'. Burke's 'peace offering' to the King burns before him: his wig (i.e. his Whig principles) and a number of papers – 'Impeachment Oriental' (of Hastings), 'Inflammatory Speeches', 'Hurled from the Throne by Providence', 'The Influence of the Crown ought to be diminished.' Notwithstanding these, his pocket still contains a crucifix and a note-book of 'Private Views'. On a neighbouring hill, a gallows beckons. 'Arise', it says, 'and be exalted'.

Meanwhile on 13 March 1791, Thomas Paine had published the first part of his *Rights of Man* in answer to Burke's *Reflections,* heralding what one historian has described as 'probably the greatest joust in the lists of political philosophy that Great Britain ever witnessed'.[34] Paine's pamphlet was celebrated by James Gillray with *The Rights of Man; – or – Tommy Paine, the Little American Taylor, taking the Measure of the Crown for a New Pair of Revolution-Breeches.* Dorothy George notes that Paine was successively stay-maker, exciseman and pamphleteer and that the London tailors were divided into Flints, who formed clubs and entered into strikes to obtain increased wages, and Dungs who accepted the statutory rates.[35] In Gillray's print Paine talks of stitching up 'the mouth of that Barnacled Edmund from making any more Reflections upon the Flints – & so Flints & liberty for ever & damn the Dungs'.

In an unusual print of 26 May 1791, attributed to F.G. Byron, eight figures – first among them Burke – give their *Contrasted Opinions of Paine's Pamphlet* (Plate 167). To the King, *The Rights of Man* 'is all abuse' and (we are reminded that he is an authority in the matter) 'Flights of madness! Flights of madness!'. The Queen deplores the book as a compound of falsehoods. To Pitt, Paine is 'a damn'd, murderous Republican'. Burke, of course, is in the same camp: Paine to him is 'an insolent fellow', his work 'an infernal book'.

The contrasted opinions are those of Fox, Sheridan, Charles Jenkinson (1727–1808, Baron Hawkesbury, a former President of the Board of Trade), and the writer Mary Wollstonecraft. Fox, in supporting Paine, attacks Burke's style: 'This is an appeal to common sense, not prose run mad, like Burke's rhapsodical Reflections!' Mary Wollstonecraft who had published her own *Vindication of the Rights of Man* in the previous year, quotes an eloquent passage from Paine:

> Not one glance of compassion, not one commiserating reflection has Mr Burke bestowed on those who lingered out the most wretched of lives, a life without hope, in the most miserable of prisons. He is not affected by the reality of distress touching his heart, but by the showy resemblance of it striking his imagination. He pities the plumage, but forgets the dying bird. His hero or his heroine must be a tragedy – victim expiring in shew, and not the real prisoner of misery, sliding into death and in the silence of a dungeon.

The caricaturists continue to harry Burke about his supposed apostasy. Dent gives him a small but significant part in a scene of wild confusion in the Commons.[36]

168. [William Dent]: *Public Credit or the State Idol.*
Published 3 June 1791, by J. Aitken. BM 7872; British
Museum.

As with many modern cartoonists, Dent's success lies in
a distinctive style and lively observation rather than in
artistic proficiency. He is blatantly scatalogical, often
with language as crude as his images and, as in this case,
happy to copy ideas from much earlier prints. Nor is
he beyond adapting images taken from his
contemporaries, Sayers (Plates 94 and 95), Rowlandson
and Gillray.

169. Anon.: *Idol-Worship or The Way to Preferment.*
Published May 1740. BM 2447; British Museum.
Through the archway on 'The Way to Preferment' lie
'The Treasury', 'The Exchequer', 'The Admiralty':
those approaching or leaving 'kissed ye Cheeks of ye
Postern', Sir Robert Walpole.

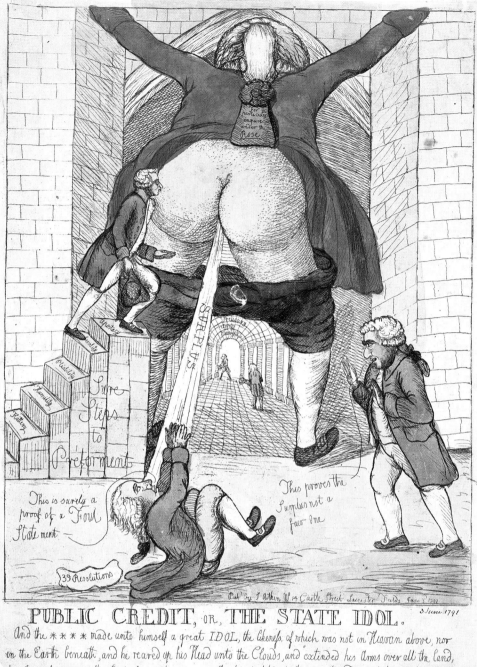

Striking a pugnacious pose, he says 'I am of no Party therefore ready to fight any Party
for any Sum not nice about the Terms'. Dent follows this up with *Public Credit, or,
the State Idol* (Plate 168), a vulgar satire on the secretary to the Treasury, George Rose.
Rose is a gigantic idol from whose bared backside a blast emits to blow Sheridan to
the ground, together with his '35 Resolutions' complaining against Pitt's financial
measures. Meanwhile, Burke has mounted a flight of steps to Rose's posterior.
Inscribed 'Sure Steps to Preferment' they are *Flattery, Humility, Pliability, Servility* and

Apostacy. His intentions, already clear, are further signalled by a description beneath the design: 'And whosoever passed in beneath with idolatrous Reverence First lifted up their Eyes, and kissed the cheeks of the Postern'. (Dent copied this image from *Idol-Worship or The Way to Preferment* (Plate 169), an anonymous print published in May 1740, in which Sir Robert Walpole had provided the postern.)

In June 1791 Louis XVI and his family tried to escape from France. In *French Flight, Or, the Grand Monarque and the Rights of Kings Supported in a Sublime and Beautiful Manner* (Plate 170), Dent lampoons Burke as the winged Mercury, bearing on his shoulders Marie Antoinette, on whose shoulders in turn is Louis XVI. 'Stop and consider', says Louis, 'my great weight, I am afraid, will overset us'. 'Indeed my dear, you are of no weight at all', replies the Queen. 'By Jasus', muses Burke, 'the only way to get what you want is to run from it. So sit easy my works and a good Conscience will bear you up'. Following their recapture, a print after G.M. Woodward depicts *An Aristocrat* weeping as he contemplates a heap of discarded (or perhaps confiscated) medals and ribbons 'sacred to the National Assemb[l]y.'[37] He holds a copy of *Burke on the French Revolution* and from his pocket emerges a paper headed 'Capture of the French King'. In a letter to Earl Fitzwilliam Burke saw the great object of Jacobinism as 'totally to root out that thing called the *Aristocrate* or Nobleman and Gentleman'.[38] Writing to Burke from Brussels in August 1791 his son Richard reported that Louis found a temporary solace in translating the *Reflections* into French.[39]

According to Isaac Cruikshank, Marie Antoinette is still on Burke's mind when he attends a levée on the marriage of the Duke of York. Queuing to meet the tiny new Duchess in *A Royal Salute*[40] he observes: 'Not unlike the French Queen but Shorter'. (He studiously ignores Fox beside him in the queue, who covers his face against the heat of a drink-blotched Sheridan and protests: 'Your nose Bardolf [Falstaff's companion in Shakespeare's *Henry IV*] may serve her the office of a Warming Pan, but approach not further, least you may Consume the Whole Court'.)

Burke's abandonment of the Whigs continues to provoke comment. In *A Uniform Whig* (Plate 171), on 16 November 1791, Gillray employs the common device of a bisected portrait, presenting a figure full face, one half contrasting with the other. Here Burke's supposed present position is reflected in his right hand side: a gold-laced coat, coins overflowing from his pockets, his hand – with copy of his book – resting on the plinth of a bust of George III. It is contrasted with his left side where, ragged, bare-footed and penniless, he holds a stick and the *bonnet-rouge* of Liberty. The face, however, is uniform; it is stern and self important. Gillray's small details are always worth looking out for: in the background a windmill – recalling Don Quixote – stands on the summit of a mountain. Fame, poised on its sail, uses two trumpets to herald the inconsistency of Burke's principles.

A Jesuitical Burke, grinning slyly as he picks a 'sinecure' from Pitt's pocket, assists the Prime Minister in another of Dent's bizarre and fascinating tableaux, *Spirit of Aristocracy enforcing Reform, or The Rights of Kings maintained* (Plate 172). Pitt, with a hatchet, has decapitated Liberty and, clutching her head, says: 'There, I have made a good Woman of you'. Louis XVI, though his hands are tied behind his back to indicate he is a prisoner of the Revolution, seeks to overturn Liberty with his foot and by a blast of air from his mouth. Burke is in full Catholic regalia, his enormous biretta labelled 'Monarchal Professor and Confessor', his crucifix 'Liberty'. 'Let the hardened Wretch die and be dam'ed', he says, 'I am for wholesome Freedom'. His vote against the proposal to repeal the Test Act has not been forgotten: one sandalled foot treads on a paper 'Protestant dissenters'. Pitt and Burke are surrounded by an enthusiastic gathering of monarchs. Prominent is Catherine II, Empress of Russia, on

170. William Dent: *French Flight, Or, the Grand Monarque and the Rights of Kings Supported in a Sublime and Beautiful Manner.* Published 26 June 1791, by W. Dent. Not in BM Cat.; collection Andrew Edmunds, London.
Burke, as Mercury, assists the flight of Louis XVI and Marie Antoinette.

A Uniform Whig.

'I preserve consistency by varying my means, to secure the unity of my end.' *Burke Reflections* (1790).

a prancing charger. 'Now cut the Strumpet's tail off', she instructs, 'for I have oft experienced Freedom to be, tho' a pleasing, a dangerous Thing'. Beside her, the devil concurs with a smile: 'Liberty! . . . there's no such thing in my Dominions, and so you may find'.

Catherine the Great appears in a number of prints around this time. She admired Fox, an effective opponent of Pitt's hostile policy to Russia in 1791, and had a bust of him made by the sculptor Nollekens. Given the appetites of both Catherine and Fox, this was bound to cause excitement: in *Black Carlo's White Bust, or The Party's Plenipo in Catherine's Closet*,[41] Sheridan, a fellow spirit, urges Fox to go to Russia. 'Your Fortune is made – she has certainly heard of your Fine Parts'.

Dent's cynicism about the conduct of government is given free rein in *Call of the [House], or, Slave Trade in a land of liberty* (Plate 173). The print derives its title from resolutions on the slave trade moved by Pitt. He now dispenses largesse from a grumbling ass, 'Poor Jack Bull', laden with loaves and fishes. Two parliamentary groups press forward to be fed, and are held back by the Treasury Secretaries, Rose and Charles Long. Pitt, naturally, is concentrating on the ministerial supporters. 'Have Patience!' he calls, 'and do as you are bid, and depend on a Call – '. Rose adds: 'Fall back till you are called you'll all have a call sooner or later'. On the ground beneath him, Brook Watson, with wooden leg, grabs at fallen fish, saying, 'My wife has a Call

SPIRIT of ARISTOCRACY enforcing REFORM, OR The RIGHTS of KINGS maintained.

171. [James Gillray]: *A Uniform Whig*. Published 16 November 1791, by H. Humphrey. BM 7913; private collection.
Burke is charged with inconsistency: the early impoverished bearer of the cap of liberty, and the later royalist author of the *Reflections on the Revolution in France*, whose pockets overflow. But Gillray gives him a uniform face, stern and unbending.

172. William Dent: *Spirit of Aristocracy enforcing Reform*. Published 23 January 1792, by W. Dent. Not in BM Cat. (but in BM, Dent folder, 1792); collection Andrew Edmunds, London. Dent indulges a taste for xenophobia as foreign monarchs rejoice at the execution of Liberty. Burke, a crucifix prominent at his waist, professes to be for 'Wholesome Freedom' as he encourages Pitt in his gruesome task, and picks a sinecure from the Prime Minister's pocket.

173. William Dent: *Call of the [House], or Slave trade in a land of liberty*. Published 2 April 1792, by W. Dent. BM 8076; British Museum. Pitt distributes the rewards of office from the panniers of 'Poor Jack Bull'. Fox and his party on the right are excluded, though Fox has empty buckets which he wishes to fill on behalf of the Prince of Wales and the 'Swinish Multitude'; and Sheridan a pot from the Crown and Anchor tavern. Burke alone has broken from their ranks and, on the ground, scrabbles for fish with Brook Watson.

174. Anon.: *The Balance of Merit*. (*c*. May 1792). Not in BM Cat.; Lewis Walpole Library, Yale University. As the balance tips in favour of Sheridan and Fox, the words from King Belshazzar's feast, (numbered, numbered, weighed and divided) foretelling and the fall of his kingdom, cause concern to the royalists. A cherub advises the King to 'stand on thine own Feet and thou wilt weigh much Heavier', and Pitt moves to dislodge Lord Chancellor Thurlow.

the BALANCE of MERIT

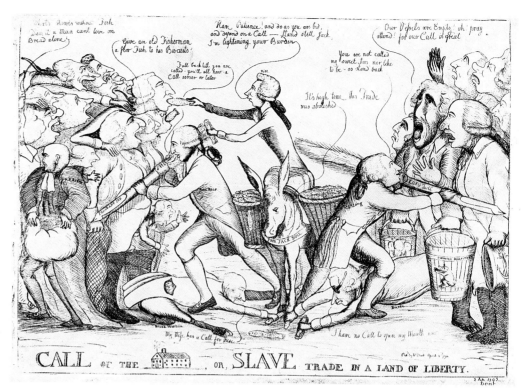

CALL OF THE [HOUSE] OR SLAVE TRADE IN A LAND OF LIBERTY.

for these'. A nice swipe by the caricaturist, this recalls an incident where Watson, having pledged as an MP for the City of London not to accept place or pension, benefitted when a pension of £500 a year was granted in 1786 to his wife. Dent was on hand to lampoon that event.[42]

If the clamour from the government side is good-natured, the Whigs are a picture of misery and vexation as Long reminds them: 'You are not called my sweet Sirs nor like to be – so stand back'. Prominent are Fox and Sheridan, Fox crying 'Our Vessels are empty! Oh! pray attend! for our Call is great'. One of the buckets he carries is for the Prince of Wales, the other for the 'swinish multitude'. (This alludes to an unfortunate phrase of Burke's considered on p. 173). Burke, like Brook Watson opposite, has ducked beneath the Treasury Secretary's legs and is clutching fish in each hand, muttering 'I have no Call to open my Mouth now'. What a mockery of the man who had sought to sweep away jobbery and placemen with his economical reform.

Thurlow's antagonism to Pitt is about to prove fatal. Standing on the King's back in *The Balance of Merit* (Plate 174)[43] in a bid to tilt the scales in his favour, Pitt will disturb the equilibrium and the Chancellor will topple. 'By God I shall be off' exclaims Thurlow. A cherub urges 'George stand on thine own Feet and thou wilt weigh much Heavier'. Thurlow, on bad terms with Pitt since 1789 but banking on the King's continuing friendship, had been opposing Pitt's measures in the Lords with characteristic sarcasm, most recently the national debt bill: (a makeweight hanging from the balance, and marked '10 Millions' alludes to this). Pitt eventually asked the King to choose between himself and the Chancellor and George, though upset, acquiesced, dismissing Thurlow with effect from June 1792.

If Thurlow is about to fall, Burke is very much on board, holding aloft his *Reflections* in an effort to counter the weight of Sheridan and Fox opposite with their revolutionary principles. The hand of God, holding the balance, warns: 'Mene Mene

175. [Attributed to Richard Newton]: *The Libertine reclaim'd*. Published ?10 August 1792, by W. Holland. Not in BM Cat.; The Pierpont Morgan Library, New York. Peel Collection No. 249.
As John Bull falls to his knees under the burden of taxes, and Paine's *Rights of Man* takes flight for America, Richmond (left), Pitt and Burke seek credit for the suppression of radical thought. 'Where are the Patriots now!' exclaims the King.

Tekel Upharsin' – numbered, numbered, weighed, divided – recalling the divine warning to king Belshazzar at his feast.

Burke's taking of sides is the subject of further satires: he is to be seen 'rigid and austere' at the side of the King in *The Grand Review of Sydenham Common*[44] as the uniformed King leads a party of officers in pursuit of the Prince of Wales and other renegades, and in *The Terrifying Comet* (a grand spectacle described by Dent and made up of the heads of the King and the Duke of Richmond), Burke is part of this 'modern planetary system' and boasts the title 'Georgium Sidus', which, as Dorothy George notes, is the name first given to Uranus by Herschel in honour of George III.[45] Burke is represented as a prisoner of Pitt's, manacled at the wrists, in a print of August 1792 attributed to Richard Newton (Plate 175). *The Libertine reclaim'd*[46] is John Bull, brought to his knees by the burden of taxation. 'Behold the wonderful effects of Gunpowder', exclaims Richmond as a winged figure, Paine's *Rights of Man*, takes flight for distant America. 'Wonderful indeed', responds the delighted King, 'ha ha where are the Patriots now!' 'It was the Proclamation annihilated them', says Pitt, alluding to the Royal proclamation of 21 May 1792 against tumultuous meetings and seditious writings. 'And my Letter', adds Burke. His *Letter to a Member of the National Assembly* (1791) had followed the *Reflections* as a form of postscript.

An episode tailor-made for the caricaturists took place in the House of Commons in December 1792: during the debate on a government bill for restricting the activities of aliens, on 28 December, Burke flung a dagger to the ground in dramatic fashion. Gillray pictures him (and, on a diet of 'loaves and fishes', he has certainly put on weight since the skeletal days of economical reform) in *The Dagger Scene* (Plate 176) as he makes his theatrical address to the House. He has discovered a plot for the manufacture of three thousand such daggers and claims that assassins 'are preparing to scour the filth from your Streets with the Blood of all who are Virtuous & Honorable!!!' Pitt responds in alarm: 'The blood of the Virtuous & Honorable? then Lord have mercy upon Me!', and Dundas echoes, 'And upon Me!' Although this is

176. James Gillray: *The Dagger Scene*. Published 30 December 1792, by H. Humphrey. BM 8147; private collection.
As if to anticipate his *Promis'd Horrors of the French Invasion . . .* of 1796 (Plate 193), Burke claims that 3,000 daggers are being manufactured with which assassins 'are preparing to scour the filth from your Streets with the Blood of all who are Virtuous & Honorable!!'. If the faceless Speaker Henry Addington (later Viscount Sidmouth) remains unmoved, Burke's theatrical gesture has startled Dundas, Pitt, Fox, Sheridan and Michael Angelo Taylor.

162

The Dagger-Scene: — or — The Plot discover'd.

Reflections on the French Revolution.

177. [Isaac Cruikshank]: *Reflections on the French Revolution*. Published 1 January 1793, by S.W. Fores. BM 8285; British Museum.
During the debate in which he had flung a dagger to the ground, Burke had spoken of the need 'to keep the French infection from this country, their principles from our minds and their daggers from our hearts'.

THE SHIFTING ORATOR,

RAGE OF PATRIOTISM, | FLOW OF LOYALTY,

OR, JOY UNNATURAL | OR GRIEF ALAMODE.

"I'll speak Daggers – but use none." | 'Hence I'll wear Sable – Like Niobe all Tears.'

178. William Dent: *The Shifting Orator*. Published 1 January 1793, by W. Dent. Not in BM Cat.; collection Andrew Edmunds, London.
Dent's bisected portrait is more explicit than Gillray's *Uniform Whig* (Plate 171): Burke's extravagant words in the regency debates are juxtaposed with his present 'Flow of Loyalty'. 'Flow tears,' he begs, 'and wash away expressions that now serve me not'.

an anti-scaremongering print, Gillray is also targeting the front bench opposite. 'Confusion!' mutters Fox ' – one of Our daggers, by all that's bloody! how the devil did he come by that?' 'O' Charley, Charley!' says a distraught Sheridan, '– farewell to all our hopes of Levelling Monarchs! – farewell to all our hopes of paying off my debts by a general Bankruptcy! . . .' Sheridan's actual response had been to enquire, amid laughter, why the spoon and fork were absent from so fine a display of theatrical cutlery?[47]

If Gillray presents a rigid, condemnatory Burke confronting parliament with his

164

chilling evidence, Isaac Cruikshank (Plate 177) is tempted to conjure up drama of a wilder kind. Burke, over-excited and with a dagger in each hand, lunges forward in the Commons, denouncing 'Plunderers Assassins Republicans Villians Cut Throats Levellers Regicides Lovers of Disorder Exporters of Treason & Rebellion These are Articles they Deal in'. Fox beats a hasty retreat, exclaiming 'D—me he's got the French Disorder'. The phrase, with its indelicate secondary meaning (alluding to syphilis) will bring a wry smile to Cruikshank's audience as they contemplate Fox's own predilections. Edward Gibbon, for one, had thought the *Reflections* 'a most admirable medicine against the French disease'.[48]

Cruikshank's satire was published on 1 January 1793. On the same day Dent offers his verdict (Plate 178). In this bisected portrait (for Gillray's, *see* Plate 171) Burke is unbalanced, an apostate, *The Shifting Orator* whose raging words against the King during the regency crisis he now deplores in a flood of loyal tears. 'Could I use such expressions?' he asks, as he casts down the famous dagger. 'God help me! sure I was mad but now I renounce my Errors! For Kings are Divine and Ministers pure!'

Meanwhile a mischievous print takes pleasure in the rebuff Burke suffered when a cabal at Oxford blocked a proposal to award him a doctorate.[49] It parodies a Henry William Bunbury design popular since the 1770s, *The Hopes of the Family – an Admission at the University,*[50] in which the aptitude of a dim young country fellow is being tested (in front of his fond parent) by a stern professor. The send-up (Plate 179) recounts *The Hopes of the State or an Hibernian Orator and Patron Meeting at the University for his Degrees as AM & Master O'F'Arts,*[51] as a smiling Burke eagerly advances, laden with tomes that attest to his scholarship, for the verdict of the Oxford academics. Pitt has turned away from the scene, clasping his hands in anxious prayer for a happy outcome. The reason for his patronage lies at Burke's feet – it is the dagger he had flung so dramatically to the floor of the Commons. Two of the gathering, one a professor, one perhaps a pageboy, raise their hands in support of Burke's candidacy but, alas, the grim professor most prominently seated keeps his hand resolutely on the

179. Anon.: *The Hopes of the State.* (*c.* 1793). Not in BM Cat.; The Pierpont Morgan Library, New York. Peel Collection No. 254.
Burke solicits, unsuccessfully, an Oxford degree, adducing as qualification the scholarship of his books, the eminence of his patron (Pitt on the right), and the dagger which he had used to such dramatic effect in the Commons (*see* Plate 176).

THE HOPES of the STATE,
Or an HIBERNIAN ORATOR and PATRON ... UNIVERSITY for his DEGREES as
... MASTER OF ARTS

TOM PAINS EFFEGY or the Rights of a ... SEDTIOUS POLTROON

180. Anon. (perhaps John Nixon): *Tom Pains Effegy or the Rights of a Sed[i]tious Poltroon*. Published 16 January 1793, by J. Aitken. Not in BM Cat.; private collection. By the same hand as Plate 158.

Thomas Paine is burnt in effigy on a bonfire of his *Rights of Man* which is stoked by Pitt. Dundas, in Scottish kilt, dances as Burke on the left directs the merriment.

table at his side. Oxford later offered the degree, which Burke declined for himself but steered to his son Richard, when the Duke of Portland was installed as chancellor of the university.[52]

In a print of 16 January 1793 (perhaps by John Nixon), *Tom Pains Effegy* (Plate 180) complete with tailor's scissors, is burned on a bonfire of the *Rights of Man* by Burke and Pitt. Dundas and others dance around excitedly. 'By Jasus,' says Burke, 'we will outlaw him & the Devil make him Dance to the tune of Ça-Ira'. 'Yes Yes', replies Pitt, 'he stirr'd us up now we will stir him up & let the Devel make a san Colotte of him.' And Burke, for so long in the other corner, is Pitt's bottle-holder (Plate 181) in another prizefight with Fox, who has been felled.[53] An anxious Sheridan, clutching a small decanter of 'Sherry', says 'Speak! Monsieur! Speak! Oh! dear! I hope he has not broke his Jaw'. Burke in contrast, holds an enormous decanter of 'Wisky'. 'By Jasus!' he asserts, 'if he offered to Rise I would knock him down'. While 'By Jasus' and 'arrah' continue to be stock-in-trade for the Irish in caricature it is noteworthy that Burke, having lived for over forty years in England, retained a marked Irish accent.

166

181. William Dent: *War! Glorious War!* Published 6 February 1793, by W. Dent. Not in BM Cat. (but in BM, Dent folder, 1793); collection Andrew Edmunds, London.

Dent has recourse, again, to the prizefight. He has in the past matched Burke against Hastings (Plate 91), and against Fox (Plate 157). Here Burke is bottleholder to Pitt ('The True Briton') who has felled 'Monsieur' Fox. The Irishman's 'By Jasus!' is echoed in the version appropriate to Dundas, 'By St. Andrew'.

Sheridan was different, having been educated at Harrow (and being son of the actor and elocution teacher who had sorted out, for one, the Scottish burr of Alexander Wedderburn, now Baron Loughborough and Chief Justice of Common Pleas).

Burke and his son Richard were among a number of members who resigned in February 1793 from the Whig Club, and whose letter of resignation was read at a meeting of the club at the famous Crown and Anchor tavern. (As headquarters of the 'Association for Preserving Liberty and Property', it gave that propagandist organisation its popular title, the Crown & Anchor Society). The incident is recorded, perhaps by John Nixon, as *A Scene in the Crown and Anchor Tavern or a Crack in the Wig Club*, and published on 17 March 1793 by S.W. Fores at No. 3 Picadilly, 'where may be had Complete Setts of Caricature on th[e] French Revolution & on every Popular Subject. An Exhibition Adm^t 1^s in which a correct Model of the Guillotine 6 feet high'.[54] A number of Whigs, one being Burke, discard their wigs on a pile (inscribed 'The Heads having Scratched out of the Club') to the consternation of Sheridan and Fox, whose 'Brother: Brother we are all in the wrong' alludes to the thieves falling out in *The Beggar's Opera* (*see* Plate 143).

A superb print by Gillray (Plate 182) portrays Burke as *The Chancellor of the Inquisition marking the Incorrigibles* outside the *Crown & Anchor*, headquarters of the 'British Inquisition'.[55] He is drawing up a 'Black List' which reads (in a parody of *Richard III*): 'Beware of N[o]rf[ol]k! P[or]tl[an]d loves us not! – the R[u]ss[el]l's [Bedford's family] will not join us. The Man of the People [Fox] has lived too long for us! The Friends of the People must be blasted by us! Sherridan, Ersk[ine]'. Burke is splendidly attired as 'Chancellor' in skull cap and robes and bearing a bag like that of the Great Seal, whose royal coat of arms has been adapted to accommodate crown, anchor and four skulls. Whatever his views about Portland, the print captures Burke's zealous marking of Fox, Sheridan and their supporters as vividly as does Burke's own prose: 'I think it one of my most serious and important public duties, in whatsoever station I may be placed for the short time I have to live, effectually to employ my best

The CHANCELLOR of the INQUISITION marking the INCORRIGIBLES

183. [William Dent]: *An Alarming Anniversary!!!* (date and publication line illegible). Not in BM Cat.; The Pierpont Morgan Library, New York. Peel Collection No. 243.
The quixotic Burke, aloft on his 'Flights of Fancy', describes for Pitt a scene where 'Hell has broke loose'.

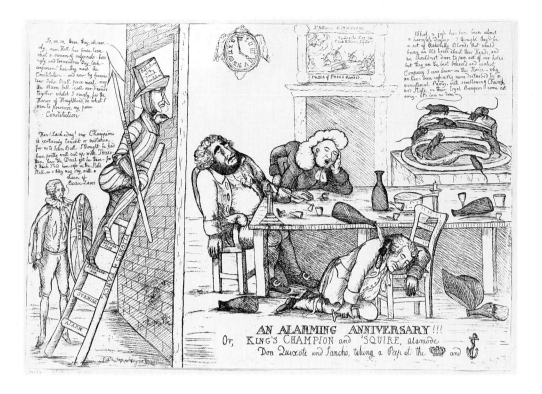

182. James Gillray: *The Chancellor of the Inquisition marking the Incorrigibles.* Published 19 March 1793, by H. Humphrey. BM 8316; private collection.
Although the Crown and Anchor tavern in the Strand had been the venue in 1791 for dinners celebrating the anniversary of the fall of the Bastille, it was from 1792 the meeting place of the 'Assocation for Preserving Liberty and Property against Levellers and Republicans'. Now it has become the sinister headquarters of Burke's 'British Inquisition', where anonymous letters may be sent about seditious behaviour.

endeavors, by every prudent and every lawful means, to traverse all their designs.'[56]

His endeavours to traverse their designs are cruelly parodied by Dent. He is Don Quixote mounting a dead-of-night reconnaisance of the Crown and Anchor tavern, scene of *An Alarming Anniversary!!!* (Plate 183).[57] Burke knows the Whigs are up to no good and, from his vantage point, reports as much to the long-suffering Pitt, his Sancho: 'So, so, so, there they all are – why, sure Hell has broke loose – what a swarm of infernals – how ugly and tremendous they look – confusion ! how they maul the Constitution – and now, by heavens! tear John Bull piece meal – ring the Alarm bell – call our Friends together' – adding, perhaps *sotto voce* – 'whilst I singly, for the Honor of Knighthood, do what I can to preserve my poor Constitution'. To see all this Burke has mounted his ladder, 'Flights of Fancy', whose rungs start with *alarm* and *surmise* and move to *apprehension* and *accusation*. The reality of the scene is quite different. Fox, Pepper Arden (Master of the Rolls) and Sheridan are sleeping off their drinking session while rats, undisturbed, nibble at a joint of roast beef on the sideboard. 'What a fuss has been about a harmless Dinner', says one rat. 'I thought they'd be a set of Rakehelly Bloods that would bring an Old house about their Heads, and we should not dare to peep out of our holes but they are the best behaved and greatest Company I ever knew in this House . . .' Pitt, at the foot of the ladder, suspects as much: 'How! Lackaday ! our Champion is certainly toucht or mistaken'. A undated print by Rowlandson bids us leave this chapter in Burke's life as we left the last, with *A Peep into Bethlehem* (Plate 184). Burke, half-naked and wearing a rosary, shares accommodation in Bedlam, the famous asylum, with John Wolcot (the satirist and poet 'Peter Pindar', who issued various satires on George III from 1785), and with the deranged woman who attempted to stab the King in August 1786, Margaret Nicholson, her head crowned with straw.[58] Pindar and Burke are associated in the print as antagonists of Thomas Paine. Verse beneath the design runs as follows:

184. [Attributed to Thomas Rowlandson]: *A Peep into Bethlehem*. (c.1793). BM 8367; British Museum.
The satirist and poet 'Peter Pindar' (John Wolcot) and Margaret Nicholson, the deranged woman who had assaulted the King, share quarters in Bedlam with the rhapsodical Burke. Rowlandson (Plate 135) had been one of the first to mock Burke's rhetoric by transferring to him the King's malady.

A PEEP INTO BETHLEHEM.

Ah! then dismounted from his spavin'd hack
To Bethlehem's walls with B[urk]e I saw him borne,
There the strait waistcoat close embrac'd his back;
While Peggy's wreath of straw, did either brow adorn,
And there they sit; two grinners vis a vis;
He writing Grub-street verse, B[urk]e ranting rhapsody.

170

CHAPTER SEVEN

PITY THE SORROWS OF A POOR OLD MAN

The Final Years, 1794–97

For a period Burke largely withdrew from public life, escaping the attention of the caricaturists. From 19 March 1793 (when Gillray created him *Chancellor of the Inquisition*) to 8 May 1795[1] he was out of their sights, returning dramatically in *The Last Scene of the Managers Farce* (Plate 185) – the outcome of the trial of Hastings. Interest in the impeachment, which had begun in such frenzy of excitement before the whole of London society, had gradually fizzled out over the years. When Pitt, on 20 June 1794, following Burke's nine-day closing speech, proposed that the thanks of the House be accorded to the managers of the trial on the conclusion of their labours, an amendment to have Burke's name excluded from the vote of thanks was defeated. As soon as the thanks had been carried Burke, a member for almost thirty years, resigned his seat. Yet I have turned up no print to record these events, even though Sumner, the MP who moved the amendment, rehearsed at length and with some vitriol the choicer epithets Burke had used in his arraignment of Hastings. Was it on account of public apathy to the impeachment? Or have the relevant prints, given that caricatures are ephemeral by nature, not survived? Or is it conceivable that the unusual reticence of the caricaturists may be partly explained by the tragedy that followed? For Burke's son, Richard, on whom all his hopes and ambitions centered, had no sooner replaced him as MP for Malton (on 18 July 1794) than he was stricken with acute tuberculosis and died on 2 August, to Burke's terrible and enduring grief. The probable answer, alas, is that the Burke-watchers (to judge their output from the British Museum collection) were either inactive or preoccupied, and public interest had moved on from this issue. Dent had made his last appearance in the BM Catalogue in May 1793. Sayers was silent between 31 May 1794 and 14 February 1795. Gillray's only production between 7 May 1794 and 1 November that year was an anti-French plate (on 25 July) that savaged Sheridan and others. Instead of Burke's nine-day speech, Isaac Cruikshank opted for the news of Admiral Howe's victory over the French. So did Richard Newton, a new and all too short-lived talent; still in his teens, he is likely to have found the ageing Indian charges tediously complicated. Much of the whiff of sulphur enlivening the Hastings affair had to do with gifts of diamonds and the King's supposed venal protection, but the King, restored from illness and a symbol of resistance to the 'French disease', had emerged as an increasingly popular figure, the affable 'Farmer George'.

Now, almost a year after Burke's closing speech, the verdict of the peers (and of Burke's old adversary Sayers) was at hand. Twenty-nine peers attended to vote on sixteen charges against Hastings; one hundred and eighty changes in the peerage had occurred since the trial began.[2] Thurlow himself had been succeeded as Lord Chancellor by Loughborough, who voted against Hastings on all charges except two. Despite this, he was acquitted on all counts and discharged, bearing his own costs. Further background to Sayers's imagined *Last Scene of the Managers Farce* is provided in Burke's own closing speech in which he had created the theatrical analogy, and had

The last Scene of the Managers Farce

laid bare the stage machinery, with which Hastings conducted the 'great Indian opera':

> You have it all laid open before you. The ostensible scene is drawn aside; it has vanished from your sight. All the strutting signors, and all the soft signoras are gone; and instead of a brilliant spectacle of descending chariots, gods, goddesses, sun, moon, and stars, you have nothing to gaze on but sticks, wire, ropes, and machinery.[3]

Now Burke is cast in Sayers's satirical production as 'One of the Managers & a principal Performer who having "out-heroded Herod" retires from the Stage in a Passion at seeing the Farce likely to be damn'd', a belated reference to Burke's retirement from the House of Commons the previous summer. 'The Scene', we are told, 'lies in an old Hall – formerly a Court of Law', a reference to Westminster Hall and to the crucial ruling by Thurlow that the rules of evidence in the courts would be followed in the hearing of evidence rather than the parliamentary rules set out in the impeachment of Strafford and argued for by the managers. On stage, an irradiated bust of Hastings rests on a pedestal inscribed in the very politicised language of Horace: *Virtus repulsae nescia sordidae incontaminatis fulget honoribus*, virtue which knows nothing of sordid rejection shines out with uncontaminated honours.[4] The bust has escaped all the smoke rising from a great cauldron where the charges, 'Ingredients mix'd up by the Managers to blacken a Character out of their reach', have been ignited by a gesticulating Burke. One column of smoke supports the winged figure of Lord Thurlow who pronounces: 'Not black upon my Honour'. He is 'a great Critic in a high situation, who has paid close Attention to the whole of the Performance, giving his Judgment'. The other column of smoke reaches up to Lord Loughborough, whose verdict is 'Black upon my Honour'. He is 'another great Critic, not quite so good a Judge, giving his Opinion on the other Side'. Fox is described as 'Another Manager a great Actor very anxious about the fate of the Farce'; he leans out of the Managers' Box as if to restrain Burke. Sir Philip Francis is not, of course, in the box itself, but close to hand as 'The Prompter, no Character in ye farce but very useful behind the Scenes'. The devil presides underneath the stage in 'a Court below to which the Managers retire upon quitting the Stage'. To indicate the length of the trial Sayers shows the progress of a snail across the managers' box, dating its trail from 1787 to 1795, and a rat who has gnawed through the box carries an admission ticket of 1787, 'renew'd 1795'.

With *The Last Scene of the Managers Farce*, Sayers was back in his anti-Burke stride. Within a few weeks Gillray had joined the attack, first, on the grounds of Burke's alliance with a warmongering Pitt, and secondly on the grounds of Burke's pension. On 4 June 1795 Gillray produces an apocalyptic image of Pitt which exploits to the full an indiscretion of Burke in his *Reflections*. There he had conjured up a scene in which learning, together with its 'natural protection and guardians' the nobility and clergy, 'will be cast into the mire and trodden down under the hoofs of a swinish multitude'. This seemingly undemocratic sentiment of the ex-Whig was seized upon by those who wished to attack him. Creamware jugs apeared, showing him with a paper inscribed *Loaves & Fishes* (to indicate that his reflections have been amply rewarded), addressing a crowd of pigs.[5] A popular song, *Burke's Address to the 'Swinish' Multitude*, begins:

Ye vile Swinish Herd, in the Sty of Taxation[6]

Gillray, too, spots the graphic potential of Burke's gaffe. In *Presages of the Millenium*

185. James Sayers: *The Last Scene of the Managers Farce*. Published 8 May 1795, by H. Humphrey. BM 8647; private collection.
Warren Hastings's 'great Indian opera' draws to a close with his acquittal. The snail on the front of the managers' box testifies to the long-drawn out nature of the case, as does the rat who nibbles an entrance ticket dated 1787 but 'renewed 1795'. The charges against Hastings vanish from view in a cloud of black smoke. Having retired from parliament, Burke too, still gesticulating, sinks on the stage mechanism into infernal regions below.

Presages of the MILLENIUM; with *The Destruction of the Faithful*, as Revealed to R: Brothers the Prophet, & attested by M.B.Hallhead Esq

"And in the Last Days began, I looked & behold, a White Horse, & his Name who sat upon it was Death: & Hell followed after him; & Power was given unto him, to kill with the Sword, & with Famine, & with Death: And I saw under him, the Souls of the Multitude, those who were destroy'd for maintaing the word of Truth, & for the Testimony —

186. James Gillray: *Presages of the Millenium*. Published 4 June 1795, by H. Humphrey. BM 8655; collection Andrew Edmunds, London.
Driven by demons – the winged figure of Dundas, with pitchfork, is followed by Loughborough, Pepper Arden and Burke – Pitt as Death on the Pale Horse (of Hanover) tramples on the swinish multitude and scatters the opposition. Sheridan has been bowled over like the swine beside him; to his right a shocked William Wilberforce clutches his 'Motion for a Peace'.

(Plate 186) a savage parody of genre paintings in vogue on the subject of 'Death on the Pale Horse', Gillray, the son of an invalided soldier, and merciless in his portrayal of war, casts Pitt as a terrifying figure of Death galloping on the usurped White Horse of Hanover over the swinish multitude.[7] Also trampled under foot are the horrified opposition leaders who had been urging peace with France. The description beneath the print continues: '& Hell followed after him: & Power was given unto him to kill with the Sword, & with Famine, & with Death'. Hell takes the form of flying furies: Dundas, as Secretary of War with the devil's horns and pitchfork, leads the Lord Chancellor, Loughborough, the Master of the Rolls, Pepper Arden, and an obdurate Burke whose attitude to the war (and, presumably, to the swinish multitude) secures his demonic presence although he holds no office.

174

187. [James Gillray] after 'Fˢ Lˢ Esqʳ': *John Bull ground down*. Published 1 June 1795, by H. Humphrey. BM 8654; collection Andrew Edmunds, London. Having provided amply for his own needs, Pitt continues to grind John Bull into guineas to pay for the Prince's extravagances, as jockey, moneylender and mistresses look on. Burke and Dundas grovel for a share, as does Loughborough behind the post.

Gillray's attack on the more personal (and more wounding) grounds of Burke's pension was made at the same time. The financial affairs of the Burke family had been in turmoil for many years, and his property at Beaconsfield heavily mortgaged. Shortly after the tragic blow of his son Richard's death in August 1794, Pitt indicated the King's intention to make 'an immediate grant out of the civil list of £1,200 per annum (being the largest sum which his Majesty is able to fix)' – a restriction imposed, ironically, by Burke's 'oeconomies' in the Civil List Act of 1782. The King also proposed to reward Burke's 'public merit' with a further annuity from the Crown's 'reserved revenue' which was not subject to such restriction. In 1795 Burke received these annuities: £1,200 for the joint lives of Edmund and his wife Jane, or either survivor, and another £2,500 for three lives.[8] Gillray anticipates his needs – and is probably aware of some lobbying on Burke's behalf – in *John Bull ground down* (Plate 187) (published on 1 June 1795) where Pitt grinds the symbol of the English taxpayer in a giant mill and converts him into coinage. Chief recipient is the Prince of Wales, the relief of whose 'Debts of Honor' will comfort his jockeys, moneylenders, and

175

False news of the defeat of the french armies in Flanders, brought to London by the Messenger. Mr Pitt fainted when the contrary account was received.

The DEATH of the Great WOLF.

_____ "We have overcome all Opposition!"___ exclaimed the Messengers.__ "I'm satisfied."___ said the Dying Hero, & Expired in the Moment of Victory.

To Beng: West Esq: President of the Royal Academy, this attempt to Emulate the Beauties of his unequalld Picture, of the Death of Gen! Wolfe," is most respectfully submitted, by the Author.

1. Mr Pitt.   3. Mr E Burke   5. Mr Fawin.   7. Mr Brook Watson   9. Lord Grenville   11. Mr Rose
2. Mr H: Dundas.   4. Mr Pepper Arden, the & &. 6. The Duke of Richmond 8. Lord Chancellor 10. Lord Mansfield 12. Mr Long   13. Lord Ch

188. James Gillray: *The Death of the Great Wolf.*
Published 17 December 1795, by H. Humphrey. BM
8704; private collection.
Gillray's parody of Benjamin West's *Death of Wolfe.*
General James Wolfe died in the course of his
victorious capture of Quebec from the French in 1759.
Burke, kneeling, occupies the position of Wolfe's aide-
de-camp in West's chauvinistic picture, his devotion
secured, suggests Gillray, by the pension referred to in
his pocket, 'Reflections upon £3700 pr. Ann.'

mistresses. Also benefitting are Burke and Dundas. Ironically Burke's pursuit of
Hastings had helped to make Dundas all-powerful in Indian affairs; as the leading
member of the Board of Control established by Pitt's India Bill of 1784 he was
practically a Secretary of State for India, and dispensed great patronage, too, as
Treasurer of the Navy. Well known for his 'gallantries', Dundas is celebrated in a
verse of 1785:

> What various tastes divide the fickle town!
> One likes the fair, and one admires the brown.
> The stately, Queensb'ry; Hinchinbrook, the small;
> Thurlow loves servant-maids; Dundas loves all.[9]

There is further reference to Burke's pension in one of Gillray's greatest parodies, *The
Death of the Great Wolf* (Plate 188) published on 17 December 1795 and lampooning

The Death of Wolfe (1770) by Benjamin West who was then President of the Royal Academy). Burke, taking the place of Wolfe's aide-de-camp Captain Hervey Smyth, kneels anxiously over the mortally wounded Pitt. His loyalty, the artist suggests, has to do with the paper projecting from his pocket: 'Reflections upon £3700 pr. Ann'. The print is a satire on the passing of the treason and sedition bills which became law on 18 December 1795. '"We have overcome all Opposition!", exclaimed the messengers [beneath the caption]. "I'm satisfied!" said the dying hero and expired in the moment of victory'. (The Victorian commentator Thomas Wright interpreted it as describing the parliamentary struggle over Pitt's estimates in December 1795, with victory purchased dearly in the blow received by the hero.[10] On another impression in a private collection, in what seems to be a contemporary hand, a different glossary is written: 'False news of the defeat of the french armies in Flanders brought to London by the Messenger, Mr Pitt fainted when the contrary account was received'.)

In November 1795, the grant of Burke's pension had been attacked in the House of Lords by the Duke of Bedford and the Earl of Lauderdale, provoking Burke to publish on 24 February 1796 *A Letter . . . to a Noble Lord,* in which he recalls 'the hunt of obloquy, which ever has pursued me with a full cry through life'.

> I was not, like his Grace of Bedford, swaddled, and rocked and dandled into a legislator. . . At every step of my progress in life (for in every step was I traversed and opposed) and at every turnpike I met, I was obliged to show my passport . . . The Duke of Bedford conceives that he is obliged to call the attention of the House of Peers to his Majesty's grant to me, which he considers as excessive and out of all bounds . . . The grants to the House of Russell [Bedford's family] were so enormous as not only to outrage economy, but even to stagger credibility. The Duke of Bedford is the leviathan among all the creatures of the crown. He tumbles about his unwieldy bulk, he plays and frolics in the ocean of the royal bounty. Huge as he is, and whilst 'he lies floating many a rood', he is still a creature. His ribs, his fins, his whalebone, his blubber, the very spiracles through which he spouts a torrent of brine against his origin and covers me all over with the spray, everything of him and about him is from the throne. Is it for *him* to question the dispensation of the royal favour?[11]

Within a day of its publication Gillray continues the 'hunt of obloquy' with a savage parody, *Pity the Sorrows of a Poor Old Man* (Plate 189). Burke, his clothes tattered but with a sack strapped to his shoulder labelled '£4,000 pr Annum', turns up to beg at Bedford's gate. He carries in his hand the 'Last Dying Speech of Old Honesty the Jesuit' and in his pocket a copy of *Reflections upon Political Apostacy*. 'Pity the Sorrows of a poor old Man', he implores, 'add a trifle to what has been bestowed by Ministry to stop my Complaints – O give me opportunity of recanting once more! – Ah! remember me in your Golden Dreams! – great Leviathan of liberty, let me but play & frolick in the Ocean of your royal Bounty, & I will be for ever your *Creature;* – my Hands, – Brains, – my Soul & Body, – the very Pen through which I have spouted a torrent of Gall against my original Friends, and cover'd you all over with the Spray, every thing of me, & about me, shall be yours – dispence but a little of your Golden store to a desolate Old Man'. Bedford smiles at the performance: 'Hark 'ee old double Face, – its no use for you to stand Jawing there, if you gull other people, you wo'nt bother us . . .'

On 7 March 1796 a versifier in the *Morning Chronicle*, perhaps inspired by Gillray's print, offers his own image of the affair:

"Pity the Sorrows of a Poor old Man." Vide. Scene in Bloomsbury Square.

189. James Gillray: *"Pity the Sorrows of a Poor old Man"*. Published 25 February 1796, by H. Humphrey. BM 8786; private collection.
Burke, his pension of £4,000 on his back, begs for another 'trifle' from the Duke of Bedford, who refuses with familiar abuse: 'Hark'ee old double face . . .' And Gillray has Burke humiliating himself further: '. . . I will be for ever your *Creature* . . . every thing of me, & about me, shall be yours . . .'

In RUSSELL's Porch low-crouching EDMUND stands,
And grasps Corinthian columns with his hands;
His huge, vast bulk the Giant sudden rears,
In hopes to pull the House about his ears.[12]

Burke's was not the first pension to provoke an uncharitable response. The caricaturists had, for instance, rounded on Pitt's father, William Pitt the elder, when in 1761 the Great Commoner accepted from the King a peerage for his wife and a pension of £3000 a year for his family. Pitt's mother, who had become Baroness of Chatham, was jeered as Lady Cheat'em, and a wit observed that:

Three thousand a year's no contemptible thing
To accept from the hands of a patriot king,
(With thanks to the bargain for service and merit),
Which he wife and son, all three shall inherit
With limited honours to her and her heirs.
So farewell to old England. Adieu to all cares.[13]

Gillray had thought fit to record *Irish Gratitude*[14] when in 1782 the Irish parliament, rejoicing in its independence, had settled a fortune on Henry Grattan. And, as we have seen, Burke's great friend Samuel Johnson (another who in his progress through life had been obliged to show his passport) had come under fire when a pension of £300 a year was found for him on the Irish civil list (*see* Plate 16). By coincidence, in this print it is the turn of Fox's mother to be mocked: she had been created, in her own right, Baroness Holland in 1762.

Isaac Cruikshank is much more sympathetic to Burke's pension. In *The Modern Leviathan!!* (Plate 190) he sits, quill in one hand and in the other a note book of 'My Feeble efforts for my countrys good'. His seat is an upturned oak tree beside the tombstone of his son Richard, which reads:

190. [Isaac Cruikshank]: *The Modern Leviathan!!* Published 8 March 1796, by S.W. Fores. BM 8788; private collection.
Cruikshank's image of the encounter between Burke and Bedford is a good deal less savage than Gillray's (Plate 189). Bedford is the leviathan frolicking 'in the ocean of the Royal Bounty'. Though weighed down by 'Pillage' and 'Confiscation' he spouts out effusions of 'Egalité,' 'Democracy', 'Leveling' and, more often, 'Envy'. Burke, at the tomb of his only son enquires of this monster, 'Why attack a Defenceless old Man?'

191. [Isaac Cruikshank]: *The Quarrell about Pensions amicably Settled*. Published 13 April 1796, by S.W. Fores. BM 8795; private collection.

It is some time since there has been any kind of amicable conjunction of Burke and Fox, here attempting to smooth over Burke's quarrel with Bedford. Burke's posture shows how their relationship has changed since, for example, 1785 and *The Orators Journey* (Plate 73). And Fox assumes an unwonted gravity, suggesting 'Take the Advice of a common friend – the less said about the matter the better!'

Take the Advice of a common friend
– the less said about the matter
the better!

The Quarrell about Pensions amicably Settled

Sacred to the Memory of an Only Son whose Manly Virtues
& well informed Mind was the only Enjoyment the Parent
Knew in his declining years but Alass – The loss of
a Finished Man is not easily supplied.

From this melancholy vantage point he envisages the Duke of Bedford as a great whale swimming in the ocean of royal bounty and spouting plumes of brine inscribed 'Cromwellism', 'Envy', 'Leveling', 'Orleanism', 'Revolutions', 'Egalite,' and 'Democracy'. 'Ah Wretch!' says Burke, 'why attack a Defenceless old Man? whose seclusion from all Public concerns & whose Irepparable loss of an only & beloved Child should have sheltered his Declining Head from the Malicious Attacks of a Monster wallowing in Luxury & Wealth Oh Orleans Oh Bedford!!!' Gillray (in a detailed design, *New Morality*, after the poem by George Canning)[15] was to come back to the leviathan theme in 1798, a year after Burke's death. Putting a barbed hook through Bedford's nose he quotes Canning:

> Thou in whose nose by Burke's gigantic hand
> The hook was fix'd to drag thee to the land.

Burke, however, had been less concerned to beach young Bedford himself than to warn of the dire consequences of the Duke's political folly: 'If a great storm blow on our coast', he wrote, 'it will cast the whales on the strand, as well as the periwinkles'.[16] Meanwhile, on 13 April 1796 Cruikshank imagines *The Quarrell about Pensions amicably Settled* (Plate 191) in a print where Burke, Fox and the Duke sit around a table, Fox, eyes lowered and the hands clasped together, offering counsel: 'Take the Advice of a common friend – the less said about the matter the better!' Burke's body-language indicates a disagreeable meeting: he sits with his back to the others, looking over his shoulder with a pained expression.

He continued to be attacked about his pension. In *A Will o' the Wisp or John Bull in a Bog*[17] John Bull flounders in the 'Slough of Despond or quagmire of War' and is offered a lantern by a will o' the wisp Pitt, above whom float other frightening spirits. Burke, naked but for his Jesuit's biretta and a bag inscribed '4000', holds a lantern which beams 'Services done the Public'; a naked woman holding in each hand a money bag inscribed '2000', and excreting a blast inscribed 'Plans', is perhaps intended for Mrs Burke.

It is March 1796, and the rays emanating from Pitt's lantern indicate that peace negotiations in the war with revolutionary France are in progress. Burke was adamant about the need to continue that war, the consequence otherwise (he wrote to Lord Auckland) 'utter and irretrievable ruin to the Ministry, to the Crown, to the Succession, to the importance, to the very existence of this country'.[18] Auckland had sent him a copy of a pamphlet he had written in October 1795 arguing that the time had come for considering a peace; Burke responded to the negotiations with *Letters on a Regicide Peace,* published in part on 20 October 1796. 'We are not at an end of our struggle', he wrote, 'nor near it. Let us not deceive ourselves: we are at the beginning of great troubles'.[19] Almost ready by early March 1796, publication had been delayed by serious illness in July, and Burke sensed he had little time to live: 'What I say I *must* say at once. Whatever I write is in its nature testamentary. It may have the weakness, but it has the sincerity of a dying declaration'.[20] By the time the work came to be published Lord Malmesbury had been despatched to Paris to negotiate with revolutionary France. Burke's text must have been available shortly before publication and on 14 October it evoked a design by his old antagonist Sayers (Plate 192): *Thoughts on a Regicide Peace* are conjured up by the author who appears to have nodded off. Sayers has come up with another clever representation of Burke grimly delighting in the 'sublime' of his great *Philosophical Inquiry.* The sensation, it will be recalled, is rooted in the feelings of passion and terror that are aroused by the contemplation of pain and danger, in this case from the comfortable distance of his armchair, inscribed *Otium cum Dignit[ate]*, leisure with dignity. Burke's overheated brain has caught fire with terrifying images that crowd the design. A French revolutionary stands astride the islands of Britain and Ireland (signalling invasion), the head of Louis XVI on his pikestaff, and leading in chains a skeletal figure with *bonnet rouge* and clay pipe representing the Dutch Republic. In his left hand he holds the key to 'Belgium' and he is offering to negotiate: 'I will retain what I have got and treat with you on fair Terms for what you have got'. The British lion, echoing one of Burke's closest associates, Earl Fitzwilliam roars angrily: 'I protest against Peace with a Regicide Directory' but Britannia, alas, is playing on the violin some music from 'A new Opera Il Trattato di Pace Overture' (in which 'Rule Britania' has been deleted in favour of the French revolutionary song 'Ca Ira', while 'God Save ye King' has given way to 'The Marsellais Hymn'). She is accompanied on the flute by an Austrian grenadier playing 'To Arms to Arms my valiant Grenadiers' ('The martial ardour of the Austrian,' notes Dorothy George, 'may well be intended ironically'.) A scroll on an empty plinth reminds us of former glories: 'Naval Victories East India Conquests &c &c' while Burke's subconscious recalls these lines from Shakespeare:

> This royal Throne of Kings this sceptred isle
> This Earth of Majesty, this Seat of Mars
> This fortress built by Nature for herself
> Against Infection and the hand of War
> This Nurse, this teeming womb of royal Kings
> This England that was wont to conquer others
> Will make a shameful Conquest of itself.

Thoughts on a Regicide Peace *Frontispiece to a Pamphlet*

Promis'd Horrors of the French INVASION, — or — Forcible Reasons for negociating a Regicide PEACE. Vide. The Authority of Edmund Burke.

193. James Gillray: *Promis'd Horrors of the French Invasion.* Published 20 October 1796, by H. Humphrey. BM 8826; collection Andrew Edmunds. This is not the first time that Gillray gives us an image of revolutionary mayhem in the west end of London: *The Butchers of Freedom* dates from 1788 (Plate 116). But this spectacular and crowded print is even more violent. Fox still leads the mob but Burke is now victim, tossed on the horns of the *Great Bedfordshire Ox.*

192. James Sayers: *Thoughts on a Regicide Peace.* Published 14 October 1796, by H. Humphrey. BM 8825; private collection. Burke, without his spectacles, lets his heated imagination develop the consequences of peace with revolutionary France. A sans-culotte, carrying the head of Louis XVI, plants his foot in Britain, having arrived from Ireland, while a compliant Britannia has erased 'God Save ye King' from her score and replaced it with the Marseillaise.

If Lord Malmesbury's peace mission has given Burke nightmares, they are as nothing to Gillray's *Promis'd Horrors of the French Invasion, — or — Forcible Reasons for negociating a Regicide Peace* (Plate 193), which the artist offers up on 'the Authority of Edmund Burke'. In his *First Letter on a Regicide Peace,* Burke had invited his readers to 'suppose a case, which after what has happened, we cannot think absolutely impossible, though the augury is to be abominated'.[20a] Gillray's fecund imagination feeds on Burke's grim vision of regicide, persecution and slaughter in the public squares to create a tableau crowded with murder, mayhem and Whig insurrection. French troops, having fired the palace, are marching up St James's Street with its fashionable gentlemen's clubs and storming White's to the cheers of the Whigs opposite, who operate a guillotine on the balcony of Brooks's. The impecunious but ever-resourceful Sheridan slopes into this second club bearing the 'Remains of the Treasury' and booty from the Bank of England. Nearby, Burke is being tossed in the air by a rampant 'Great Bedfordshire Ox' (the Duke) goaded on by the republican

183

orator John Thelwall. As he tumbles he loses his glasses and wig, and two pamphlets, 'Letters to the Duke of Bedford' and 'Reflections upon a Regicide Peace' fall to the ground. And maybe, because this is Gillray at the height of his powers of invention and invective, we should digress for a moment to indulge in some more of the extraordinary wealth of detail contained in the print. In the foreground, Pitt has been tied to a pole representing the 'tree of liberty' (planted wherever the French troops established themselves) and is being flogged unmercifully by Citizen Fox, urged on by a tiny chicken with the head of Michael Angelo Taylor who is perched on a blood stained axe.[21] Behind the ox the head of William Grenville hangs on scales held aloft by Earls Lauderdale and Stanhope. As Draper Hill puts it, they 'weigh Grenville's head against his hind quarters, finding another expression of *Égalité* in the result'.[22] On the balcony of White's the King's sons are being overwhelmed by French soldiers: the Duke of Clarence recoils from the daggers of his assailants, the Prince of Wales has been thrown head-first over the side, and the Duke of York is about to topple over and will pass the bodies of two young MPs (both future prime ministers) who have been hanged together from a lampstandard, Robert Jenkinson (Lord Hawkesbury) and George Canning. Thus Canning makes his keenly awaited début in a Gillray plate.[23] Whether or not solicited, it is Jenkinson's début as well, and Gillray has a problem – how is he to identify them for the print shop customers? He resolves it ingeniously by juxtaposing a poster: 'New March to Paris, by Betty Canning & Jenny Jenkison'. Jenkinson's claim in 1794 that 'marching to Paris was practicable; and he for one would recommend such an expedition'[24] was clearly still remembered. Betty Canning was a name plucked from folklore (of a servant girl notorious for her perjured evidence in a trial in 1753) to provide a clue to George Canning's identity. On Brooks's balcony we have noted the guillotine; it is being operated by the Marquis of Lansdowne (formerly Lord Shelburne) who holds aloft Lord Loughborough's wig, while Thomas Erskine has set fire to 'Magna Charta' and flourishes instead his 'New Code of Laws'. In front of him, a platter contains the heads – 'Killed off for the Public Good' – of the former Home Secretary Lord Sydney, William Windham and Pepper Arden; looking on with pleasure are the Dukes of Grafton and Norfolk and the Earl of Derby. It is speculated that the dwarfish drummer might be intended to resemble Gillray himself.[25] In the gutter we see the head of the retired Master General of the Ordnance, the Duke of Richmond, alongside a 'Treatise upon Fortifying the Coast', testimony to the inadequacy of his arrangements. A basket in the foreground to the right holds the head and the bagpipes of Dundas and is labelled 'To the care of Citizen Horn Tooke'. Beside it the bundle of 'Waste Paper' comprises 'Acts of Parliament', 'Statutes' and the 'Bill of Rights'. In using the subtitle, *Forcible Reasons for negotiating a Regicide Peace*, Gillray is perhaps pointing to Fox's efforts to achieve peace forcibly by flogging Pitt into submission, rather than wilfully misunderstanding Burke's warnings against such negotiations,[25a] for when it comes to Jacobinism the bellows might as well be applied to Gillray's brain as to Burke's.

Burke is involved in two further Gillray plates on the cost of the war and of defending the anticipated invasion. In *Opening of the Budget: – or – John Bull giving his Breeches to save his Bacon*[26] Pitt is agitating for more money to defend John from the 'cannibal French' who will strip him to the very skin. Burke, grubbing for guineas with Dundas and Grenville echoes Pitt's cry that the French are coming. An unhappy Fox cries '. . .Vite Citoyens! . . . or we shall be too late to come inn for any Snacks of the l'argent!'. Cruikshank thinks it safe (and profitable) to plagiarise the print for Fores's customers a few days later on 20 November 1796, (Plate 194). In *Begging no*

194. Isaac Cruikshank: *The Budget or John Bull Fright[e]ned out of his wits.* Published 20 November 1796, by S.W. Fores. BM 8837; private collection. As Fox signals unpatriotically to 'Citoyens' across the channel, Pitt and his follow alarmists – Windham, Grenville, Burke and Dundas – persuade an agitated John Bull to give all in Britain's defence.

Robbery; – i.e Voluntary Contribution – or – John Bull, Escaping a Forced Loan (Plate 195) Gillray satirises the 'loyalty loan' of £18m raised by a public appeal made on 1 December 1796. In his *Third Letter on a Regicide Peace* (1797) Burke will hail the loan as a great success, proving that 'there exists, though not always visible, a spirit which never fails to come forth whenever it is ritually invoked' and displaying an abundant confidence in the government's prosecution of a war 'in defence of that very property which they expend for its support'.[27] Gillray, not surprisingly, sees it differently: Pitt and his beggar gang of Dundas, Lord Grenville and Burke level their blunderbusses at John Bull, whose mount, if it is intended for the White Horse of Hanover, has become a very sorry nag. 'Good Sir', calls Pitt, 'for Charity's sake have Pity upon a poor ruin'd Man; – drop if you please, a few bits of Money into the Hat, & you shall be rewarded hereafter'. A document on the ground indicates that a voluntary contribution will 'save the Distress'd from taking worse Courses', an allusion to Pitt's meeting with directors of the Bank of England at which he threatened that, failing

185

BEGGING no ROBBERY; _i.e._ Voluntary Contribution; _ or _ John Bull, escaping a Forced Loan. _ A hint from Gil Blas.

195. James Gillray: *Begging no Robbery*. Published 10 December 1796, by H. Humphrey. BM 8842; collection Andrew Edmunds, London.
Gillray denounces as blackmail Pitt's 'loyalty loan', seeking voluntary subscriptions to finance the war with France. Though not in government, Burke's writings qualify him as one of the gang.

196. Richard Newton: *Cries of London* (detail). Published 3 May 1797, by W. Holland. Not in BM Cat.; private collection.
Following the model, perhaps, of Francis Wheatley's *Cries of London* engraved in 1795, a down at heel Burke is peddling 'fine Shillalees for Jacobin backs and Irish Brogues for the French Clergy'.

197. [Attributed to Isaac Cruikshank]: *This is the House for Cash Built!!* (detail). Published 1 December 1797, by S.W. Fores. BM 9044; private collection.
In a previous parody of *The House that Jack Built* (Plate 70), Burke had been characterised as the cock whose crowing set events in motion. Now he is 'a Blade in a Jesuit rug, who wrote a Book to make himself snug . . .'

voluntary subscriptions, 'a peremptory mode of drawing forth the resources of the kingdom must be adopted . . . in the last resort'.[28] Burke has a quill pen in his hat: with this weapon, implies Gillray, he has whipped up public fears and is party to the emotional blackmail involved in the 'loyalty loan'. Draper Hill cites a memorandum by Gillray in his possession in which the caricaturist described the *Reflections* as 'another Pamphlet with which Mr Burke has threatened us'.[29] Burke was well aware of this criticism. Writing in 1793 of a general war against Jacobins and Jacobinism as 'the only possible chance of saving Europe (and England is included in Europe) from a truly frightful revolution', he continues: 'For this I have been censured, as receiving through weakness, or spreading through fraud and artifice, a false alarm'.[30]

By now Burke was dying, yet he continued until the end to take a passionate interest in the war against revolutionary France. In possibly the last caricature before his death on 9 July 1797, Richard Newton refers to his activity on behalf of French refugee clergy in England. Depicting him as one of a number of street sellers crying their wares (Plate 196) Newton dresses him in slippers and old patched clothes, with a large hat perched on his old fashioned wig. Bent under the load of sticks or 'shillele[es]' borne on his head, a bundle of stout shoes attached to his waist trailing

behind him as he shuffles along, he calls: 'Here's my fine shillelees for Jacobin backs! and Irish Brogues for the French Clergy. Who buys! who buys, ho!'.

Burke's death in July 1797 did not prevent his inclusion as one of ten political figures in a rhyming satire on 1 December 1797, *This is the House for Cash Built!!* (Plate 197).[31] Burke is No. 8: 'This is a Blade in a Jesuit rug, who wrote a Book to make himself snug [*Reflections* is seen as an act of apostasy], but frowned on the lad for dashing away [Sheridan], who on every subject had something to say, who stuck close to the Boy for speech complete [Fox], who spent all his money before it was meete, who smiled at the Patriot shatter'd and shorn [Wilkes] once in esteem but now forlorn, a friend to the Scot of fortunate lot [Dundas] who flattered the Youth [Pitt] who to speak the truth, look'd after the Cole that lay in the hole, in the midst of the house for Cash built! [the Treasury]'. Burke is followed by Loughborough – 'the Judge with eyes like a Hawk and is highly delighted to hear himself talk, that shook hands with the blade in the Jesuit rug' – and by Lord Thurlow, 'the Nobleman govern'd by Gall – who grumbled look'd black and Damn'd them all – not excepting the Judge with eyes like a Hawk . . .' Burke, looking severe and censorious is dressed in biretta and cassock and holds a book, the 'Ans[wer] to Pain[e's] Rights of [Man].'

What of other posthumous references? We have already noted the Duke of Bedford as leviathan – 'Thou in whose nose by Burke's gigantic hand / The hook was fix'd to drag thee to the land'. A radical print, undated but of around 1798, shows Pitt supporting his elbows on 'Burke's Refl[ections]' in a design featuring symbols of liberty and oppression.[32] In *The Tale of a Tub!!!*[33] an 1802 print on the corrupt competition for the loaves and fishes of office (one of the supplicants being Sheridan), Burke, as Janus, is one of four lifelike statues standing in the background.

A Gillray print that year caricatures the Duke of Bedford, famous as a breeder of cattle, examining a prize specimen.[34] 'Ah, here's your sort!' he exclaims, '– here's your Nine-Inch Fat my boys! "O how he will cut up! (as my old friend Burke said) – "how he will Tallow in the cawl and on the Kidneys!"' It is Gillray, however, who is doing the cutting. On the face of it, a jolly print innocuously celebrates the first president of the Smithfield Club, the great breeder of fat cattle whose prize winners are being bought up for fancy sums by the carcass butchers. But Gillray remembers – and hopes now in 1802 that most of his audience does as well – the context in which Bedford's 'old friend' Burke had been speaking: it was not in his capacity as agricultural improver. Having ridiculed the Duke as the leviathan tumbling about his unwieldly bulk, playing and frolicking in the ocean of the royal bounty, Burke had then switched metaphor . The *sans-culottes*, he had said, were Bedford's natural hunter and he, poor herbivore, their natural game. They 'will not care a rush whether his coat is long or short, – whether the color be purple, or blue and buff . . . Their only question will be . . . : How he cuts up; how he tallows in the caul or on the kidneys'. The passage continues – and Gillray himself could not have surpassed the imagery conjured up by the angry pensioner:

> Is it not a singular phenomenon, that, whilst the sans-culotte carcass-butchers and the philosophers of the shambles are pricking their dotted lines upon his hide, and, like the print of the poor ox that we see in the shop-windows at Charing Cross, alive as he is, and thinking no harm in the world, he is divided into rumps, and sirloins, and briskets, and into all sorts of pieces for roasting, boiling and stewing, that, all the while they are measuring him, his Grace is measuring *me*, – is invidiously comparing the bounty of the crown with the deserts of the defender of his order, and in the same moment fawning on those who have the knife half out

198. [Charles Williams]: *Spectres visiting John Bull*. Published 23 February 1808, by Walker. BM 10968; British Museum.

As late as 1808, more than ten years after his death, Burke (like Fox and Pitt) is still to be recognised: the 'caricaturer's stock in trade' for Burke remains the spectacles, the biretta, a haughty and didactic demeanour and, under his arm, the 'Sublime and Beautiful'.

of the sheath? Poor innocent!

> Pleased to the last, he crops the flowery food,
> And licks the hand just raised to shed his blood.[35]

In 1805, Burke's friend William Windham (one of the managers of the Hastings impeachment and Secretary for War, 1794–1801) was lampooned by Charles Williams in *Political Astronomy* as 'The Windhamerian Star'.[36] He 'belong'd to the Burkean constellation which has disappear'd – this is a most Eccentric planet and partakes of the nature of the Comet. Astronomers are strongly of Opinion – that if he be not closely confined to his orbit, he must end in the destruction of the world'. One of Burke's pallbearers, Windham, is said to have thought Burke 'the great god of his idolatry'.[37] and ungenerously opposed a motion in the House to give Pitt a public funeral in 1806 partly because Burke in 1797 had not received such an honour.[38]

There is passing reference in a Gillray print of 5 April 1806 to Burke's *Letter to a Noble Lord*: it emerges from the pocket of Bedford's brother (who had succeeded him as the Duke) labelled 'a serious Ballad Burke to Duke', as his Grace plays the 'Harp of St Patrick'.[39] He had been sworn in as Lord Lieutenant of Ireland only days earlier. The regency crisis is recalled in an 1807 print, frontispiece to *The Rising Sun,* volume 1,[40] a scurrilous satire on the Prince, whose features constitute the rising sun. Supporters like Sheridan are kneeling before the sun but Burke, in biretta and gown, and Grey (Viscount Howick) look away. In a Williams print of February 1808, Burke, Fox and Pitt are invoked as *Spectres visiting John Bull* (Plate 198) to denounce a vote of thanks for effecting the surrender of the Danish navy. John Bull asks, in exasperation: 'Why dont you come then and transact the business yourselves? – it is impossible I can please every body – it is come to such a pitch now that I have no peace either with the living or the dead!!!' William Heath appealed to the same three apparitions in 1810, as *The Last Recorce or Supernatural Committee Employ'd*.[41] Spencer

Perceval, Chancellor of the Exchequer, is Macbeth consulting the witches, behind whom emerge the ghosts of Burke, Pitt and Fox. The satire concerns Sir Francis Burdett's defiance of the warrant of the Speaker of the House of Commons and his committal to the Tower by motion of the House. Burke, identified thirteen years after his death to a new generation of caricature customers by his biretta, inscribed *Sublime and Beautiful*, says: 'Laugh to Scorn the Power of Man'. Eight years later, in 1818, *The Rehe[a]rsal*[42] by George Cruikshank (son of Isaac, and most famous of the Cruikshank family of caricaturists), is a small vignette in *Tegg's Prime Jest Book*, illustrating an anecdote of Burke as a youth. Finally, in 1819 comes another small print,[43] an illustration to *The Real or Constitutional House that Jack Built*, which, against the backdrop of – beloved Burkean metaphor – a sturdy oak, portrays national heroes of which the three most prominent are Nelson, Wellington and Edmund Burke: *These are The Patriots of high renown* . . .

SUBLIME AND BEAUTIFUL REFLECTIONS

In the course of this account of Edmund Burke's treatment at the hands of the caricaturists a range of images has been assembled, from the mildly amusing and quirky to the outrageously offensive and defamatory. It is important, therefore, to emphasise that Burke, like other leading figures, was handsomely represented in the printsellers' stocks in conventional plates such as John Jones's mezzotint (1790) after George Romney's portrait of 1776 (Plate 199). 'So much so, that, introducing Vol. VI of the British Museum's great catalogue of satirical prints, Dorothy George observes that, throughout, 'the prints are a corrective to the suavity of official portraiture'. She has Burke specifically in mind, and continues:

> Burke is depicted as irritable and unbalanced, verging at times on madness in his attacks on Hastings . . . , in his praise of Marie Antoinette, in his quarrel with Fox, in the dagger scene, and especially during the Regency crisis, when he spoke wild words that were long remembered against him . . . This aspect of Burke was politically important, and is often forgotten by historians who marvel at his exclusion from high office.[2]

This is only part of the composite picture of Burke to emerge from the prints, but, before considering that picture further, a caveat should be entered: Edmund Burke, with his commanding intellect, exemplary diligence and attention to detail, with his great gifts of writing and oratory, might have aspired to the intellectual leadership of the Whig party and, indeed, have achieved it. But, however exceptional his talents, as an outsider of narrow means and modest background he faced enormous, perhaps insurmountable, difficulties in seeking one of the great offices of State, even had he enjoyed the populist support of the printsellers. The historian Christopher Hobhouse put it nicely: 'the motive power, the moral force of the Rockingham party, came from him. It was in recognition of this important obligation that they always excluded him from their cabinets'.[3] So it must be remembered where Burke came in the Whig pecking order: not with the aristocratic grandees of vast landed wealth and social influence – the Marquis of Rockingham, dukes such as Portland, Devonshire, Richmond, Bedford, or earls such as Fitzwilliam; nor with the influential commoners of great estates such as Sir George Savile; nor yet with the less wealthy but well connected country gentlemen, also eligible for high office, typified by Fox. It was some way below them that the workers of the party, such as Burke, joined the queue, rarely achieving cabinet rank.[4] As Burke himself summed it up in that famous passage in his *Letter to a Noble Lord,* 'I was not, like his Grace of Bedford, swaddled and rocked and dandled into a legislator; "Nitor in adversum" [I struggle against obstacles placed in my path] is the motto for a man like me'.[5]

Among these obstacles must have been the taunts of the caricaturists that he was, at different times, a pauper, a Jesuit, an Irishman, a subversive, a pension-seeker, a man who saw what he wanted to see through those absurd spectacles.

No doubt he could have taken steps to ease the adversity, to jump part of the queue, and this may have prompted him to borrow beyond his means in acquiring

199. [John Jones] after George Romney: *Edmund Burke MP, Statesman and Writer*. Mezzotint, published 10 December 1790, by John Jones. Collection National Gallery of Ireland.

and maintaining his estate at Beaconsfield and prompted, too, the speculative stock investments that proved so disastrous. But Burke's bottom line was his adherence to deeply held convictions, and he was not going to build a fortune from the opportunities office provided. 'I attest heaven and earth', he said, 'that in all places, and at all times, I have steadfastly shoved aside the gilded hand of corruption, and endeavoured to stem the torrent which threatens to overwhelm this island'.[6] Indeed, if Fox's father was suspected of accumulating 'unaccounted-for millions' as Paymaster General, Burke, by his policy of economical reform is said to have disadvantaged himself in that post by some thousands. And if his principled actions led to the disapproval of his electors in Bristol he stood his ground: 'I knew that you chose me, in my place, along with others, to be a pillar of the state, and not a weather-cock on the top of the edifice, exalted for my levity and versatility, and of no use but to indicate the shiftings of every popular gale'.[7] If advancement was to be gained through royal favour he gritted his teeth and denounced the King's unconstitutional intermeddling in legislative affairs. In like manner he addressed another great purveyor of patronage, the East India Company. Choosing his path on American taxation he knew, he said, the map of England as well as the noble Lord North or any other person, 'and I know that the way I take is not the road to preferment. My excellent and hon. friend [William Dowdeswell] . . . has trod that road with great toil for upwards of 20 years together. He is not yet arrived at the noble lord's destination. However, the tracks of my worthy friend are those I have ever wished to follow; because I know they lead to honour.'[8]

But how powerful were the prints and what enduring impact did they have on Burke's reputation? We are familiar nowadays with the cartoonist's role in the creation of a politician's persona – we have a sense, for instance, of the impact on President Richard Nixon's image of his invariably being given the swarthy stubble, the 'five-o'clock shadow'. But what was the impact of this very same treatment on Fox's career? Fox, by far the most caricatured man of his period, seems to have been good humouredly impervious to public opinion, treating even the most antagonistic and outrageous prints as after-dinner amusements for his guests and, by his voracious appetites in gambling, carousing and womanising, fuelling the very contents of those amusements. Secure in his world, maybe in the end he did not want office badly enough to care what effect these prints might have. But for Burke, the outsider who never lost (nor ditched) his Irish brogue, they must have been part of 'the hunt of obloquy', dogging him at every turn.

Some of the taunts may be discounted as made in the heat of battle. Many are ephemeral. Others, more insidious, linger to build up a composite caricature. From earliest outlines in the days of 'Junius' a picture emerges and is worked up by the print trade: of someone too clever by a half, an Irish adventurer whose push for upward mobility makes him a danger to his elders and betters, whose crypto-Catholicism makes suspect his views on the great constitutional issues of the day (though it is conceded that he speaks out for reform and stands up to George III), a longwinded, quixotic tilter at windmills whose overheated rhetoric tends to obsessiveness and even mental unbalance. Inconsistency becomes a theme, as does apostacy: here is a man, it is suggested, who will snitch on his friends for place and pension, and ingratiate himself with the monarch he has so long opposed. But then the xenophobic Gillray takes up his cause, albeit ambiguously, because if there is something Gillray loathes more than (Burke's) popery it is anything French, so imposed on the picture, and partly rescuing it, is the sense of a stern senator whose grim and insightful reading of revolutionary France marks him out as a true, if austere, elder statesman.

If this is what has filtered through the murky waters of propaganda and prejudice, it should not upset us. Clearly, from such a source, an honest or sympathetic verdict on so crucial a combatant could not be expected. Yet in an age when such extraordinary licence is afforded to Grub-Street gravers we can take comfort in what the composite caricature does *not* say. No mud labelled 'sleaze' thrown against him sticks. No dubious financial transactions are seized upon. Even where he is present when the spoils of office are shared out he is seen to be preoccupied with his 'plans of economy', and one mocking print concedes:

> To tempt with Money were a Crime;
> Thine are the Riches of the Mind.

Nor does any print that I have found allude to disreputable kinsmen, let alone his being dragged down in their wake. These are accusations put to rest by historians;[9] my point is that they were not peddled in the caricatures, not even in the plates of those briefed to do him down. As for the prints retailing titbits of amorous scandal, piled high as they are in the Print Room of the British Museum, none may be enlisted to enliven the composite Burke. His were passions of a different kind and provoked in turn the passions of others: on the influence of the Crown, relations with America, the governance of India, economical reform, Irish affairs, the regency crisis, the French Revolution. And (with the exception of America) the caricaturists were on hand – specialists like Gillray, consultants like Sayers, and, to continue the medical analogy, quacks and medicine men as well, and some early practitioners in the fashionable profession of spin doctoring – to mock and traduce and, occasionally, applaud this *Knight of the Wo[e]ful Countenance*.

Caricature could be a powerful weapon to arouse such political passions, but ultimately, its most effective – and enjoyable – role was to allow all the lilliputians to poke at, and poke fun at, Gulliver. And, if not always beautiful, was it not occasionally sublime?

PERSONS MOST CARICATURED, 1778–97

The extensive collection of political and personal satires indexed in the British Museum Catalogue allows us to gauge which figures were most caricatured during the last twenty years of Burke's life. In the Museum's listed holding of 3,686 prints of this period the following appearances are recorded:

Charles James Fox	821
William Pitt	457
George III	441
Lord North	355
George, Prince of Wales	294
Edmund Burke	293
Richard Brinsley Sheridan	200
Lord Thurlow	144
Queen Charlotte	118
Henry Dundas	114
Duke of Richmond	103
Duchess of Devonshire	100
Earl of Shelburne	90
Mrs Maria Fitzherbert	79
Warren Hastings	77
Louis XVI	72
Duke of Portland	68
Duke of York	67

John Wilkes	63
George Hanger	62
Earl of Sandwich	60
Admiral Keppel	59
Admiral Samuel Hood	54
Earl of Derby	52
Cecil Wray	49
Catherine II of Russia	45
Mrs Albinia Hobart (Countess of Buckinghamshire)	44
Mary 'Perdita' Robinson	41
Earl Stanhope	41
Earl of Bute	40
Sam House	40
Richard Pepper Arden	39
Baron Loughborough	38
Duke of Norfolk	38
Thomas Paine	38
Duke of Clarence	37
Earl of Mansfield	35
Dr Samuel Johnson	33
Lord John Cavendish	31
Oliver Cromwell	31
Lord George Gordon	31
Marie Antoinette	31
Lord George Sackville	31

Thomas Erskine	30
Viscount Sydney	30
Lady Archer	29
James Boswell	29
Charlotte Augusta, Princess Royal	29
William Grenville	29
Joseph Priestley	29
Louis Weltje	29
Duke of Grafton	28
Admiral Rodney	27
Dorothea Jordan	26
Duc d'Orléans	26
Duke of Bedford	25
Marquis of Buckingham	25
Michael Angelo Taylor	25
The Revd John Horne Tooke	25
William V of Orange	25
Duchess of York	25
Charles Cornwall, Speaker of the House	24
Admiral Howe	24
George Rose	24
Viscount Stormont	24
Edward Topham	23
Brook Watson	21
Thomas Powys	20
Dr Richard Price	20

PRINTSELLERS' AND PUBLISHERS' ADDRESSES

Listed below are addresses given for publishers of prints referred to in the text. Not all prints contain addresses. Square brackets denote those obtained from other prints.

Aitken, J.	14 Castle Street, Leicester Fields (or Leicester Square); 2 Jan 1789; Bear Street, Leicester Square.
Asperne, J.	Cornhill
Barrow, J.	[(from 1783) White Lion, Bull Stairs, Blackfriars Bridge]
	[(1782) St Bride's Passage, Fleet Street]
Bentley & Co.	–
Berry, J.	129 Oxford Road
Blofield, R.	2 Craven Court, Craven Street, Strand
Boyne & Walker	11 Great Turnstile, Lincolns Inn Fields
Bradshaw, J.	Coventry Street
Bretherton Charles	New Bond Street
Bretherton, James	134 New Bond Street
Brown, D.	–
Brown, J.	Holborn; Mayfair
Brown, J.	Rathbone Place
Brown, Tom	Spa Fields, Chelsea
Burke, J.	–
Buttens, R.	? 79 Fleet Street
Carter J.	Oxford Street
Clarkson, F.	73 St Paul's Church Yard
Colley, Thomas	257 High Holborn
Cornell, Thomas	Bruton Street
Crawford, J.	[7] Middle Row, Holborn
D'Archery (or D'Achery) Eliz.	St James's Street
Darly, M.	[39] Strand
Dent, William	116 Strand

Dickie, W.	195 Strand (opposite Exeter Change)
Doughty, J.	19 Holborn
Evans, T.	Oxford Street
Fielding & Walker	[20] Paternoster Row
Fores, S (or S.W. or W.)	3 Piccadilly; (moved during 1795): 50 Piccadilly
Grant, T.	Oxford Street
Hamilton, Archibald jr	near St John's Gate
Harmar, T.	164 Piccadilly
Hedges, E.	92 Cornhill
Hedges, [J]	Under the Royal Exchange
Holland, William	66 Drury Lane; (moved during 1786): 50 Oxford Street; (1803) 11 Cockspur Street
Holloway, W.	Strand
Hone, William	45 Ludgate Hill
Humphrey, G.	48 Long Acre
Humphrey, H.	[51] New Bond Street; (moved during 1790): 18 Old Bond Street; (moved during 1794): 37 New Bond street; (moved during 1797): 27 St James's Street
Humphrey, W.	227 Strand; 1786: Lancaster Court
Johnston, J.	98 Cheapside
Langham, J.	84 Dorset Street
Laurie & Whittle Macintosh, W.	53 Fleet Street
– (M.D. George suspects name fictitious, BM 5644)	
McKenzie, Alexander	101 Berwick Street, Soho
Macklew, E.	9 Haymarket

Macphail, H.	68 High Holborn
Maynard, W.	St Martin's Court, Leicester Fields
Moore, William	Oxford Street; (from 1785): 48 New Bond Street
Nill, George	Fleet Street
Nunn, J.	Queen Street
Owen, R.	Fleet Street
Phillips, R.	Southwark
Pownall, B.	6 Pall Mall
Rich, E.	55 Fleet Street
Richardson, W.	near Surrey Street, Strand
Ridgway (or Ridgeway) James	196 Piccadilly
Robinson, G & Co.	Paternoster Row
Sams, W.	St James's Street
Sherlock, A.	Princes Street, Lambeth
Sidebotham, James	24 Lower Sackville Street, Dublin
Smith, M.	46 Fleet Street
Smith, 'Mr' (initials unknown)	45 Long Acre, near Drury Lane
Symonds, H.D.	Paternoster Row
Tegg, Thomas	111 Cheapside
Todd, E.	–
Walker (initials unknown)	7 Cornhill
Wallis, J.	16 Ludgate Street
Walwyn, B.	2 Pedlars Acre, Westminster Bridge
Wells, W.	132 Fleet Street
Whitaker, J.	Ave Maria Lane
Wiggins, T.	9 Founders Court, Lothbury
Williamson, T.	20 Strand
Wright, J.	169 Piccadilly

ABBREVIATIONS

Ayling   Stanley Ayling, *Edmund Burke – His Life & Opinions* (London 1988)

BM Cat.   *Catalogue of Political and Personal Satires preserved in the Department of Prints and Drawings in the British Museum*, F.G. Stephens, Vols I–IV; M.D. George, Vols V–XI (London 1870–1954)

Carretta   Vincent Carretta, *George III and the Satirists from Hogarth to Byron* (Georgia 1990)

Corr.   T.W. Copeland and others (ed.), *The Correspondence of Edmund Burke,* 10 vols (Cambridge and Chicago 1958–78)

Cruise O'Brien   Conor Cruise O'Brien, *The Great Melody: A Thematic Biography of Edmund Burke* (London 1992)

Ehrman   John Ehrman, *The Younger Pitt* Vol. 1: *The Years of Acclaim* (London 1969, paperback ed. 1984)

George   M.D. George, *English Political Caricature* Vol. 1 (Oxford 1959)

Godfrey   Richard Godfrey, *English Caricature 1620 to the Present* (V & A, London 1984)

Haydon   Colin Haydon, *Anti-Catholicism in eighteenth-century England* (Manchester and New York 1993)

Hill   Draper Hill, *Mr Gillray the Caricaturist* (London 1965)

Magnus   Philip Magnus, *Edmund Burke* (London 1939)

Mitchell   L.G. Mitchell, *Charles James Fox* (Oxford 1992)

Parl. Hist   W. Cobbett (ed.), *The Parliamentary History of England from the Norman Conquest in 1066 to the year 1803* (London 1806–20)

Prior   James Prior, *Memoir of the Life and Character of the Right Hon. Edmund Burke* (London 1824)

Reynolds   Nicholas Penny (ed.), *Reynolds* (Royal Academy of Arts, London 1986)

Watson   J. Steven Watson, *The Reign of George III* (Oxford 1960)

Westminster Election *History of Burke* Vols II, V, VI, VIII, IX (Oxford 1981–91)

Works   *The Writings & Speeches of Edmund Burke in Twelve Volumes* [The Beaconsfield Edition] (London *c.* 1901)

Wraxall   Sir Nathaniel W. Wraxall, *Posthumous Memoirs of His Own Time* 3 Vols (London 1836)

Writings and Speeches Paul Langford and others (ed.), *The Writings and Speeches of Edmund Burke* Vols II, V, VI, VIII, IX (Oxford 1981–91)

NOTES

INTRODUCTION
THE CARICATURER'S STOCK IN TRADE

1. An unnamed contemporary's account quoted by Thomas Wright in *The Works of James Gillray, the Caricaturist* (London 1851) p.12.

2. In *Punch,* by John Leech, in 1843, though an anonymous print entitled *The Political Cartoon for the Year 1775* (BM 5288) anticipates Leech in this.

3. From the Italian, *caricare,* to charge or to load.

4. Quoted in E.H. Gombrich and E. Kris, *Caricature* (London 1940) pp. 11–12.

5. *Ibid.,* pp. 12, 13.

6. George, pp. 11,13. For an account of graphic satire from early times *see* pp. 3–13.

7. Quoted in Thomas Wright, *A History of Caricature and Grotesque* (London 1875) p. 412.

8. Herbert M.Atherton, *Political Prints in the Age of Hogarth* (Oxford, 1974) p. 65.

9. *Ibid.,* p. 69.

10. *Ibid.,* p. 82.

11. 28 June 1729, quoted in *ibid.,* p. 71.

12. When Gillray and the print seller Fores were charged with blasphemy in 1796 it is possible that George Canning – a member of Pitt's administration who quietly fed material for many satirical plates – interceded to have the action dropped, though Draper Hill thinks it much more probable that it died a natural death: Hill, p. 62.

13. 5 June 1765, quoted by F.G. Stephens, BM 3847. The 'great General' referred to is the Duke of Cumberland, portrayed by his fellow officer Townshend as *The Recruiting Serjeant,* BM 3581.

14. The pose struck by Bute is reminiscent of his portrait by Allan Ramsay, 1758, in the National Trust for Scotland, Bute House, Edinburgh.

15. Hill, p. 45.

16. George, p. 3.

17. Anon., BM 5295, 26 October 1775, published by W. Humphrey.

18. John Brewer, *Party ideology and popular politics at the accession of George III* (Cambridge 1976) p. 154.

19. Robert William Buss, *English Graphic Satire* (London 1874) p.127. Draper Hill, however, observes that by 1792 'progressively there is less to suggest that designs were etched directly [by Gillray] on the copper without preliminary sketches'. Hill, p. 41.

20. Translated from *A View of England towards the close of the eighteenth century* (1791) by M.D. George, BM Cat. Vol. v, p. xiv.

21. Godfrey, p. 16.

22. *Ibid.,* p. 58.

23. H.T. Dickinson, *Caricatures and the Constitution 1760–1832* (Cambridge 1986) p. 13.

24. Matthew Darly, No. 39 Strand, preface to *Caricatures Macaronies and Characters,* quoted in M.D. George, Introduction to BM Cat. Vol. v, p. xxxiv.

25. Noted by William Bates, 1879: Hill, p. 138.

26. *See* p. xxx., and Pl. 119.

27. The attribution by Calabi, *Bartolozzi.* (1928) is noted by M.D. George, BM 5318.

28. M.D. George, BM Cat. Vol. vi, p. xi, fn. i.

29. George, p. 175.

30. *Frontispiece to Reflections on the French Revolution,* BM 7675.

31. *See,* for example, Richard Earlom (after Charles Brandoin), *The Exhibition of the Royal Academy of Painting in the year 1771,* in *Reynolds,* p. 365; and Pietro Martini (after Johann Ramberg), *The Exhibition of the Royal Academy, 1787,* in *Reynolds,* pp. 368-69.

32. An addition to the publication line in *Cooling the Brain or – The Little Major, shaving the Shaver,* BM 7529, James Gillray, 8 May 1789. Great latitude in the publication of caricature did not preclude other hazards; Aitken was imprisoned for two years (1795–97) for selling a directory of prostitutes: Hill, p. 54.

33. George, p. 176.

34. *Very Slippy Weather,* BM 11100, 10 February 1808.

35. Quoted by M.D. George, BM Cat. Vol. viii, p. xli.

36. Quoted in E. McSherry Fowble, *Two Centuries of Prints in America 1680–1880* (Virginia 1987) p. 11.

37. *Ibid.,* p. 12.

38. Diana Donald, 'Character and Caricatures', in *Reynolds,* p. 355.

39. The print, reproduced in *Reynolds* p. 298, was executed in 1782; the painting was exhibited in the RA in May 1782.

40. Diana Donald, *The Age of Caricature* (New Haven and London 1996) pp. 1, 19.

41. John Brewer, *The Common People and Politics 1750–1790s* (Cambridge 1986) p. 46.

42. BM 3579 (1757): M.D. George, BM Cat. Vol. v. p. xviii. For Henry Fox with one of his cubs, probably Charles, *see* Pl. 21.

43. For a list of those most caricatured, 1778–97, *see* Appendix 1.

44. Francis Grose, *A Classical Dictionary of the Vulgar Tongue* (3rd ed. 1796).

45. Another is the Whig apothecary Edward Hall whose face and figure are plumper than Burke's and who is often depicted with a pestle and mortar, symbols of his calling. He kneels in front of Burke in Pl. 124. In 1808, of the fifteen senators portrayed by John Kay in *The Last Sitting of the old Court of Session* no fewer than six are wearing spectacles: Hilary and Mary Evans, *John Kay of Edinburgh* (Edinburgh 1973, 1980 ed.) Pl. 83.

46. BM 6978, anon., *c.* 1786; *see* pp. 107–8.

47. Mitchell, p. 97.

48. At her benefit at Covent Garden on 10 February, 1786: M.D. George, BM 7053.

49. *Essays on Physiognomy* (English translation, London 1788–98) quoted in Godfrey, p. 38

50. *Printmaking in Britain* (Oxford 1978) p. 75. For Canning's debut in 1796, in *Promis'd Horrors of the French Revolution, see* p. 184, and Pl. 193.

51. BM 6328, July 1783, G.B. Hill (ed.), *Johnsonian Miscellanies* (New York 1897) Vol. ii, pp. 419–20.

52. *Writings and Speeches,* ix, p. 153.

CHAPTER ONE
THE FLOWERS OF ORATORY

1. *Works* I, 4–5.

2. Cruise O'Brien, p. 450, and *see* pp. 448–50.

3. *Works* I, p. 125.

4. James Barry, *Works*, I, p. 182.

5. David Berman, 'The culmination and causation of Irish philosophy'. *Archiv für Geschichte der Philosophie*, 64, Band 1982 Heft 3, p. 275.

6. *An Analytical Inquiry Into the Principles of Taste* (London, 2nd ed. 1805) p. 377.

7. David Berman, *op.cit.*, p. 275.

8. Owen Dudley Edwards, in a communication to Conor Cruise O' Brien, cited in Cruise O'Brien, p. 49 fn. 2.

9. In April 1770.

10. *Corr.,* II, p. 101.

11. 5 December 1769, *Writings and Speeches*, II, pp. 246–47.

12. Cruise O'Brien, p. 51.

13. *Public Advertiser* 27 September 1769, and *see ibid.*, 1 May 1770, 27 August 1770, 12 October 1769, 28 September 1769; cited by Paul Langford in *Writings and Speeches,* II, p. 9.

14. Recalling Lucius Junius Brutus who drove out Tarquin the Proud and established the Roman Republic in 510 BC, and his descendant Marcus Junius Brutus who slayed Caesar.

15. The *London Magazine* Vol. XXXIX p. 98. It is stated on the title page to this volume that it contains a 'Portrait of the Celebrated Junius'.

16. In particular, the engraving for *Memoirs of Sir P. Francis,* Vol. I, 1867, by Joseph Parkes: note by F.G. Stephens to BM 4314.

17. Sackville (who assumed the name Germain in 1770 and later became Viscount Sackville) was MA 1734, Burke, BA 1748, Philip Francis senior, BA 1728.

18. Prior, p. 122.

19. *Writings and Speeches*, II, pp. 75 and 87.

20. Dr William Markham to Burke, November 1771, cited in Isaac Kramnick, *The Rage of Edmund Burke* (New York 1977) p. 110.

21. Quoted in Cruise O'Brien, p. 276 fn. 2. For a print purporting to identify Burke as 'Junius' *see*, for example, *Opposition Defeated,* Pl. 17.

22. T. Bonnor (his first name, like those of many caricaturists of the time, is no longer known) worked *c.*1763–1807: M.D. George, BM Cat. Vol. V. p. 840.

23. *See* Alvar Ellegaard, *A Statistical Method for Determining Authorship; the 'Junius' Letters* (1962).

24. Cruise O'Brien, pp. 276-80.

25. Its full title is *Political Electricity; or, an Historical & Prophetical Print in the Year 1770.*

26. For an engraving depicting Burke as 'The British Cicero', *see* Pierpont Morgan Library, New York. Peel Collection No. 17.

27. Paul Langford (ed.) *Writings and Speeches,* II, p. 55.

28. *Writings and Speeches*, II, p.80.

29. They are: William Dowdeswell (former Chancellor of the Exchequer), Colonel Isaac Barré (another Irish candidate for Junius), the lawyer Charles Cornwall MP (later Speaker of the House), Lord John Cavendish (MP for York and son of the Duke of Devonshire) and Richard Whitworth (MP for Stafford, who wrote against the government under the name 'Veridicus').

30. For this account of the *Town and Country Magazine* I am grateful to Rosemary Baker.

31. *Writings and Speeches* II, p. 458.

32. *See too Coalition Dance* (Pl. 34) in which Burke holds a book inscribed 'Little Red Riding Hood'.

33. Published shortly after Burke's *Reflections on the Revolution in France,* with its famous passage on the Queen of France and the passing of the age of chivalry.

34. James Boswell, *The Life of Samuel Johnson, LL.D* (1791, ed. G.B. Hill, Oxford 1887) vii, p. 250.

35. Paul Langford (ed.) *Writings and Speeches,* II, p. 407.

36. *See* Godfrey, p. 58, and George, p. 135.

37. For an analysis, *see* Cruise O'Brien, pp. 102-103.

38. George, pp. 134-35.

39. F.G. Stephens suggests the Rockinghams are doing this, citing *The Repeal* as well as three sequels which he lists as [18 March 1766]: BM 4141, 4142, 4143; BM Cat. Vol. IV, p. xxxvii.

40. George, p. 134.

41. Godfrey, p. 74. The drawing is in the Yale Center for British Art, Paul Mellon Collection, B1975. 4.1346.

42. The incident is described in John Wain, *Samuel Johnson* (New York 1975) p. 268.

43. John Wain (ed.), *The Journals of James Boswell* (London 1991) p. 301 (5 April 1776).

44. John Cannon, *Samuel Johnson and the Politics of Hanoverian England* (Oxford 1994) p. 296.

45. The description of the cooks is taken from the accompanying text. A show carried about in a box, a peep show, the phrase 'raree-show' was also used to mean a spectacle of any kind.

46. Ehrman, p. 37.

47. *Ibid.*, p. 42.

48. *Ibid.*, p. 61.

49. Watson, p. 208.

50. *Works*, II, p. 267.

51. *Ibid*, II, p. 273.

52. *Ibid*, II, pp. 288–89.

53. Katherine C. Balderston (ed.), *The Diary of Mrs. Hester Lynch Thrale . . . 1776-1809* (Oxford 1942, reprinted 1951) Vol. 1, pp. 329-30.

54. *Works*, II, p. 303.

55. *Ibid*, II, pp. 303–304.

56. *Ibid*, II, pp. 338–39.

57. *Ibid*, II, p. 354.

58. It was abolished under the Establishment Act (22 Geo III, *c.* 82), but was reconstituted in 1786.

59. *Works,* II, pp. 340–41.

60. *Ibid*, II, p. 341.

61. 'Teague' was slang for an Irishman; in Ulster for a Roman Catholic.

62. M.D. George, note to BM 5644.

63. *Corr.,* III, p. 388, Burke to William Baker, 12 October 1777.

64. *Ibid.,* III, p. 107, 24 January 1775.

65. BM 5645, 1 March 1780 (perhaps after George, fourth Viscount and later first Marquis Townshend).

66. E.g. *The Thing in a Nasty Situation* [*c.* 1780] BM 5709: Fox and others are playing a game of handball, using Lord North as the ball. One of the smaller figures identifies himself as Burke by saying 'This is sublime & Beautiful'. In *War of Posts* BM 5984, 1 May 1782, Burke holds a paper inscribed 'economy'.

67. In *Cincinnatus in Retirement* (Pl. 29). *See also* Pl. 22 [*Edmund Burke*] by James Sayers.

68. Quoted by Paul Langford in his Introduction, *Writings and Speeches*, II, p. 9.

69. BM 5650, 16 March 1780, published by T. Cornell.

70. Irish bulls are attributed to Burke in three other prints: *The F-x, Goose and Primier* (1783) BM 6180; *A Peep Below Stairs a Dream,* 8 June 1784, BM 6616; *French Flight* (Pl. 170). They had become a popular source of amusement in England from the appearance of a collection of *Bog-Witticisms* in the 1680s: Michael Duffy, *The Englishman and the Foreigner* (Cambridge 1986) p. 22.

71. Luis Vicente de Velasco Isla (1711–1762); I am grateful to Professor Nigel Glendinning for suggesting this possibility.

72. As M.D. George suggests, note to BM 5854, 21 November 1781. Perhaps she takes her cue from an old print of Beaconsfield reproduced in Magnus, opposite p. 42. *See too* BM 5842, *The Late Auction at St Eustatia* (attributed to T. Colley) 11 June 1781, published by E. Hedges where Rodney and Vaughan are satirised for dallying at St Eustatius to auction off their booty.

73. *Works,* I, p. 444.

74. In *The Ghost,* quoted (p. 98) in Carretta, p. 98, a valuable study of verbal and visual satire relating to the King.

75. Quoted by M.D. George, note to BM 5132, BM Cat. Vol. V, p.128.

76. Quoted in Ehrman, p. 52.

77. BM 5972, 12 April 1782.

78. The BM's impression (5979) bears the publication line of Eliz D'Achery, St James's Street. In the impression illustrated (Pl. 70) this line has been cut and in manuscript is written, beside the title, 'Pub. 23rd April 1782 by T. Grant Oxford St'.

79. M.D. George, note to BM 5979. Burke's speech was on 15 April 1782.

80. *See,* for example, *Edmund Burke,* 'Engraved by O'Keeffe from a painting by Sir Joshua Reynolds Published by Thomas Kelly', Pierpont Morgan Library, New York, Peel Collection No. 20. *See too* Peel Collection No. 35.

81. Reproduced in Lucy Sutherland, *Politics and Finance in the Eighteenth Century* (London 1984) p. 298.

82. *Reynolds,* p. 227.

83. *Corr.,* V, p. 70.

84. James Burke, *The Speeches of the Right Hon. Edmund Burke* (Dublin 1865 edition) p. 214.

85. BM 6162, 1783, published by W. Humphrey.

86. Quoted by M.D. George, note to BM 6162.

87. Watson, p. 248.

88. Ayling, pp. 110–11.

89. Lucy Sutherland, *op. cit.,* pp. 416, 417. She and J. Binney analyse. Henry Fox's tenure as Paymaster pp. 415–43; *Works,* II. p. 319, 320.

90. *Works,* II, pp. 319–20.

91. Lucy Sutherland, *op. cit.,* p. 422.

92. *Ibid.,* p. 422.

93. *Ibid.,* pp. 427–29.

94. *Ibid.,* p. 418.

95. Letter to Barry, in Rome, 16 Sept. 1769, quoted in William L. Pressly, *The Life and Art of James Barry* (New Haven and London 1981), p. 15.

96. William L. Pressly, *op. cit.,* p. 72.

97. In his *Letter to the Dilettanti Society,* 1798; *ibid.,* p. 76.

98. William L. Pressly, *op. cit.,* p. 75.

99. Published December 1776; Yale Centre for British Art, Paul Mellon Coll. B 1977.14.11067.

100. *Letter to the Dilettanti Society,* 1798, quoted in Godfrey, p. x.

101. *A History of Caricature and Grotesque* (London 1875) p. 466.

102. *Ibid.,* p. 455.

103. E.H. Gombrich, *Meditations on a Hobby Horse* (London 1963, reprint of 4th ed., 1994) p. 131.

104. Quoted by M.D. George in BM Cat. Vol. V, p. xxvii.

105. *See* BM 5968, *Lord No[rt]h in the Suds,* [?T.Colley], published by T. Evans, 27 March 1782; and note by M.D. George.

106. *Dictionary of National Biography* xlviii, p. 304.

107. *War of Posts,* BM 5984.

108. BM 5986, 10 May 1782.

109. *Works,* I, p. 524.

110. Stripped naked in *The Whipping Post,* for example, she is being flailed with a thistle by Bute: BM 3945, 1762.

111. Quoted by M.D. George in her note to BM 5987. Draper Hill says the piece 'sounds suspiciously like a paid advertisement': Hill, p. 23.

112. BM 6007, *c.* June 1782, published by W. Humphrey.

113. *Visiting the Sick.* Published 28 July 1806, by H. Humphrey BM 10589.

CHAPTER TWO
PARADISE LOST, PARADISE REGAINED

1. Cruise O'Brien, p. 239; his analysis of Burke's loathing of Shelburne should be read in full, pp. 234–42.

2. Carl Philip Moritz, *Journeys of a German in England (*1783) translated Reginald Nettel (London 1983 edition) p.183.

3. *Ibid.,* p. 184.

4. Francis Hardy, *Memoirs of the Political and Private Life of James Caulfeild, Earl of Charlemont* (London 1810) p. 177.

5. BM 7150 *A Noble Lord, on an approaching Peace, too busy to attend to the Expenditure of a Million of the Public Money;* 12 March 1787; published by R. Phillips. As the crafty Shelburne deals with his Jewish financiers, the portraits that hang behind him are of John Calvin (alluding to his nonconformist connections as patron of Dr Price and Dr Priestley) and of Edmund Burke as the Jesuit Ignatius Loyola. Gillray probably knows that this association with Shelburne, however mocking, will infuriate Burke.

6. But *see* the caveat of Owen Dudley Edwards, noted on p. 11.

7. Cruise O'Brien, p. 49.

8. Haydon, p. 253.

9. Quoted in Haydon, p. 76.

10. *Ibid.,* p. 25.

11. Quoted in Haydon, p. 196.

12. *See also, The Royal Ass,* BM 5669, 20 May 1780, published by M. Darly, where the King is driven to Rome by Bute.

13. Paul Wright (ed.) *The New and Complete Book of Martyrs* [1785?] p. iii, quoted in Haydon, p. 29.

14. Prior, p. 243.

15. Cruise O'Brien, pp. 147–48.

16. The description is that of Thomas Wright, *The Works of James Gillray the Caricaturist* (London 1851) p. 41.

17. BM 6042, 5 December 1782, published by J. Langham.

18. Quoted in Watson, p. 151.

19. Bernard Falk, *Thomas Rowlandson: His Life and Art* (London 1949) p. 64.

20. BM 6165, 9 January 1783, published by W. Humphrey.

21. BM 6180, [1 March 1783].

22. Cruise O'Brien, p. 241 fn. 2.

23. For Dance's involvement, *see* Hill, p. 24.

24. The presence of a dog in the print alludes to North's riposte on being interrupted by a barking dog: 'Sir, I was interrupted by a new Speaker, but as his argument is concluded I will resume mine'.

25. BM 6199, 1 April 1783, published by E. Hedges.

26. BM 6195, 24 March 1783, published by E. D'Achery.

27. *See* Pls 75, 76 and 85: *The Impeachment,* BM 6925, 17 March 1786, by James Sayers; *Impeachment,* BM 6926, 19 March 1786, by William Dent; *Poor Vulcan and his Cyclops . . .,* BM 6948, 29 April 1786, by William Dent.

28. BM 6203 (anon., perhaps John Boyne) published by W. Humphrey.

29. *Correspondence of George III,* VI, p. 262.

30. Essay in *Reynolds,* p. 362.

31. Lewis Walpole Library, LWL 783. 6.6.1.

32. Although the style is Dent's, the name of [Thomas] Colley beneath the image suggests possible collaboration.

33. R. Willis, *The Way to Stable and Quiet Times* (1715) p. 25, quoted in Haydon, p. 93. The notion of a priest as Little Red Ridinghood's wolf was to persist: *Punch* 1851, Vol XX, p. 139, for example, has a cartoon of that name.

34. BM 6212, 16 April 1783.

35. Quoted in Oscar Sherwin, *Uncorking Old Sherry* (London 1960), pp. 184-85.

36. Quoted in Lewis Gibbs, *Sheridan* (1947, reissued 1970) p. 17.

37. Quoted in Madeleine Bingham, *Sheridan: The Track of a Comet* (New York 1972) p. 16.

38. Lewis Gibbs, *Sheridan,* p. 64.

39. *Ibid.,* p. 14.

40. 11 February 1780, quoted in James Burke, *op. cit.,* p. 172.

41. BM 6214, 17 April, 1783, published by E. Dachery .

42. *Razor's Levee or ye Heads of a new Wig A[dmin-istratio]n on a Broad Bottom,* BM 6217, 21 April 1783, published by Thomas Cornell.

43. September 1781, quoted by John Brooke, *King George III* (London 1972, paperback ed. 1985) p. 226.

44. BM 6256, 9 August 1783, published by B. Pownall.

45. October 1781, p. 537, quoted in James Raven, *Judging New Wealth* (Oxford 1992) p. 174.

46. *A Curious Collection of Wild Beasts,* BM 6269, 1 November 1783.

47. *Portland Sharks or the Ministry Upon a Broad Bottom,* BM 6238 [1 June 1783] from the *Rambler's Magazine.*

48. BM 6251, 24 July 1783, [perhaps by and] published by J. Barrow, White Lion, Bull Stairs.

49. Cruise O'Brien, p. 277.

50. P.J. Marshall, In his introduction to *Writings and Speeches,* V, p. 19.

51. *Ibid.,* p. 18.

52. Quoted in Cruise O'Brien, p. 336.

CHAPTER THREE
CARLO KHAN

1. Quoted by P.J.Marshall (ed.) in *Writings and Speeches,* V., p. viii.

2. *Ibid.,* p. 4.

3. Mitchell, p. 63.

4. Two bills, in fact, were involved, one vesting the Company's affairs in the commissioners, the other dealing with the governance of its territorial possessions.

5. 25 November 1783; BM 6271, published by Thomas Cornell.

6. *Memoirs* 1884, III p. 254 cited in M.D. George's note to BM 6271.

7. BM 6277, 12 December 1783, Anon, published by William Holland. The other print sympathetic to the coalition is *To Day Disliked . . . ,* BM 6291, *see* p. 56.

8. BM 6279, [18] December 1783, published by T. Wiggins.

9. BM 6280, 21 December 1783, published by E. D'Archery.

10. BM 6281, 22 December 1783, John Boyne, published by E. Hedges.

11. Quoted in Ehrman, p.127.

12. Mitchell, p. 67.

13. BM 6291 [1783, after 18 December].

14. West exhibited *The Death of Wolfe* in 1771.

15. For Perdita Robinson's affair with the Prince of Wales see, for example, BM 5767 *Florizel and Perdita,* 10 November 1780; for her affair with Fox, see, for example, BM 6117, *Perdito and Perdita,* 17 December 1782.

16. BM 6361, 1 January 1784, published by W. Wells.

17. BM 6398, 2 February 1784, published by B. Walwyn.

18. He and Richmond were caricatured on 12 January 1784 in *Ordnance See-Saws,* BM 6373, published by E. Darchry [sic].

19. A sequel will follow, *c.* March 1784: *Satan Harangueing his Troops after their Defeat,* BM 6482.

20. The theme is taken up in *Coalition Arms* the description of which, beneath the design, includes: 'First Quarter. A Standard with the Thirteen Stripes of the American States; Base, Edmund St Omer's, like a skilful Dentist, drawing the Teeth of a Lion'.

21. *Cromwell ye 2nd Exalted or the Poison Bag out-done by the Halter.* The poison bag refers to an incident in which a leather bag with noxious contents was thrown into Fox's face on 14 February in Westminster Hall: a spectator cries 'Huzza! what the Poison Bag could not effect the Halter has'.

22. *Guy Vaux or F— Blowing up the Par—t House!!!* BM 6389, 30 January 1784, published by B. Walwyn. Pitt's bill was defeated on 23 January.

23. *George and the Dragon,* BM 6405, 7 February 1784, published by B. Walwyn.

24. Pierpont Morgan Library, New York. Peel Collection No. 107. The dragon python has the heads of Fox, North and Burke (who disgorges a turban marked *Economy*).

25. Carretta, p. 162.

26. BM 6446, 11 March 1784, published by W. Humphrey.

27. BM 6380, *The Mirror of Patriotism,* 20 January 1784, published by James Bretherton.

28. *The Dividend or Half a Crown in the Pound,* BM 6409, 12 February 1784.

29. *The Times – or a View of the Old House in Little Brittain – with Nobody Going to Hannover,* BM 6384, 23 January 1784, published by W. Humphrey.

30. For Robinson as rat catcher, and his rats see BM 6427 and 6431.

31. Oscar Sherwin, *Uncorking Old Sherry* (London 1960) p. 184.

32. BM 6449 [*c.* March 1784].

33. BM 6454, 18 March 1784, published by T. Cornell.

34. BM 6455, 19 March 1784, published by E. Hedges.

35. M.D. George, note to BM 6455.

36. *The Eclipse*, BM 6467, 26 March 1784, published by H. Macphail.

37. BM 6486, 1 April 1784, published by W. Humphrey.

38. Mitchell, p. 67.

39. *Westminster Election*, p. 320. George Nugent-Temple-Grenville (1753-1813) had succeeded as second Earl Temple in 1779 and was created first Marquis of Buckingham in 1784.

40. BM 6528.

41. BM 6604 (*c*. May 1784).

42. *Westminster Election*, p. 290.

43. *Ibid.*, p. 291.

44. *Ibid.*, p. 324.

45. *Ibid.*, pp. 324–25. It appears that Mountmorres thereupon paid his taxes on the furnished house he rented, had his name entered in the parish books, and voted next day: *Ibid.*, p. 190.

46. *Ibid.*, p. 314.

47. *Ibid.*, p. 329.

48. *Ibid.*, p. 229.

49. *Ibid.*, p. 223.

50. *Ibid.*, p. 225.

51. *Ibid.*, p. 352.

52. *Ibid.*, p. 326.

53. *Ibid.*, p. 244.

54. *Ibid.*, p. 253.

55. *Ibid.*, p. 269. Burke was installed as Lord Rector of Glasgow University on 10 April 1784, in succession to Henry Dundas.

56. *Ibid.*, p. 247. The reference is to Thomas Gray's *Elegy in a Country Churchyard*, 1751.

57. *Westminster Election*, p. 151.

58. *Ibid.*, pp. 100 and 125.

59. *Ibid.*, p. 307.

60. BM 6484 (*c*. March–April 1784), [attributed to Samuel Collings].

61. BM 6481, 31 March 1784, published by H. Humphrey.

62. *The General Election*, BM 6507, 7 April 1784, published by J. Brown, Rathbone Place. In *The Heads of the Mutiny Bill, Laid on the Table* (20 February 1784, Anon, published by E. Darchery) Lord Thurlow, pointing to the heads of Fox, North and Burke, asks: ' Is it your lordships opinion that these Heads be now Committed to the Polls in Temple Bar? The Ayes have it'.

63. BM 6512 (*c*. 8 April 1784), [?J. Barrow], published by E. Rich.

64. For a table showing the daily state of the poll from 1 April to 17 May 1784 *see Westminster Election*, p. 410.

65. *Westminster Election*, p. 321.

66. BM 6540, 17 April, 1784.

67. Mitchell, pp. 97 and 93–4.

68. *Britons: Forging the Nation 1707–1837* (New Haven and London 1994) p. 244.

69. Cited by M.D. George in her note to BM 6588. *See* Horace Walpole, *Letters,* Vol. xiii, p. 142.

70. E.g. *Madam Blubber on her Canvass,* BM 6544, 22 April 1784, published by Mrs H. Humphrey.

71. BM 6561, *Madam Blubber's Last Shift or the Aerostatic Dilly* (probably after Viscount Townshend) 29 April 1784, published by H. Humphreys [*sic*] Bond Street.

72. *Westminter Election,* pp. 103-4, (12 April 1784). Francis Grose, *A Classical Dictionary of the Vulgar Tongue* (3rd. ed. 1796) defines stallion as 'a man kept by an old lady for secret services'.

73. George, p. 184.

74. *Britons: Forging the Nation 1797–1837,* p. 245.

75. Anon., reproduced in *ibid.,* p. 245; not in BM Cat; Lewis Walpole Library, 5 May 1784, published by [H.]McPhail.

76. 'J.M.W.', BM. 6625, published by J. Wallis.

77. *Westminster Election,* p. 253.

78. *Ibid.,* p. 336.

79. *Ibid.,* p. 345.

80. *Ibid.,* pp. 341-42.

81. *Ibid.,* p. 363. Townshend lived at 9 Hanover Square; the original sketch for BM 6561 is in the Print Room of the BM and resembles, says M.D. George, sketches by Townshend in the Department.

82. *Ibid.,* p. 502.

83. Mitchell, p. 70.

84. 15 June 1784, published by W. Holloway, described in BM Cat. Vol. vi, p. 150.

85. BM 6629, 28 June 1784, published by G. Humphrey.

86. *Hi nostri Reditus, expectatique triumphi!* [These are our returns, and our awaited triumphs!] BM 6657, (before September 1784) published by J. Whitaker, Ave Maria Lane. It is the frontispiece to *Fox's Martyrs,* 2nd Edition. For Burke's epitaph-writing, *see* Prior, pp. 198–200 and 327–28.

87. Quoted by M.D. George in her note to BM 6659.

88. BM 6671, published by J. Brown, Rathbone Place.

89. R.B. McDowell, in *Writings and Speeches* ix, p. 405.

90. *Ibid.*, pp. 405–406.

91. *Ibid.*, p. 586.

92. Charles Jenkinson (1727–1808), first Earl of Liverpool and first Baron Hawkesbury, had also been Vice-Treasurer of Ireland.

93. *See A Picturesque View of the State of the Nation for February 1778,* BM 5472, 1 March 1778, engraved for the *Westminster Magazine*.

94. Michael Wynne Jones, *The Cartoon History of the American Revolution* (London ed., 1977) p. 184.

95. An earlier and less elaborate form of the design is BM 6792, 25 April 1785.

96. An Irish secret agrarian society.

97. Ehrman, p. 207.

98. Composed by Captain Morris: M.D. George, note to BM 6795.

CHAPTER FOUR
ASSAILING THE 'SAVIOUR OF INDIA'

1. Quoted in Robin Reilly, *Pitt the Younger* (1978) p. 274.

2. *Ibid.*, p. 274.

3. Quoted by M.D George, note to BM 6770 *The Fall of Achilles,* 7 January 1785, [Thomas Rowlandson].

4. Wraxall, I, p. 320.

5. From his mock elegy *Retaliation* (1774).

6. William Le Fanu (ed), *Betsy Sheridan's Journal* (London 1960) pp. 31 and 198.

7. P.J. Marshall, in his introduction to *Writings and Speeches*, vi, p. 2.

8. In articles between 6–15 February 1786.

9. The lakh (100,000 rupees) was worth about £10,200: Robin Reilly *op. cit.*, p. 148.

10. (1756–1815); *Dictionary of National Biography*, Vol. lv, p.116; I am indebted to Andrew Edmunds for this attribution.

11. M.D. George, note to BM 6937.

12. BM 6943, 11 April 1786, published by S.W. Fores.

13. Hugh Elliott to William Pitt, 17 October 1785, quoted by M.D. George, note to BM 6493.

14. Anon., BM 6968, 18 July 1786, published by S.W. Fores.

15. Wraxall, III, p. 133.

16. BM 6980, 23 August 1786, published by E. Macklew.

17. A sequel is *Landing at Botany Bay*; BM 6992 (16 November 1786, John Boyne, published by E. Hedges, and by H. Humphrey). Burke is a ruffian in the *Hibernian Magazine* print, *The First Parliament of Botany Bay in High Debate*, 1786, p. 685, (BM 7122, published in January 1787). The Prince and his supporters, one of which is Burke, another Fox as 'Carlo Crusoe', are *The Poor Blacks Going to their Settlement*, the phrase implying they are paupers: BM 7127 (12 January 1787, William Dent, published by E. Macklew).

18. Also left behind is Perdita Robinson (*see* Pl. 43). Those pushing off from Execution Dock are (from left) Sheridan, Captain Morris, Erskine, Hanger, Prince of Wales, Fox, Portland, North and Burke.

19. A companion plate to *Morning Preparation* [25 April 1785, published by W. Humphrey].

20. BM 7158, 28 April 1787, published by S.W. Fores. The figures of Fox, North and Burke are copied from Gillray's *Political Banditti Assailing the Saviour of India* BM 6955 (Pl. 86).

21. BM Cat. Vol. VI, p. 1073.

22. BM 7160 *The Insults of the Brave I have borne with Some Degree of Patience . . .*, [May 1787], published in *The Bristol Mercury*.

23. M.D. George, note to BM 7160.

24. *The Prince at Grass*, BM 7167, 2 June 1787, published by S.W. Fores, Piccadilly.

25. *The Prince in Clover*, BM 7168, 2 June 1787 [published by S.W. Fores, Piccadilly].

26. *Parl. Hist.* XVII, p. 819, quoted in Ayling, p. 187.

27. BM 7170, 16 June 1787, published by S.W. Fores.

28. BM 8485, published by S.W. Fores, 'who has jus[t] fitted up his Exhibition in an entire Novel stile admittance one shill[in]g'.

29. 24 August 1794, quoted in W.H. Wilkins, *Mrs. Fitzherbert and George IV* (London 1905, reprinted 1914) p. 217.

30. P. J. Marshall in his introduction to *Writings and Speeches*, VI, p. 6.

31. BM 7131, 23 January 1787, published by S.W. Fores.

32. *See,* for example, *Knave of Diamonds*, BM 6966, 11 July 1786, published by J. Burke.

33. In *A Shot at the Min . . . . r* [*Minister*] Burke is seen gesticulating with an angry scowl and urging Fox to discharge a blunderbuss at the 'Commercial Treaty': BM 7137, 6 February 1787, James Sayers, published by Thos Cornell.

34. BM 7132, 23 January 1787, published at 164 Piccadilly. This is the address of T. Harmar: *see* Pl. 93.

35. BM 7136, 2 February 1787, published by George Nill.

36. P.J. Marshall in his introduction to *Writings and Speeches*, VI, p. 10.

37. *See also* [*The Governor of Rue Peas*] BM 7272, involving Thurlow, Hastings and Burke.

38. *See,* for example, Gillray's *Paddy on Horse-Back*, 1779, BM 5605, in which an Irish fortune hunter rides towards London, back-to-front on a bull. Pitt is similarly mounted in *Paddy O'Pitt's Triumphal Exit!!* BM 6799, 1785, a satire on his Irish propositions.

39. *See,* for example, BM 7152 James Gillray, *The Board of Controul, or the Blessings of a Scotch Dictator*, 20 March 1787, published by R. Phillips.

40. *Writings and Speeches* VI, p. 121, fn. 3.

41. *The Impeachment*, BM 7268.

42. Pierpont Morgan Library, New York. Peel Collection No. 81.

43. The BM's impression lacks date and publication line.

44. George, p. 14.

45. The lawyer's rapacity is a constant theme in caricature, discussed by J.A. Sharpe in *Crime and the Law in English Satirical Prints 1600–1832* (Cambridge 1986) pp. 25–30.

46. 15 February 1788, quoted in B.W. Hill (ed.), *Edmund Burke on Government Politics and Society* (Glasgow 1975) pp. 270-72.

47. Lewis Walpole Library, LWL 788.4.22.1.

48. The phrase, 'I hate Alonzo' used by Sayers, casts Francis as Zanga in Edward Young's play, *The Revenge*, produced at Drury Lane in 1721.

49. Dubbed 'the Palinurus of the north', Lord North was often depicted in caricature nodding off, like the careless pilot Palinurus in Virgil's *Aeneid* who nodded off at the helm and fell overboard. *See,* for example, *Wife & No Wife* (Pl. 77).

50. Samuel Johnson's Dictionary defines Rareeshow as 'A show carried in a box'.

51. Quoted in Oscar Sherwin, *Uncorking Old Sherry* (London 1960) pp. 224–25.

52. Mitchell, p. 102.

53. Wentworth Woodhouse MSS; noted by Paul Langford, *A Polite and Commercial People* (Oxford 1989, paperback 1992) p. 687.

54. *See* M.D. George, notes to BM 6966, 7287; the gift was made on 14 June 1786, Sheridan's imputation on 21 June.

55. BM 7295, [? March 1788] published by [J] Crawford.

56. BM 7302, 13 April 1788, published by Thos Cornell.

57. *A Reverie of Prince Demetrius Cantemir, Ospidar of Moldavia*, BM 7307, 26 April 1788, published by Thos Cornell.

58. *The Princess's Bow alias the Bow Begum*, BM 7309, 1 May 1788. The Vizier's mother was the Bahu or Bow-Begum, his grandmother the Burra Begum, begum denoting a married Muslim lady of high rank.

59. BM 7300, 11 April 1788, published by Thos Cornell.

60. Magnus, p. 302.

61. BM 7308, 27 April 1788, published by S.W. Fores.

62. BM 7310, 2 May 1788.

63. — *Coaches*, BM 7324, [James Gillray], 20 May 1788, published by S.W. Fores.

64. *English Slavery; or a Picture of the Times*, BM 7301, April 1788, published (in four sheets) by W. Holland.

65. Thurlow is cast as Father Paul in Sheridan's *Duenna* and his words are adapted from the play.

66. BM 7330, 4 June 1788, published by S.W. Fores.

67. P.J. Marshall in his introduction to *Writings and Speeches*, VI, p. 8.

68. To what purpose is not clear. Sayers's rendering of Sheridan would itself be hostile. For examples of Gillray's 'J.S.' prints *see* Pls 99, 105, 106; for Rowlandson's *see* Pl. 132.

69. Pierpont Morgan Library, New York. Peel Collection No. 236.

70. Diary of the Duchess of Devonshire, 20 November 1788, quoted in Mitchell, p. 86.

71. Hill, p. 32.

72. BM 7344, 21 July 1788, published by H. Humphrey (price 5s.3d).

73. M.D. George, note to BM 7344.

74. A charge also made in 1784: *see The West[minste]r Candidate Coming North about the Geese,* BM 6480, where North is dispensing 'Treasury Grains'. Anon., 31 March 1784.

75. William LeFanu, *Betsy Sheridan's Journal* (London 1960) p. 111, Betsy Sheridan to Alice LeFanu, 1 August 1788.

76. BM 7356, 29 July 1788, [James Gillray], published by H. Humphrey (price 1s.).

77. Mitchell, p. 95. He quotes from the *Diary of Lady S. Lyttleton,* 5 December 1813.

78. *Charons Boat: – or – Topham's Trip, with Hood to Hell,* BM 7371, 22 August 1788.

CHAPTER FIVE
FIGHTING FOR A CROWN

1. Ehrman, p. 647.

2. For an account of the regency crisis and some relevant prints, *see* Nicholas Robinson, 'Caricature and the Regency Crisis: an Irish perspective', *Eighteenth-Century Ireland* Vol. 1, (Dublin 1986) pp. 157–76.

3. Lewis Walpole Library, LWL 788. 9.1.1. *See also The Frolick or a New-Market, Race,* BM 7338. Burke, in fact, does not seem to have met Orléans on his visit in 1788: L.G. Mitchell, introduction to *Writings and Speches,* VIII, pp. 2–3.

4. The date given in ms. to the print in the BM collection. BM 7375.

5. James Marwood, *The Life and Works of Richard Brinsley Sheridan* (Edinburgh 1985) p. 125.

6. *Ibid.,* p. 127.

7. Prior, p. 252.

8. M.D. George, note to BM 7381.

9. W. Pitt to Prince of Wales, 30 Dec. 1788, quoted in Ehrman, p. 658.

10. Ehrman, p. 658.

11. Shane Leslie, *George the Fourth* (London 1926) p. 48.

12. George, p. 197.

13. Quoted in Thomas Wright, *op. cit.,* p. 103.

14. *Invocation,* BM 7397 [December 1788], sold by W. Moore.

15. Not in BM Cat.; Library of Congress, Washington D.C. (ref PC 2- B -1789), 11 January 1789, published by W. Dent. The great collection in the Library of Congress, incorporating the Royal Collection formerly at Windsor and purchased in 1921, contains nearly 10,000 prints, about 2,000 of which are not in the BM Cat.

16. BM 7477, January 1789, published by William Holland.

17. For the depiction of Richmond as Uncle Toby (from Sterne's *Tristram Shandy*) *see,* for example, *Unkle Toby and Corporal Trim,* BM 6921, 8 March 1786.

18. Lewis Walpole Library, LWL 789.1.14.2.

19. *See,* for example, *The Corsican Crocodile dissolving the Council of Frogs!!!* BM 9427, anon., published Nov.1799 by W. Holland.

20. *Preceptor and Pupil,* 18 May 1784, BM 6585, published by G. Humphrey.

21. *See* John Baskett and Dudley Snelgrove, *The Drawings of Thomas Rowlandson in the Paul Mellon Collection* (London 1977), p. 84 and illustration 336.

22. BM 7495, Anon., 27 January 1789.

23. Eric Partridge, *A Dictionary of Slang* (1937).

24. BM 7492, 21 January 1789.

25. M.D. George, note to BM 7627.

26. M.D. George, note to BM 7499.

27. *See* Pls 99, 105 and 106.

28. John Wardroper, *Kings, Lords and Wicked Libellers* (London 1973) p. 134.

29. Not in BM Cat.; Pierpont Morgan Library, New York. Peel Collection No. 206.

30. In *The Tories and the Whigs Pulling for a Crown* he is shown on Pitt's side, against Burke and Fox, his words echoing his preoccupation: 'Damme to the[i]r tugg or Billy I shall lose the Seals': Not in BM Cat., Lewis Walpole Library; LWL 789.1.2.2 . 2 January 1789; published by J. Aitken.

31. *The Eclipse at an End – and Political Tilting Discovered,* undated, 'pub. for R Blofield.' Not in BM Cat.; Pierpont Morgan Library; reproduced in Carretta, p. 286.

32. Wraxall, p.53.

33. BM 7509, 19 February 1789, published by Thos. Cornell.

34. Wraxall, III, p.318.

35. 3 December 1788, quoted by John Brooke, *King George III* (London, 1985 edition), p. 329.

36. Ida Macalpine and Richard Hunter, *George III and the Mad-Business* (London 1969, 1993 ed) p. 26.

37. Wraxall, III, p. 270.

38. Pierpont Morgan Library, New York. Peel Collection No. 209.

39. Rowlandson neatly parodies an incident that arose during the five day examination (beginning 7 January 1789) of Willis's views. Burke had censured the physician for allowing the King access to a dangerous razor, demanding to know what power he had of ensuring the patient's immediate obedience. It was reported that Willis's piercing gaze when replying 'There, Sir, by the EYE! I should have looked at him *thus,* Sir', had caused Burke to avert his head: Ida Macalpine and Richard Hunter, *op. cit.,* p. 272.

40. BM 7513, published by W. Dent.

41. The collected letters, an attack on the viceroy by Henry Flood (1732–1791) and others, were published as *Baratariana* (1773).

42. *The Death, Dissection, Will and Funeral Procession of Mrs Regency,* printed for John Walter, 1789.

43. Huntington Library, California, ref HEH Pr. Box 206/1.

44. A contemporary print by Dent caricatures Frith as *Frith the Unfortunate Stone-Thrower . . .* contrasting him with *. . .Wm* [Hastings] *the Fortunate Stone* [i.e. Diamond] *Thrower.* BM 7626, (c. January–April 1790).

45. Cruise O'Brien, p. 398.

CHAPTER SIX
THE KNIGHT OF THE WOEFUL COUNTENANCE

1. Townshend had caricatured Newcastle and Henry Fox (Lord Holland) as Peachum and Lockit in 1756: BM 3371.

2. *Life and Letters,* I, p. 357, quoted by M.D. George in her note to BM 7631.

3. Chatsworth MSS fo.1037, quoted in Mitchell, p. 294.

4. Anon. (perhaps Henry Kingsbury), BM 7633, in which it is entitled [*Fragment of a Strip Design*]*;* from the first caption on the left it may be identified as *Old Bluff Has Paid Me Many Compliments . . .*

5. Quoted in Ayling, p. 198.

6. Lewis Walpole Library, LWL 790.3.4.2; published by W. Dent, ?4 March 1790.

7. They are, perhaps, branches from the burning bush 'Ardens sed Virens'.

8. *A Discourse on the Love of our Country,* in which Price welcomed recent events in France and likened them to Britain's 'Glorious Revolution' of 1688.

9. Cruise O'Brien, p. 400.

10. M.D. George tentatively attributes the print to 'H.W.' while E.B. Krumbhaar (some of whose attributions might be treated with caution) publishes the original pencil sketch signed by Isaac Cruikshank and suggests he etched it as well: *Isaac Cruikshank* (Philadelphia 1966) pp. 70, 71 and illustration 401. The writer has been guided by Andrew Edmunds who attributes the print, part of a group by the same hand, to Frederick George Byron (private communication).

11. *Corr.* VI, pp. 85–7.

12. *See* Cruise O'Brien pp. 407–409.

13. Pierpont Morgan Library, New York. Peel Collection No. 233.

14. (1743–1825) teacher and writer.

15. Its full title is: *Observations on the Reflections of the Right Hon. Edmund Burke on the Revolution in France, in a Letter to the Earl of Stanhope.*

16. Another holding a scourge is the writer Helen Maria Williams 1762–1827, a supporter of the revolution. Imprisoned by Robespierre she narrowly escaped execution: *Dictionary of National Biography* LXI, p. 404.

17. Hill, p. 42.

18. BM 7688, 10 December 1790.

19. For the inscription in full, *see* Pl. 147. 'Cauldron of the Old Jewry' alludes to Price's sermon ('on The Love of our Country') having been preached at the Meeting House in the Old Jewry.

20. *See* Anon.: *Sawney's Defence against the Beast, Whore, Pope and Devil.* 1 April 1779, BM 5534.

21. *Letter to William Elliott Esq.* 1795, *Works,* V, p. 116.

22. *Parl. Hist.,* XXIX, p. 249, quoted in Cruise O'Brien, p. 414. For his analysis of Burke's quarrel with Fox, *see* pp. 414–31.

23. Quoted in Cruise O'Brien, p. 419.

24. Quoted in ibid., p. 425.

25. *Ibid.,* p. 415.

26. *See ibid.,* p. 430.

27. A photograph is in the reading room, National Portrait Gallery, London.

28. *Parl. Hist.,* XXIX, p. 396.

29. Note to BM 7856. Townshend had been last credited with a BM satire in April 1784: BM 6713.

30. John Monro, physician at Bethlehem hospital since 1751, died in 1791. His son Thomas (MD 1787) became physician to the hospital in 1792. Another House of Commons scene is depicted in *The Scholar lamenting the Departure of his Master,* BM 7870 [1 June 1791] from the *Bon Ton Magazine,* i, 106: while Fox weeps, Sheridan sits clapping his hands.

31. BM 7864, 17 May 1791, published by W. Holland. In *The Ghost of Mirabeau's Address to the London Revolution Society!!!* published by W. Holland on 1 July 1791 (BM 7888) Mirabeau opines 'A fig for *Burke's Book* and the Noise it has made'.

32. BM 7866, 22 May 1791, published by W. Holland.

33. The following lines are contained beneath the title: 'And it may be asked what credit ought to be given to his East India oratorical Representations, when mere apprehension provokes him, in a manner equally solemn, to Accuse his dearest Friends of a Design against the Constitution of this Country.'

34. R.B. McDowell, *Irish Public Opinion 1750–1800* (London 1944) p. 163.

35. BM 7867, 23 May 1791, published by H. Humphrey.

36. *A Hasty Sketch of the Debates,* BM 7871, 1 June 1791, published by W. Dent.

37. Not in BM Cat., private collection, 2 September 1791, published by S.W. Fores.

38. *Corr.,* VI, p. 451, 21 November 1791. Burke's *emigré* acquaintances supplied him with French news, 'often biased and embittered': R.B. McDowell, in his introduction to *Writings and Speeches,* IX, p. 2.

39. Magnus, p. 195.

40. BM 7920, published by S.W. Fores. Another levée scene, in which Burke stands in silence, is depicted in BM 7935: *The Duchess's First Levee,* anon., 19 December 1791, published by W. Holland.

41. BM 7902, William Dent, 14 September 1791, published by W. Dent.

42. *The Gentlemen Pensioners,* BM 6965, 13 July 1786, published by J. Carter.

43. Lewis Walpole Library, LWL + 792.5.0.5.

44. BM 8110, 28 June 1792; the description of Burke is M.D. George's.

45. BM 8115, 24 [?] July 1792.

46. Pierpont Morgan Library, New York. Peel Collection No. 249.

47. Alice Glasgow, *Sheridan of Drury Lane* (New York 1940) p. 205.

48. R.E. Prothero (ed.) *Private Letters of Edward Gibbon* (London 1896) Vol II, pp. 236–37.

49. Members of the convocation of the university had proposed the degree of LL.D. to Burke 'in Consideration of his very able Representation of the true Principles of our Constitution Ecclesiastical and Civil': quoted from a undated petition, in John Keane, *Tom Paine: A Political Life* (London 1995) pp. 289–90. Ironically Sheridan was opposed, years later, when he went to Oxford to receive a doctorate, and withdrew his name. Gillray parodies the affair in *Tentanda via est qua me quoque possim Tollere humo,* BM 11570, 8 August 1810, published by H. Humphrey.

50. BM 4727, 3 January 1774, designed by H.W. Bunbury, engraved and published by J. Bretherton.

51. Pierpont Morgan Library, New York. Peel Collection No. 254.

52. In the summer of 1793. His alma mater, Trinity College, Dublin, had awarded him an honorary LL.D. on 1 January 1791 and afterwards voted him an address in a gold box: Prior, pp. 426 and 365.

53. Dent enjoys the prize fighting analogy. e.g. Fox against Pitt in the regency crisis: *The Meeting of Parties or Humphreys & Mendoza fighting for a Crown,* 22 December 1788; not in BM Cat., Lewis Walpole Library, LWL 788.12.22.1. The scrap takes place before the Speaker and an audience of bottle-holders, seconds, and members of the front benches. Burke, for once, appears to be sleeping.

54. BM 8315; *see too The Patent Wigg,* BM 8338, Wetherell, 1 August 1793, also published by Fores: a barber offers Fox a new wig (the design containing beneath it a 'hidden' profile of George III) which 'vill fit any loyal subject'. Burke looks through the door, wearing his one.

55. The 'Friends of the People' was an association formed to promote parliamentary reform.

56. *Observations on the Conduct of the Minority,* 1793, *Works,* V, p. 55.

57. [Date and publication line illegible]; Pierpont Morgan Library, New York. Peel Collection No. 243.

58. Catalogued by M.D. George as '?1793 or perhaps earlier', and probably a plate to a book. Bedlam originated in the priory of St Mary of Bethlehem outside Bishopsgate, which was founded in 1247 and began to receive 'lunatics' in 1377.

CHAPTER SEVEN
PITY THE SORROWS OF A POOR OLD MAN

1. Except for the minor print of 1 August 1793 referred to in Chapter 6, note 54, the undated *Peep into Bethlehem* (Pl. 184) and passing reference to his book in *Nouvelles de la Cour de la Grande Bretagne*, BM 8631, *c.* March 1795.

2. Magnus, p. 257.

3. *Works,* XI, p. 413.

4. Horace, *Odes,* Book III. 2. Lines 17–18.

5. 'Ye pigs who never went to college, You must not pass for pigs of knowledge'; illustrated and described in David Bindman, *The Shadow of the Guillotine* (London 1989) p. 109.

6. M.D. George, note to BM 8500.

7. Diana Donald points out the schizophrenic nature of Gillray's activity as a political satirist in producing this (4 June 1795) hardly more than a month after *Light Expelling Darkness* (30 April 1795, BM 8644) proclaims Pitt as Apollo in his sun chariot: *The Age of Caricature* (New Haven and London 1996) pp. 163–65.

8. Ayling, p. 257.

9. From *Rose, or The Complaint*, a parody of Virgil, quoted in Wraxall, I, p. 165.

10. Thomas Wright, *op. cit.,* p. 195.

11. *Works,* V., pp. 193, 198–99.

12. Quoted in R.B. McDowell's introduction to *Writings and Speeches,* IX, p. 13.

13. Quoted in Alan Lloyd, *The Wickedest Age* (Newton Abbot 1971) p. 114.

14. BM 6003, published 13 June 1782 by H. Humphrey.

15. *New Morality; – or – The Promis'd Installment of the High Priest of the Theophilanthropes, with the Homage of Leviathan and his Suite,* BM 9240, 1 August 1798, published by J. Wright, for the *Anti-Jacobin Magazine & Review.*

16. *Works,* V, p. 211.

17. BM 8792, Isaac Cruikshank, 28 March 1796, published by S.W. Fores .

18. *Corr.,* VIII, p. 335.

19. Quoted in Cruise O'Brien, p. 554.

20. *Ibid*, p. 559.

20a. *Writings and Speeches,* IX, p. 253.

21. Taylor (1757–1834), an MP, was ridiculed as 'the Chick of the Law' in a Westminster incident in 1785: *see* note by M.D. George to *The Old Hen and Chicken of the Law,* BM 6777, [W. Dent].

22. Draper Hill, *Fashionable Contrasts* (London 1966) pp. 142-45.

23. *See* p. 9; for an account of Canning's involvement with Gillray and the satirical journal the *Anti-Jacobin Magazine & Review, see* Hill, p. 56–72.

24. Draper Hill, *Fashionable Contrasts* p. 142.

25. Hill, p. 134.

25a. As Diana Donald suggests: *The Age of Caricature* (New Haven and London 1996) p. 170.

26. BM 8836, 17 November 1796, published by H. Humphrey.

27. *Writings and Speeches,* IX, p. 346.

28. M.D. George, note to BM 8842, quoting the *London Chronicle* of 29 November 1796.

29. Draper Hill, *Fashionable Contrasts,* p. 142.

30. 'Observations on the Conduct of the Minority, particularly in the Last Session of Parliament', *Works,* V, p.3.

31. A parody of *The House that Jack Built; see also* Pl. 70.

32. BM 9286, untitled.

33. BM 9888, 30 September 1802, published by T. Williamson.

34. *Fat-Cattle,* BM 9912, 16 January 1802, published by H. Humphrey.

35. *Works,* V, p. 221.

36. BM 10411, May 1805 published by William Holland.

37. Henry Edward, Lord Holland (ed.), *Memoirs of the Whig Party during My Time* by Henry Richard Lord Holland (London 1854) II, p. 207.

38. James J. Sack, *From Jacobite to Conservative* (Cambridge 1993), p. 98.

39. BM 10549, *Pacific-Overtures-or-A Flight from St Cloud's,* published by H. Humphrey.

40. BM 10702, [?] 20 February 1807, J. Brown Sculp., O'Keefe del.

41. BM 11555, 12 May 1810, published by Walker.

42. BM 13169, a plate from *The Wits Magazine and Attic Miscellany,* Vol. 1, printed for Thomas Tegg [1818].

43. BM 13311 printed for J. Asperne, W. Sams, and J. Johnston, 1819, a reply to William Hone's parody – *see* BM 13292, *The Political House that Jack Built* [G. Cruikshank].

CONCLUSION
SUBLIME AND BEAUTIFUL REFLECTIONS

1. National Gallery of Ireland, NGI Inv. 10442. For a group of prints portraying Burke, *see* Pierpont Morgan Library, New York. Peel Collection, Nos. 4–39. In No. 17, entitled *The British Cicero,* Burke holds a copy of 'Magna Charta'.

2. BM Cat. Vol. VI, p. XXIV.

3. Christopher Hobhouse, *Fox* (London 1934, reprinted 1964) p. 15.

4. G.H. Guttridge, *English Whiggism and the American Revolution* (Berkeley and Los Angeles 1966) pp. 51–3.

5. *Works,* V, p. 193.

6. Prior, p. 159.

7. Quoted in Prior, p. 181 (to electors of Bristol on 6 September 1780).

8. (19 April 1774), James Burke, *The Speeches of the Right Hon. Edmund Burke* (Dublin, 1865 edition) p. 71.

9. *See* Cruise O'Brien, p. lvi.

INDEX OF CARICATURES

Alarming Anniversary III, An **Pl. 183,** 169
All Alive or the Political Churchyard 51–2
Apollo and the Muses Inflicting Pennance on Dr Pomposo Around Parnassus 9
April Fool or the Follies of a Night, The **Pl. 78,** 84
Aristocrat, An 159
Aristocratic Crusade, The **Pl. 155,** 146–47

Balance of Merit, The **Pl. 174,** 161
Banco to the Knave 28
Bandelures **Pl. 125,** 4, 122
Banditti 55
Barataria **Pl. 137,** 131
Battle of Bow-Street, The **Pl. 118,** 115, 117
Battle of Hastings, The **Pl. 89,** 93–4, 101
Battle of St Stephen's, The 123
Battle of Whigs, or the Meal-Tub Plot discovered, The **Pl. 157,** 96, 149–50
Battle Royal, or who wears the Breeches, The **Pl. 45,** 57–8
Begging no Robbery **Pl. 195,** 184–86
Black Carlo's White Bust 160
Blessings of Peace, The 49
Block for the Wigs, A **Pl. 38,** 51, 68
Blood & Co. Setting Fire to the Tower **Pl. 115,** 113, 136, 155
Board of Controul, or the Blessings of a Scotch Dictator, The 202(n.39)
Bottom Snout & Quince **Pl. 61,** 69
Britania's Assassination **Pl. 26,** 37
British Titans, The **Pl. 50,** 58–9
Bubbles of Opposition **Pl. 114,** 110, 113
Budget or John Bull Fright[e]ned out of his Wits, The **Pl. 194,** 184
Bull Broke Loose, The 26
[*Burke, Edmund*] **Pl. 22,** 32, 198
★★★★★ [*Burke*] *on the Sublime & Beautiful* **Pl. 72,** 34, 79, 98, 155
[*Burke's Two Consciences*] **Pl. 142,** 136, 152, 161
Butchers of Freedom, The **Pl. 116,** 114, 147, 183

Call of the [*House*], *or Slave Trade in a land of liberty* **Pl. 173,** 160–61
Camera-Obscura **Pl. 105,** 106
Canterbury Tale, A (first state) **Pl. 122,** 118
Canterbury Tale, A (second state) **Pl. 123,** 118–20
Captive Prince – or – Liberty run Mad, The **Pl. 20,** 29
Caricaturers Stock in Trade, The **Pl. 1,** 8, 81
Carlo Khan's triumphal Entry into Leadenhall Street **Pl. 39,** 34, 53, 55, 56, 78, 101
Chancellor of the Inquisition, The **Pl. 182,** 167, 171
Charley's Return from over the water **Pl. 124,** 120–21, 197(n.45)
Charons Boat: – or – Topham's Trip 203(n.78)
Cicero Against Verres **Pl. 87,** 82, 93
Cincinnatus in Retirement **Pl. 29,** 39, 68, 198(n.67)
— *Coaches* 202(n.63)
Coalition Arms 200 (ch. 3, n.20)
Coalition Dance **Pl. 34,** 46–7, 198(n.32)
Coalition Party Beating up for Recruits, The 69
Cock of the Walk Distributing His Favours, The **Pl. 80,** 85
Comet, The **Pl. 134,** 128
Common Stage Wagging from Brooke's Inn, The **Pl. 84,** 89

Concerto Coalitionale **Pl. 71,** 78
Confucius the Second 53–5
Congress or The Necessary Politicians, The **Pl. 9,** 17
Constitution, The **Pl. 15,** 23
Constitution of England, The **Pl. 14,** 22–3
Contrasted Opinions of Paine's Pamphlet **Pl. 167,** 157
Convention of Not-Ables, A 87
Corsican Crocodile dissolving the Council of Frogs!!!, The 203(n.19)
Cooling the Brain **Pl. 140,** 133–34, 197(n.197)
Countryman's Dream of Coalescing Virtue And Vice, The **Pl. 54,** 63
Cries of London **Pl. 196,** 186–87
Cromwell ye 2ⁿᵈ Exalted **Pl. 48,** 58, 136, 200(ch.3, n.21)
Crumbs of Comfort **Pl. 31,** 32
Curious Collection of Wild Beasts, A 200(n.46)

Dagger Scene, The **Pl. 176,** 162–64
Death of the Great Wolf, The **Pl. 188,** 176–77
Devonshire Amusement, The (LWL) 70
Devonshire Amusement, The (BM6625) 70
D[evonshire] rout or Reynard in his Element, A **Pl. 63,** 70
Dido Forsaken **Pl. 83,** 88–9
Different Sensations **Pl. 144,** 137–40
Disappointment, or, The King's Evidence, The **Pl. 166,** 157, 204(n.33)
Dissolution **Pl. 57,** 66
Dividend or Half a Crown in the Pound, The 200(ch.3, n.28)
Doctor Lasts Examination **Pl. 135,** 130, 170
Don Dismallo, After an Absence of Sixteen Years, Embracing His Beautiful Vision! **Pl. 150,** 16, 143–44
Don Dismallo among the Grasshoppers in France 145
Don Dismallo running the Literary Gantlet **Pl. 151,** 143–44
Don Volaseo The Famous Spanish Partizan **Pl. 18,** 27
Duchess's First Levee, The 204(n.40)

East India Reformers 55
Ecce Homo **Pl. 3,** 5, 66
Ecce Homo versatilis! **Pl. 156,** 147
Eclipse, The 201(n.36)
Eclipse at an End, The 127
Election-Troops, bringing in their accounts, to the Pay-Table **Pl. 119,** 117, 123, 197(n.26)
Employment During Recess **Pl. 88,** 93, 132
English Slavery; or a Picture of the Times 202(n.64)
Evacuation Before Resignation **Pl. 27,** 37
Evening Consolation **Pl. 82,** 86–7
Every Man in His Humour **Pl. 59,** 68
Examination of S[i]r Elijah Impey, The **Pl. 112,** 110, 133

Fall of Achilles, The 79
Fall of Carlo Khan, The **Pl. 41,** 55–6
Farmer George Deliver'd of a most Grevous S[peec]h 93
Fat-Cattle 205(n.34)
Father Paul & The Lay Porter **Pl. 108,** 7, 108–109
First Charge-Exit in Fumo, The 105
First Parliament of Botany Bay in High Debate, The 202(n.17)
Florizel and Perdita 200(n.15)
For the Trial of Warren Ha[stings] **Pl. 98,** 101
Fox & Badger Hunting the K[in]g's Hounds, The **Pl. 52,** 60–62

[*Fox and Burke as Hudibras and Ralpho*] 70(n.66)
F[o]x, Goose and Primier, The 44, 199(n.70)
Fox's Fool 66
[*Fragment of a Strip Design*], *see Old Bluff Has Paid Me Many Compliments . . .*
[*Francis, Philip*] **Pl. 95,** 34, 99
Free Regency, The **Pl. 128,** 124
French Flight, Or, the Grand Monarque . . . **Pl. 170,** 159, 199(n.70)
Frith the Madman Hurling Treason at the King **Pl. 141,** 134–35
Frith the Unfortunate Stone-Thrower 203(n.44)
Frogs Chusing a King **Pl. 127,** 123
Frolick or a New-Market, Race, The 203(ch.5, n.3)
Frontispiece **Pl. 47,** 58
Frontispiece to Reflections on the French Revolution **Pl. 147,** 140, 197(n.30)
[*Frontispiece to The Rising Sun, Vol.1*] 188
Funeral Procession of Miss Regency, The **Pl. 138,** 132
Funeral Procession of Mrs Regency, The **Pl. 139,** 132–33

Galante Show **Pl. 104,** 106
Ganders addressing the Lion, The 63
General Blackbeard wounded at the Battle of Leadenhall **Pl. 43,** 56, 68
General Election, The 201(n.62)
Gentleman Pensioners, The 204(n.42)
George and the Dragon 200(ch.3, n.23)
Ghost of Mirabeau's Address to the London Revolution Society!!!, The 204(n.31)
Ghosts of Mirabeau and Dr Price Appearing to Old Loyola, The 156
Golden Image that Nebuchadnezzar the King had set up, The **Pl. 51,** 59–60
Golden-Pippin Boys, on the Branches of State 52
Gorgon **Pl. 53,** 63
[*Governor of Rue Peas, The*] 202(n.37)
Grand Irish Air Balloon **Pl. 67,** 75
Grand Pitch Battle, The **Pl. 91,** 96
Grand Review of Sydenham Common, The 162
Guy Vaux 37
Guy Vaux Discovered in his Attempt . . . **Pl. 163,** 154–55
Guy Vaux or F[ox] Blowing up the Par[liamen]t House!!! **Pl. 58,** 155, 200(ch.3, n.22)

Harry Jenkins, the Masculine & Feminine Bellows Mender 116
Hasty Sketch of the Debates, A 204(n.36)
Heads of the Mutiny Bill, Laid on the Table, The 201(n.62)
Hibernia In the Character Of Charity **Pl. 68,** 76
Hi nostri Reditus, expectatique triumphi! **Pl. 65,** 72–3, 201(n.86)
Holland's Caricature Exhibition **Pl. 4,** 6
Holy Benidiction, The **Pl. 35,** 47–8
Hopes of the Family – an Admission at the University, The 165
Hopes of the State, The **Pl. 179,** 165
Host of Dissenters and St Charles their Black Convert routed by the Church Canon, The **Pl. 146,** 139
House Breaking, before Sun-Set **Pl. 113,** 127, 154
[*House that Jack Built, The*] **Pl. 70,** 76–8, 186
Hudibrass and his 'Squire' 56
Hungry Mob of Scriblers and Etchers, The **Pl. 2,** 2

Idol of the People 72
Idol-Worship or The Way to Preferment **Pl. 169,** 159
Ignatius **Pl. 58,** 68
Impeachment (Dent) **Pl. 76,** 63, 82–3, 200(ch.2, n.27)
Impeachment, The (Sayers, BM6925) **Pl. 75,** 82, 93, 200(ch.2, n.27)
Impeachment, The (Sayers, BM7268) 202(n.41)
Impeachment, – or – "The Father of the Gang turn'd Kings Evidence", The **Pl. 162,** 152
Impeachment Ticket **Pl. 99,** 101
Indian Prince on a visit to a Friendly Court, An **Pl. 103,** 105
Installation-Supper, The 109
Insults of the Brave I have Borne with Some Degree of Patience . . . The 202(n.22)
Introduction of F[itzherbert] to St James's, The **Pl. 79,** 84–5
Invocation 203(n.14)
Irish Audience, The 131
Irish Gratitude 179
Irish Stubble alia[s] Bubble Goose **Pl. 16,** 23–4, 179

John Bull ground down **Pl. 187,** 175–76
Joint Motion or the Honey-Moon of the Coalition, A **Pl. 37,** 50
Jovial Crew or Merry Beggars, The 86
Junius **Pl. 6,** 12–13

Knave of Diamonds 202(n.32)
Knight of the Wo[e]ful Countenance, The **Pl. 148,** 140–43, 193
Knight of the Woeful Countenance, The (sketch), **Pl. 149,** 143

Landing at Botany Bay 202(n.17)
Last Recorce or Supernatural Committee Employ'd, The 188
Last Scene of the Managers Farce, The **Pl. 185,** 171–73
Last Sitting of the old Court of Session, The 197(n.45)
Late Auction at St Eustatia, The 199(n.72)
Late Bombardment of Government Castle, The **Pl. 25,** 36
Launce and his Dog Crab 157
Learned Coalition, A **Pl. 36,** 16, 48
Libertine reclaim'd, The **Pl. 175,** 162
Light Expelling Darkness 205(ch.7, n.7)
Literary Characters Assembled Around a Medallion of Shakespeare 20
Loaves and Fishes, The 44
Long Pull, Strong Pull and A Pull All Together, A 43–44
Long-Winded Speech, The **Pl. 109,** 109
Loose Principles 127
Lord No[rt]h in the Suds 199(n.105)

Madam Blubber on her Canvass 201(n.70)
Madam Blubber's Last Shift 201(n.71)
Managers in Distress, The 106
Market Day 106
Mason, the Duke's Confectioner, Disposing of the Trinkets 113
Meeting of Parties or Humphreys & Mendoza fighting for a Crown 204(n.53)
Meeting of the Legion Club, The 93
Minister's Bull, The **Pl. 69,** 76
Mirror of Patriotism, The 200(ch.3, n.27)
Miss S–r. The Hibernian Demosthenes **Pl. 8,** 16
Modern Leviathan!!, The **Pl. 190,** 179–80
Monster, The 44
Monstrous Hydra or Virtue Invulnerable, The **Pl. 126,** 123
More Ways than One or The Patriot turn'd Preacher **Pl. 66,** 73–4
Morning Preparation 202(n.19)
Mr Burke's Pair of Spectacles for short sighted Politicians **Pl. 161,** 63, 152
Mr S[herida]n's Speech **Pl. 110,** 109–110
My Grandmother, Alias The Jersey Jig 89

Neddy's Black Box **Pl. 132,** 127
Neither[r] War nor Peace! **Pl. 33,** 44
Newmarket Humane Society! The **Pl. 121,** 118

New Morality 180
No Abatement **Pl. 113,** 63, 110–11, 152
Noble Lord, on an approaching Peace . . ., A 199(n.5)
Non Commission Officers Embarking for Botany Bay **Pl. 81,** 86
Nouvelles de la Cour de la Grande Bretagne 205(ch.7, n.1)

Old Bluff Has Paid Me Many Compliments . . . 203(ch.6, n.4)
Old Hen and Chicken of the Law, The 205(n.21)
Opening of the Budget 184
Opposition ——— **Pl. 107,** 108
Opposition Defeated **Pl. 17,** 25–6, 118, 198(n.21)
Opposition Music or Freedom of Election **Pl. 117,** 114
Orators Journey, The **Pl. 73,** 79–81, 98
Ordnance See-Saws 200(n.18)

Pacific-Overtures – or – A Flight from St Cloud's 205(n.39)
Paddy on Horseback 202(n.38)
Paddy O'Pitt's Triumphal Exit!! 202(n.38)
Paddy Whack's First Ride in a Sedan **Pl. 60,** 69
Paradise Lost **Pl. 28,** 38–9
Parliamentary Meeting 1786 **Pl. 74,** 81–2
Patent Wigg, The 204(n.54)
Patriotic Song for Poor Old England 27
Peachum and Lockit **Pl. 143,** 136, 161
Peep Below Stairs a Dream, A 199(n.70)
Peep into Bethlehem, A **Pl. 184,** 169–70, 205(ch.7, n.1)
Perdito and Perdita 200(n.15)
[Philip Francis], see [Francis, Philip]
Phoenix or the Resurrection of Freedom, The 32–3
Picturesque View of the State of the Nation for February 1778, A 201(n.93)
Pit of Acheron, The **Pl. 42,** 56
Pity the Sorrows of a Poor Old Man **Pl. 189,** 137, 177
Political Astronomy 188
Political-Banditti Assailing the Saviour of India, The **Pl. 86,** 91, 202(n.20)
Political Cartoon for the Year 1775, The 197(n.2)
Political Cerberus, The 69
Political Cluster in terrorem, The **Pl. 64,** 72
Political Contest, The 93
Political Electricity **Pl. 7,** 13–15, 198
Political House that Jack Built, The 205(n.31)
Political Mirror, The **Pl. 24,** 35
Political Playthings For Prostitute Patriots **Pl. 165,** 156
Political Raree-Show, The **Pl. 12, Pl. 13,** 20
Political Sampson in Revenge sets fire to the Country, The 72
Poor Blacks Going to their Settlement, The 202(n.17)
Poor Vulcan and his Cyclops Preparing Impeachment Proof **Pl. 85,** 89–91, 200(ch.2, n.27)
Portland Sharks or the Ministry Upon a Broad Bottom **Pl. 52,** 200(n.47)
Preceptor and Pupil 203
Presages of the Millenium **Pl. 186,** 4, 173–74
Priest at his Private Devotion, A **Pl. 30,** 41
Prince at Grass, The 202(n.24)
Prince in Clover, The 202(n.25)
Princess's Bow alias the Bow Begum, The 202(n.58)
Promenade in the State Side of Newgate 6
Promis'd Horrors of the French Invasion **Pl. 193,** 162, 183–84, 197
Prospect Before Us, The **Pl. 129,** 124–26
Prospect Before Us, The (sketch) **Pl. 130,** 124
Public Credit or the State Idol **Pl. 168,** 158–59
Puerile Attack upon an old Servant, A **Pl. 90,** 95
Puke-ation in Answer to the Late State of the Nation 44
Purging Draught for Extracting Diamonds, A 105

Quarrel between the Political Builders, The **Pl. 160,** 150
Quarrell about Pensions amicably Settled, The **Pl. 191,** 180
Queen of Hearts Cover'd with Diamonds, The 8

Race for a Crown, A **Pl. 55,** 63
Raising the Royal George **Pl. 32,** 42–3

Raree Show, The **Pl. 96,** 99–101
Razor's Levee 50–51, 75, 200(n.42)
Recruiting Serjeant, The 197(n.13)
Reflections on the French Revolution **Pl. 177,** 165
Regency Twelfth Cake not cut up, The 128
Rehe[a]rsal, The 189
Renard Stating his Accounts **Pl. 21,** 31, 197(n.42)
Repeal, Or the Funeral of Miss Ame-Stamp, The **Pl. 11,** 5, 17–19, 198(n.39)
Retreat of Carlo Khan from Leadenhall St., The **Pl. 40,** 55
Reverie of Prince Demetrius Cantemir, A 202(n.57)
Revolutionists **Pl. 120,** 118, 136
Reynard caught at last or the [Fox] in a Pitt 63
[Richard Brinsley Sheridan], see [Sheridan, Richard Brinsley]
Rights of Man; – or – Tommy Paine, the Little American Taylor, The 157
Rival Quacks, The 57
Royal Ass, The 199(n.12)
Royal Hercules Destroying the Dragon Python, The **Pl. 49,** 58
Royal Hunt, or a Prospect of the Year 1782, The **Pl. 19,** 28
Royal Salute, A 159
Royal Society, The 84

Satan Harangueing his Troops after their Defeat 200(n.19)
Satan harangueing his Troops Previous to Action **Pl. 46,** 58
Sawney's Defence against the Beast, Whore, Pope and Devil 204(n.20)
Scene in the Crown and Anchor Tavern, A 167
Scene in the School for Scandal, A 86
Scholar lamenting the Departure of his Master, The 204(n.30)
Screen, The 3
Sedition and Atheism Defeated **Pl. 145,** 139
[Sheridan, Richard Brinsley] **Pl. 111,** 110, 136
Shifting Orator, The **Pl. 178,** 165
Shot at the Min[iste]r, A 202(n.33)
Sick Prince, The 89
Sixpence a Day 4
Slow and Sure Deliverance, A **Pl. 102,** 105
Smelling out a Rat **Pl. 152,** 63, 144
Soliloquy of Reynard, The 69
Solomon in the Clouds 64
Spectres visiting John Bull **Pl. 198,** 188
Spirit of Aristocracy enforcing Reform **Pl. 172,** 159–60
State-Jugglers **Pl. 106,** 7, 107–108
S[ta]te Miners 55
Struggle, for a Bengal Butcher and an Imp-Pie, The **Pl. 100,** 101–102, 133
St Stephen's Mad-House; or, The Inauguration of King William The Fourth 126
Sublime and Beautiful Reflections on the French Revolutioh [sic] **Pl. 153,** 145, 150
Sublime Oratory – a Display of it **Pl. 93,** 97–8
Such things may be. A tale for future times. **Pl. 101,** 93, 102–103
Suitable Restrictions **Pl. 131,** 126–27
Surrender of Government Castle, The 36–7
Sweating for Opposition by Dr W[i]llis, Dominisweaty and Co., A 130

Tale of a Tub!!!, The 187
Tell Tale in High Credit With The State Gossips, The **Pl. 154,** 145–46, 149, 156
Tentanda via est . . . 204(n.49)
Terrifying Comet, The 162
These are The Patriots of high renown . . . 189
Thing in a Nasty Situation, The 198(n.66)
This is the House for Cash Built!! **Pl. 197,** 187
Thoughts on a Regicide Peace **Pl. 192,** 181
Thunder, Lightning and Smoke **Pl. 94,** 34, 99
Times – or a View of the Old House in Little Brittain 200(ch.3, n.29)
To Day Disliked, and yet perhaps Tomorrow Again in favour 56, 200(n.7)
Tombs of the Worthies, The **Pl. 56,** 64, 147
Tomb-Stone, The **Pl. 10,** 17

Tom Pains Effigy or the Rights of a Sed[i]tious Poltroon **Pl. 180,** 166
Tories and the Whigs Pulling for a Crown, The 203(n.30)
Tottering Pyramid, The **Pl. 62,** 89
Transfer of East India Stock, A 53
Triumph of Virtue, The 63
Tryumph of Pitt, The **Pl. 44,** 57

Unfortunate Ass, The 60
Uniform Whig, A **Pl. 171,** 136, 159, 164, 165
Unkle Toby and Corporal Trim 203(n.17)
Up & Down or Wheel of Admi-ration, The 50

Very Slippy Weather (Gillray) 197(n.34)
Very Slippy Weather (Sidebotham) **Pl. 5,** 7
Visiting the Sick 199(n.113)
Volcano of Opposition, The **Pl. 164,** 155–56

War **Pl. 33,** 44, 99
War! Glorious War! **Pl. 181,** 166
War of Posts 199(n.107)
West[minste]r Candidate Coming North about the Geese, The 203(n.74)
Westminster Hunt, The 106
Whig Club, or the State of the Blue and Buff Council, The 75

Whipping Post, The 199(n.110)
Wife & No Wife – or A Trip to the Continent **Pl. 77,** 83–4, 202(n.49)
Will o'the Wisp or John Bull in a Bog, A 180–81
Wonders Wonders & Wonders 30
Wrangling Friends or Opposition in Disorder, The **Pl. 158,** 150
Wrangling Friends or Opposition in Disorder, The (sketch) **Pl. 159,** 150

GENERAL INDEX

Abington, Frances ix, 8
Accountants 31
Addington, Henry 156, 162
Admission ticket for the trial of Warren Hastings 101, Pl. 97
Aesop 123–24
Air-balloons 59–60, 70, 72, 75
Aitken, James, publisher 7, 132, 195, 197(n.32), 203(n.30), Pls 139, 140, 168, 180
Alchemist, The 49
Allestree, Richard 46
America and the Americans 41, 147, 162, 193, 200(ch.3, n.20)
    American Congress 16, 17
    Boston Tea Party 15, 16
    independence 33
    loss of 8, 28, 36, 78, 91, 98, 99
    print trade 7
    Secretary of State and 25
    St Eustatius 27
    taxation 16, 17–19, 192
    uniform 75
    war with, 20, 21, 22, 25, 28, 37, 70, 72, 75, 77, 78
Annual Register 11
Anti-Jacobin Magazine & Review 205(n.15, n.23)
Archer, Sarah, Lady 194
Arden, Richard Pepper 81, 82, 136, 169, 174, 184, 194
Armistead, Mrs Elizabeth 120, 121
Army, soldiers 4, 20, 25, 51, 57, 67, 115, 117, 174, 177, 181
Ashburton, Baron, *see* Dunning, John
Asperne, J., publisher 195, 205(n.43)
Association for Preserving Liberty and Property 167, 169
Auckland, Lord, *see* Eden, William
Austin, William 5, 66, 133
Australia 86, 87
Austria 181
Ayliffe's ghost 31

Bank of England 68, 183, 186
'Barataria' 131, 203(n.41)
Barbauld, Anna Letitia 144
Baretti, Giuseppi 20
Barré, Colonel Isaac, MP 15, 25, 26, 27, 28, 35, 39, 44, 60, 75
Barrington, William, second Viscount 31
Barrow J., caricaturist and publisher 66, 195, 200(n.48), 201(n.63), Pl. 25
Barry, James 10, 32–3, 44, Frontispiece, Pl. 23
Bartolozzi, Francesco 5, 7
Bastille Prison 87, 144, 169
Beaux' Stratagem 8
Bedford, Francis Russell, fifth Duke of 167, 177–80, 183, 184, 187–88, 190, 194
Bedford, John Russell, fourth Duke of 11, 17, 18, 19
Bedford, John Russell sixth Duke of 188
Bedlam, *see* Bethlehem Hosptial
Beggar's Opera, The 9, 20, 136, 137, 167, 203(ch.6, n.1)
Belgium 159, 181
Belshazzar, King 161, 162
Bembridge, clerk 44
Bentley & Co., publishers 195
Berman, David 10–11

Berry, J., publisher 104, 105, 194, Pl. 103
Bethlehem Hospital 5, 169, 170, 204(n.30), 205(n.58)
Bible, The 2–3, 41, 68, 83, 84, 139, 152
Binney, John 31
Blofield, R. 195, 203(n.31)
Blood, Captain Thomas (*d.* 1680) 113, 136, 155
Board of Trade 11, 25, 198(n.58)
Board of Works 25
Bolingbroke, Henry St John, Viscount 10, 13
Bonnor, T. 13, 198(n.22), Pl. 6
Bon Ton magazine 204(n.30)
'Boreas', *see* North, Frederick
Boston Gazette 7
Boswell, James 13, 16, 20, 194
'Bout-de-Ville, George' 2
Boyne, John 55, 66, 68, 69, 82, 93, 200(n.10), 202(n.17), Pls 40, 58, 61, 62, 66, 87, 88
Boyne & Walker, publishers 195, Pl. 87
Bradshaw, J., publisher 124, 194, Pl. 128
Bretherton, Charles, publisher 195, Pls 22, 28, 95
Bretherton, James publisher 195, 200(ch.3, n.27), 204(n.50)
Bridgwater & Orkney, constituency of 72
Bristol, Electors of 41–2, 59, 191–92
Bristol Mercury 202(n.22)
Britain, symbols of, *see* Britannia; British lion; Bull, John; Magna Carta; Oak
Britannia 17, 35, 36, 37, 52, 55, 75, 76, 93, 123, 181, 183, 199(n.110)
British lion 1, 55, 58, 59, 123, 181
British Museum, London, satirical print collections ix, 19, 44, 66, 123, 190, 193, 194
Brooks's Club 68, 89, 183, 184
Brown, D., publisher 195, Pl. 41
Brown J., publisher, Holborn; Mayfair 195, Pls 85, 102
Brown J., Rathbone Place 195, 201(n.62, n.88), Pls 64, 67, 68, 76
Brown, Tom, publisher 195, Pl. 129
Buck, Adam 6
Buckingham House 89
Buckingham, Marquis of, *see* Temple, George Nugent
Bull, John 25, 26, 51, 76, 77, 78, 160, 161, 162, 169, 175, 180–81, 184–85, 188
Bunbury, Henry William 165, 204(n.50)
Burdett, Sir Francis 189
Burgoyne, General John 20
Burke Edmund ix, 7, 8, 9, 15, 24, 198(n.17, n.66), 202(n.33), 204(n.40, n.53, n.54)
    accused of alarmism 182–86
    and America 15, 16, 17, 192, 193
    and anti-Irish sentiment 11–12, 13, 26, 93, 190, 192
    and James Barry 32–3
    and Beaconsfield 11, 27, 69, 156, 175, 191
    breach with Fox and Whigs 136, 139–40, 148–57, 159, 161, 167, 180, 190
    Burke's Civil List Act 30
    charges of inconsistency, apostacy 136–37, 144, 145, 147, 148, 149, 150, 154, 157, 158–59, 161, 162, 164, 165, 169, 177, 179, 187, 192
    and 'The club' 20
    composite caricature 192
    and dagger plot 162–65, 190

    and Dissenters 139, 159
    and 'economical reform' 20–5, 26, 28, 29–32, 36, 37, 42, 49, 50, 51, 52, 55, 56, 60, 68, 69, 73, 75, 87, 147, 161, 162, 191, 192, 193
    and electors of Bristol 41–2, 191–92
    epitaph writer 72–3, 201(n.86)
    Fox's East India Bill 52, 53–6, 60, 73, 75, 79, 192, 193, 204(n.33)
    Fox's friend and mentor 47, 56, 81, 135, 149–50, 152–55, 156
    and Francis 12–13, 52, 94, 95, 96, 140
    French ideas and French Revolution 10, 135, 136–70 *passim*, 173, 174, 180, 181, 183–84, 185, 186–87, 192, 193, 204(n.31, n.38)
    and George III 24–5, 27–8, 29, 37, 42, 52, 58–60, 134, 135, 145–46, 157, 159, 161, 162, 164, 165, 192, 193
    and Warren Hastings 44, 52, 78, 79–83, 89–111, 137, 147, 157, 171–73, 176, 190
    and Mrs Humphrey 1, 2
    'hunt of obloquy' 9, 135, 177, 192
    as husband 16, 193
    'inspires' designs 5, 17–19
    and Ireland 10, 11, 50–51, 75, 136, 193
    and Marie Antoinette 16, 140, 143, 190
    'Mnemon' and 'Tandem' 13
    much caricatured 8, 194
    and North 28, 29, 35, 43, 44, 93, 98, 99, 103
    and Nullum Tempus 13, 15
    and oratory 13, 20, 21, 32, 38, 52, 79–81, 82, 95, 98–9, 101, 127, 135, 147, 155, 170, 192
    and Oxford University 165–66, 204(n.49)
    Paymaster General 28, 29–32, 44, 50, 82, 191
    pension 173, 175, 176–81, 184, 186, 187, 190, 192
    personal finances 11, 27, 31, 50, 51, 68, 69, 86, 87, 93, 94, 105, 108–109, 111, 175, 177, 190–91, 202(n.17)
    and Pitt 28, 59, 63, 122, 146, 149, 150, 151, 156, 157, 165, 169, 175
    portraits of Frontispiece, Pl. 199; 29, 30, 32, 36, 190, 199(n.80), 205(concl. n.1)
    posthumous references 187–89
    and Powell 44, 82, 83, 93
    and Prince's secret marriage 83–5, 88–9
    prolixity 79–81, 98, 109, 110, 155
    Rector of Glasgow 68, 201(n.55)
    Regency crisis 118–24, 126–27, 128, 129, 130, 132, 133, 147, 165, 190, 193, 203(n.30, n.39)
    resigns office 1782 38–42
    retires as MP 171, 173
    and Reynolds 32
    rise to prominence 3, 10–12, 19, 40–41
    and Rockingham 11, 17, 19, 20, 21, 22, 25–6, 37, 38, 40–1
    and Shelburne 22, 38, 40, 43–4, 46, 47, 199(n.1, n.5)
    and Sheridan 49, 93, 109, 110, 114, 120–21, 123, 135, 136, 137, 139, 144, 166–67
    and Sarah Siddons 8, 81, 98
    and son Richard 159, 167, 171, 175, 179–80
    spectacles, *see* Burke's spectacles
    and 'swinish multitude' 147, 161, 173–74, 205(n.5)
    Westminster election 1788 113–16

and John Wilkes 13, 15
writings 10–11, 13, 28, 36, 56, 139–40, 157, 162, 177, 181, 185–86
  as Chancellor of the Inquisition 167
  as Cicero 13, 82, 83, 93, 198(n.26), 205(concl. n.1)
  as Cincinnatus 39–40
  as Crab 157
  as Don Dismallo 143, 144
  as Don Quixote, quixotic 91, 140, 146–47, 159, 169, 192
  as 'Georgium Sidus' 162
  as 'Hibernian Demosthenes' 16
  as 'Hippocrisy' 69
  as Janus 136–37
  as Jesuit etc. 16, 26, 39–41, 46, 47, 48, 51, 53, 55, 57, 59, 63, 66, 68, 69, 83, 84, 86, 87, 89, 97, 118, 121, 132, 133, 137, 139, 140, 144, 155, 156, 157, 159, 161, 186, 187, 188, 189, 190, 192, 199(n.5), 200(ch.3, n.20)
  as 'Junius' 12–13, 26
  as Man in the Moon 145
  as Mercury 159
  as Moloch 58
  as old woman 73–5, 136
  as parson 102, 103, 108
  as Peachum 136, 137
  as Pegasus 147, 148
  as Prince Demetrius 105–106
  as prizefighter, bottleholder 96, 149, 166, 167
  as Quince 69
  as Ralpho 56, 70
  as serpent 63, 66, 79, 123
  as showman 55, 56, 106
  as street vendor
  as touched with madness 8, 127, 129, 130, 132, 133, 134, 145, 150, 155, 165, 169–70, 181, 188, 190, 192
  as weather vane
  as wolf in sheep's clothing 16, 46, 47, 48
  as zany 57, 101, 144
Burke, Edmund Frontispiece
Burke Edmund, M.P. Statesman and Writer Pl. 199
Burke, J., publisher 195, 202(n.32)
Burke, Mrs Jane (*née* Nugent) 11, 143, 156, 175, 181
Burke, Mrs Mary (*née* Nagle)
Burke, Richard (father) 10
Burke, Richard (brother) 11, 41
Burke, Richard (son) 159, 166, 167, 171, 175, 179–80
Burke, William 32
Burke's address to the 'Swinish' Multitude 173
Burke's Spectacles ix, 8, 32, 35, 40, 63, 72, 73, 83, 96, 111, 123, 136, 144, 152, 188, 190
Burney, Fanny 123
Burrell, Sir Peter 101
Buss, Robert 4
Bute, John Stuart, third Earl of 2, 3, 15, 17, 18, 19, 22, 23, 35, 194, 197(n.14), 199(n.110, n.12)
Butler, Samuel 56
Buttens, R., publisher 195, (Pl. 133)
Byron, Frederick George 108, 140, 143, 155, 156, 157, 204(n.10) Pls 121, 147, 148, 150, 151, 164, 165, 167
Byron, George, Lord 49

Cade, John, 'Jack' (*d.* 1450) 146
Calcroft, Fox 105
Calvin, John 199(n.5)
Camden, Sir Charles Pratt, Earl 35, 136
Canada 41, 148, 176
Canning, Betty 184
Canning, George 9, 180, 184, 197(n.12), 205(n.23)
Cantemir, Demetrius 105
Carey, W.P. 66
Caricature, satirical prints
  audience for, customers 6, 7, 9, 18, 19, 37, 184
  and cartoons 1, 4, 8, 13, 34, 135, 158, 192, 200(n.33)
  copyright, plagiarism, piracy 4–5, 7, 18–19, 87, 95, 158, 184

  exhibitions of, 6, 7
  exportation 5, 7
  freedom and licence of 2, 3, 197(n.32)
  and history painting 9, 33, 46, 88, 176–77
  Italian and Dutch influences 1
  and libel 2, 3, 6, 34
  main targets of 7–8, 194
  nature and development of Ch.1 *passim*, 13, 135, 143, 193
  and physiognomy 7, 8
  prices of 4, 6, 7, 18, 115
  print runs 5, 18
  pursuit for amateurs 1, 4, 5, 44
  suppression of 2, 114–15
Carlton House, 84, 86, 87–8, 89
Caroline of Brunswick, Princess 89
Carracci, Annibale 1, 61
Carter, J., publisher 195, 204(n.42)
Cartoons, *see* Caricature and
Catherine II of Russia 159–60, 194
Catholic Relief Act, 1778 20, 21, 41, 42, 68
Catholicism 2, 20, 41, 48–9, 68, 75, 83–4, 198(n.61)
  symbols of 39–40, 46, 48, 88–9, 137, 140, 147, 156
  and *see* Burke as Jesuit; No-Popery riots, Catholic Relief Act; Fitzherbert, Maria
Cavendish, Lord John 15, 29, 30, 37, 38, 50, 56, 60, 194
Cervantes, Miguel de 132
Chait Singh, Rajah of Benares 53, 105
Charlemont, James Caulfeild, first Earl of 40
Charles I of England 126, 127, 144
Charlotte, Queen ix, 8, 63, 106, 107–108, 123, 124, 125, 145, 146, 157, 194
Charlotte Augusta, Princess Royal 194
Chatham, Baroness of 179
Chatham, Earl of, *see* Pitt, William the elder
Chelsea Hospital 67
Church, Established (Church of England) 19, 41, 48–9, 73, 75, 118–20, 139, 140, 147
Churchill, Charles 28
Cicero 13, 82, 83, 93, 198(n.26), 205(concl. n.1)
Cincinnatus 39–40
Civil List 23–5, 30–31, 175
Clare, Lord 15
Clarence, Prince William, Duke of 130, 184, 194
Clarkson, F., publisher 195, Pl. 63
Claudius 122
Clive, Robert, Baron 15, 95
Club, The 20
Colley, Linda 70
Colley, Thomas, caricaturist and publisher 27, 35, 47, 195, 199(n.105), 200(n.32), Pls 18, 35
Collings, Samuel 56, 66, 201(n.60), Pls 50, 51, 133
Congreve, William 133
Constitution, British, symbolised in prints 13, 22–3, 55, 118, 152, 169
Conway, General Henry Seymour 17, 29, 30, 35
Cooper, Grey 17
Copyright Act, 1735 4–5, 7, 18
Cornell, Thomas, publisher 195, 200(n.42, n.5, ch.3, n.33), 202(n.33, n.56, n.57, n.59), 203(n.33), Pls 39, 71, 72, 74, 104, 134, 137, 161
Cornwall, Charles, Speaker 15, 35, 95, 96, 194
Covent Garden Theatre 49, 84
Craftsman, The 2
Crawford, J., publisher 195, 202(n.55).
Critic, The 49
Cromwell, Oliver 38, 58, 59, 60, 118, 136, 144, 152, 180, 194
Crown and Anchor tavern 161, 167, 169
Crown, influence of 20, 22–3, 24–5, 28, 29–31, 38, 39, 42–3, 145, 157
  'backstairs' intriguing 66, 67
Cruikshank, George 4, 5, 135, 189, 205(n.43)
Cruikshank, Isaac 66, 89, 134–35, 146, 151, 159, 165, 171, 179, 180, 184, 189, 204(n.10), 205(n.17), Pls 141,

155, 177, 190, 191, 194, 197
Cruikshank, Isaac Robert 135
Cruise O'Brien, Conor ix, 13, 38, 41, 150
Cumberland, William Augustus, Duke of 17, 18, 197(n.13)

Dallas, Sir Robert 79
Dance, George the younger 44
D'Archery or D'Achery, Elizabeth, publisher 195, 199(n.78), 200(n.26, n.41, n.9, n.18), 205(n.62), Pls 26, 29
Darly, Mary, publisher 5
Darly, Matthew, publisher 2, 3, 5, 195, 199(n.12)
Death of Dido, The 88
Death of Wolfe, The 25, 26, 56, 176, 200(n.14)
Deccan, Nizam of 105
Decline and Fall of the Roman Empire, The 25
de Grey, William 15
Denbigh, Basil Feilding, Earl of 30
Denmark 188
Dent, William, caricaturist and publisher 4, 16, 34, 48, 63, 66, 69, 74–6, 82, 89, 96, 98, 99, 105, 109, 110, 118, 123, 131, 136–37, 139, 144, 145, 156, 157, 158, 159, 160, 161, 162, 165, 169, 171, 195, 200(n.32), 202(n.17), 203(n.44, ch.6, n.6), 204(n.36, n.41, n.53), 205(n.21), Pls 36, 54, 64, 67, 68, 69, 74, 76, 85, 91, 94, 96, 102, 108, 109, 110, 113, 120, 124, 126, 143, 146, 153, 154, 166, 168, 170, 172, 173, 178, 181, 183
Derby, Edward Stanley, twelfth Earl of 73, 114, 123, 184, 194
Derry, Earl Bishop of, *see* Hervey, Frederick
Devonshire, Georgiana, Duchess of ix, 8, 56, 69, 70–2, 85, 115–17, 139, 194
Devonshire, William Cavendish, fifth Duke of 20, 70, 113, 190
Dickie, W., publisher 195, Pls 91, 94, 96, 102
Dido, Queen of Carthage 88
Dissenters 139, 144, 159
Dodsley, James 140
Dodsley, Robert 11
Dominicetti (quack doctor) 130
Donald, Diana 47
Don Quixote 9, 131–32, 144, 146–47
Doughty, J., caricaturist and publisher 101–102, 194, Pls 100, 101
Dowdeswell, William 15, 192
Draper, Sir William 12
Drury Lane Theatre 49, 81, 202(n.48)
Dublin print trade 5, 7, 86
Duenna, The 49, 202(n.65)
Dundas, Henry 52, 88, 94, 107, 149, 150, 162, 166, 167, 174, 175, 176, 184, 185, 187, 194, 202(n.55)
Dunning, John 39, 43
Dyson, Jeremiah 15

East India Company 52, 53–7, 68, 79, 91, 93, 192, 200(n.4)
Economical Reform; 20–5, 26, 29–32, 49, 72, 73, 147, 175
Eden, William 78, 181
Ehrman, John 22
Eldon, John Scott, first Earl of 34
Elections, *see* Middlesex; Westminster 1784; Westminster 1788
Ellenborough, Baron, *see* Law, Edward
Elliot, Sir, Gilbert, MP 102, 139
Elliott, Hugh 202(n.13)
Erskine, Sir James, MP 94–5
Erskine, Thomas, MP 56, 87, 167, 184, 194
Evans, T., publisher 195, 199(n.105)

Fame 159
  Temple of 28, 29
  Farquhar, George 8
Fawkes, Guy 37, 58, 152, 154

Fielding & Walker, publishers 195, Pls 12, 13
Fitzherbert, Mrs Maria 8, 83–5, 88–9, 121, 122, 130, 139, 194
Fitzpatrick, General Richard, MP 72
Fitzwilliam, William Wentworth, second Earl 159, 181, 190
Flood, Henry 203(n.41)
Flying machine, see Air-balloons
Fores, Samuel William, publisher 7, 85, 86, 167, 184, 195, 197(n.12), 201(n.12), 202(n.14, n.20, n.24, n.25, n.27, n.28, n.31, n.61, n.63, n.66), 204(n.37, no.40, n.54), 205(n.17), Pls 48, 73, 78, 80, 83, 105, 106, 111, 122, 123, 125, 131, 132, 136, 138, 141, 144, 145, 155, 158, 162, 177, 190, 191, 194, 197
Fox, Charles James ix, 1, 12, 20, 28, 31, 34, 57, 81, 82, 188, 189, 190, 202(n.33)
    and Mrs Armistead 120, 121
    and Dissenters 139
    and Duchess of Devonshire 8, 56, 70–2
    Fox's East India bill 52, 53–7, 66, 72, 73
    Fox–North coalition 44, 46, 47, 50, 56, 73
    and French Revolution 135, 148–69 passim, 183, 184, 185, 204(n.54)
    and George III 28, 29, 43, 51, 53, 58–60, 115, 161
    and impeachment of Hastings 89–93, 110, 173
    and Ireland 75–8
    much caricatured 7–8, 117, 192, 194
    and North's administration 35, 44, 198(n.66)
    opposed by Burke 162–69, 181
    personal life and finances 7–8, 31, 42, 56, 64, 79, 86, 87, 103, 105, 139, 160, 161, 165, 187, 192, 200(n.15), 202(n.17)
    and Pitt 38, 57
    quarrel and breach with Burke 96, 135, 148–57, 159, 204(n.30)
    Regency crisis 118–24, 126, 127, 128, 130, 132, 134, 203(n.30), 204(n.53)
    resigns, 1782 38, 39, 42
    and Shelburne 38, 43–4
    Westminster election 1784 111–17
    1784 struggle 57–66, 201(n.62)
    as Bottom the Weaver 69
    as Capt. Blood 113
    as Carlo Khan 53, 55, 70, 84
    as Cromwell 58, 59, 60, 118, 136, 152
    as Gorgon 62
    as Guy Fawkes 37, 58, 154, 155
    as Hudibras 56, 70
    as Launce 157
    as 'Man of the People' 30, 53, 72, 93, 167, 183
    as Mason 113
    as prizefighter 166, 167
    as Satan 58
    as toad 124
    as Typhon 60
    as Vulcan 89
Fox, Henry, first Baron Holland 7, 23, 24, 31, 102–103, 191, 203(ch.6, n.1)
Fox, Lady Caroline, Baroness Holland, 12, 179
    Fox, Stephen 31
Foxe, John 41, 72
Fragonard, Jean Honoré 122
France and the French 18, 21, 23, 24, 25, 27, 36, 37, 40, 41, 124, 174
    French invasion threat to Britain 181–86
    French Revolution 135, 136–69, 170, 177, 183–88
    peace negotiations 174, 181, 183
Francis, Sir Philip
    'Junius' 12–13, 52, 94, 99
    and Reflections 140
    and Warren Hastings 13, 52, 89, 91, 94, 95–6, 98, 99, 101, 106, 110–111, 173
Freeman's Journal 131
Frith, John 134, 203(n.44)
Fuseli, Henry 9

Garrick, David 20, 49
Gazeteer and New Daily Advertiser 18
General Warrants 13, 14–15, 17
Gentleman's Magazine 66
Goerge, M. Dorothy ix, 4, 72, 87, 150, 157, 181, 190
George III ix, 8, 17, 28, 35, 38, 44, 102, 117, 162, 169, 179, 194, 204(n.54)
    and Burke 28, 29, 37, 49, 52, 58–60, 134, 135, 145–46, 157, 175, 192
    and Catholicism 41, 199(n.12)
    and see Crown, influence of
    and Fox 28, 29, 37, 51, 58, 73, 115, 161
    and Fox–North coalition 46–7, 51, 53, 55, 56, 58–60, 79
    and Hastings 91, 93, 104, 105, 106, 107, 133, 134, 171
    illness 118, 123, 127, 128, 129–30, 131, 132, 133, 135, 157, 170, 171, 203(n.39)
    and Paine 157, 162
    and Prince's debts 85–6
    and Prince's secret marriage 84, 89
    and Rockingham 28–9, 36–7
    royal prerogative 15, 58, 59–60
    and Thurlow 43, 60, 106, 161
    1784 struggle 56–67, 136
George, Prince of Wales
    and Mrs Fitzherbert ix, 8, 83–5, 88–9, 139
    French Revolution 184
    and Lady Jersey 89
    much caricatured 8, 194
    and Opposition 25, 58, 63, 69, 70, 113, 118, 152, 161, 162
    and Perdita Robinson 56, 87, 200(n.15)
    personal life 69–70, 85–6, 87–9, 118, 175, 202(n.17)
    possible succession 46
    Regency crisis 118–132, 134, 188
Germain, Lord George, see Sackville
Germany and Germans 5, 60, 108
Ghiberti, Lorenzo 10
Gibbon, Edward 25, 165
Gillray, James (1757–1815) 4, 5, 32, 33, 44, 84, 106, 134, 136, 158, 164, 171, 179, 188, 193, 197(n.12), 202(n.39), 203(n.76), 204(n.49)
    and Bedford 187
    and Burke 26, 36, 39–40, 41, 42, 46, 51, 68, 86–7, 89, 91, 133, 144, 159, 161, 162, 173, 175, 177, 179, 183, 186, 199(n.5)
    and Fox 29, 37, 42
    hiring of 4, 34, 66, 111–113, 116, 117
    and Mrs Humphrey 5, 7
    and J.H. Mortimer 20, 91
    and Paine 157
    parodies Reynolds 46, 47, 88
    parodies Sayers 101, 106, 107, 127, Pls 99, 105, 106
    parodies West 56, 176–77
    and Pitt 117, 174
    and Regency crisis, 132, 133
    and revolutionary France 183–84, 185–86, 192, 205(n.23)
    and Rockingham 36, 37
    and royal family 51, 106–108, 122
    Pls 26, 27, 29, 31, 34, 38, 77, 82, 86, 99, 105, 106, 114, 115, 116, 118, 119, 125, 138, 140, 152, 162, 163, 171, 176, 186, 195
    and Shelburne 40
    skills 4, 39, 51, 83, 134, 144, 184, 197(n.19), 205(n.7)
'Glorious Revolution', 1688 2, 139, 152
Godfrey, Richard 9
Goldsmith, Oliver 15, 20, 40, 79
Gombrich, Ernst 34
Gordon, Lord George 38, 41, 68, 194
Gower, Granville Leveson, second Earl 20
Grafton, Augustus Henry Fitzroy, third Duke of 12, 17, 184, 194
Graham, Catherine Macaulay 144

Grant, T., publisher 195, 199(n.78), Pl. 20
Grattan, Henry 179
Gray, Thomas 68, 201(n.56)
Greenwich Hospital 20, 21
Grenville, George (1712–70) 11, 13, 15, 17, 18, 19
Grenville, William 184, 185, 194
Grey, Charles (later Viscount Howick and second Earl Grey) 70, 149, 150, 188
Guildhall Library, London 72

Habeas Corpus Act 13, 14
Halifax, George Montagu Dunk, second Earl of 17, 19
Hall, Edward 75, 118, 121, 197(n.45)
Hamilton, Archibald jr, publisher 194, Pl. 8
Hamilton, William Gerard 11, 12, 40
Hanger, George ix, 8, 83, 84, 85, 86, 87, 113, 115, 118, 120, 194
Hanover, White Horse of 174, 185
Hardwicke, Earl of ix
Harmar, T., publisher 195, 202(n.34), Pl. 93
Harrow School 49, 167
Hastings, Mrs Anna Maria Appollonia 108
Hastings, Warren 13, 44, 52, 55, 78, 79, 81–2, 89–111, 125, 133–34, 147, 157, 167, 171–73, 176, 190, 194, 203(n.44)
Hawkesbury, Lord, see Jenkinson, Charles
Haydon, Colin 41
Heath, William 188
Hedges, E., publisher 195, 200(n.25, n.10), 201(n.34), 202(n.17), Pls 40, 43, 53, 58
Hedges, J., publisher 195, Pl. 49
Herschel, Sir William 162
Hervey, Frederick, Earl Bishop of Derry 75, 76
Hibernia, as symbol of Ireland 20, 75, 76, 78 (and 'Ireland' 77
Hibernian Magazine 202(n.17)
Hill, Draper 4, 144, 184
Hinchcliffe, Bishop John 70
Hinchinbroke, John Montague, Viscount 176
History and genre painting 9, 32, 46–7, 88, 174, 176–77
History of the Westminster Election, The 68
Hobart, Mrs Albinia 67, 70, 72, 194
Hobhouse, Christopher 190
Hogarth, William 2, 3, 4, 5
Holland and the Dutch 1, 27, 36, 37, 181
Holland, Lord, see Fox, Henry
Holland, William, publisher 5–6, 7, 144, 195, 200(n.7), 202(n.64), 203(n.16, n.19), 204(n.31, n.32, n.40), 205(n.36), Pls 77, 86, 121, 135, 147, 148, 150, 151, 164, 165, 167, 175, 196
Holloway, W., publisher 195, 201(n.84)
Homer 32
Hone, William 195, 205(n.43)
Hood, Admiral Samuel 67, 68, 69, 72, 111, 117, 194
Horace 16, 173
Horne Tooke, Revd John 144, 184, 194
House of Commons, scenes in 32, 38, 44, 79, 81, 82, 91–2, 93–4, 95, 109, 110, 121, 126, 129–30, 133, 148–52, 155–56, 157–48, 162–65; outside 60–62
House, Sam 194
Howe, Admiral Richard 171, 194
Howe, General Sir William 20
Howick, Viscount, see Grey, Charles
Hudibras 9, 56
Humane Society, The 120
Humphrey, George, publisher 195, 201(n.85), 203(n.20), Pls 55, 62
Humphrey, Mrs Hannah, publisher 1, 2, 5, 7, 44, 195, 199(n.113), 20(n.61, n.70, n.71), 202(n.17, n.72), 203(n.76), 204(n.35, n.49), 205(n.14, n.26, n.34, n.39), Pls 27, 33, 81, 115, 116, 118, 119, 152, 163, 171, 176, 182, 185, 186, 187, 188, 189, 192, 193, 195
Humphrey, William, publisher 195, 199(n.112), 200(n.20, n.28, n.26, n.29), 201(n.37), 202(n.19), Pls 1, 34, 38, 45, 46, 52

Humphries and Mendoza, prizefighters 96, 204(n.53)

Impey, Sir Elijah 102, 110, 133
India and Indians 8, 13, 52, 53–7, 60, 73, 75, 78, 79, 81, 82, 83, 89–91, 93–111, 133–34, 171–73, 176, 181, 192, 193, 204(n.33)
Ireland and the Irish 10, 11, 12, 13, 25, 51, 68–9, 72, 75–8, 113–14, 131–32, 136, 137, 166, 181, 183, 188, 198(n.61), 202(n.38), (and see Hibernia)
    Irish Bulls 27, 44, 132, 159, 199(n.70), 202(n.38)
    Irish Civil List 3, 11, 23–4, 17
    Irish identified in caricature 10, 25, 26–7, 166–67
    Irish Trade 20, 21, 42, 75–8
Islamic religion attacked 105–106
Italy and Italians 1, 20, 32

Jacobite rebellions 17, 121
James II 41
Jenkinson, Charles, first Baron Hawkesbury 77, 78, 79, 123, 157, 201(n.92)
Jenkinson, Robert 184
Jersey, Frances, Countess of 89, 139
Jews and anti-Jewish sentiment 20, 87, 199(n.5)
Johnson, Dr Samuel 2, 3, 9, 11, 13, 17, 20, 23, 24, 127, 179, 194
Johnston, J., publisher 195, 205(n.43)
Jones, John 190, Pl. 199
Jonson, Ben 49
Jordan, Dorothea 130, 194
'Junius' 12–13, 15, 26, 35, 131, 192, 198(n.14)
Justice, symbols of 22, 23, 57, 123, 144

Kay, John 197(n.45)
Kelly, Thomas, publisher 199(n.80)
Kenyon, Sir H. Lloyd 67
Keppel, Admiral Augustus, first Viscount 29, 30, 44, 51, 56, 58, 59
Kingsbury, henry 87, 203(ch.6, n.4)
Knight, Richard Payne 11

Lambeth Palace 118, 120
Langham, J., publisher 195, Pl. 32
Lansdowne, Marquis of, see Shelburne, Earl of
Lauderdale, James Maitland, eighth Earl of 177, 184
Laurie & Whittle, publishers 195, Pl. 60
Lavater Johann 8
Law, Edward, KC 96, 104, 105
Lawyers 33–4, 35, 52, 96–7, 104, 105, 106, 110, 147, 202(n.45)
Lee, John 56
Leech, John 197(n.2)
Lefanu, Alicia 49
Leinster, William Robert Fitzgerald, second Duke of 131, 132
Letter to a Member of the National Assembly 162
Letter to a Noble Lord 177, 184, 188, 190
Letters on a Regicide Peace 181, 183, 184, 185
Liberty, symbols of 13, 22, 23, 32–3, 144, 159, 161, 187
Licensing Act, 1737 49
Little Red Ridinghood 16, 46, 47, 48, 200(n.33)
'Loaves and Fishes' 44, 67, 81, 82, 149, 150, 160–61
Locke, John 41
London butchers 113–14
London chairmen 68–9, 72, 113–114
London Chronicle 205(n.28)
London Evening Post 17
London Magazine 12
London print trade, see print publishers
London tailors 157
Long, Charles 160, 161
Longinus 56
Loughborough, Alexander Wedderburn, first Baron 19, 95, 167, 171, 173, 174, 175, 184, 187, 194
Louis XVI 147, 159, 181, 183, 194
Lowther, Sir James 15, 20

Loyola, Ignatius 68, 69, 199(n.5)
Luther Martin 41

Macartney, George, first Earl 82
Macbeth 50, 56, 81, 156, 189
Macintosh, W., publisher 194, Pl. 17
'Mackenzie, Alexander' 2, Pl. 2
McKenzie, Alexander 195, Pl. 84
Macklew, E., publisher 195, 202(n.16, n.17)
MacNally, Leonard 84
MacPhail, H., publisher 195, 201(n.36, n.75)
Magna Carta (or Charta) 13, 23, 184, 205(concl. n.1)
Mahon, Lord, see Stanhope, Earl
'Malagrida' 40
Malmesbury, James Harris, Baron 181, 183
Malton, constituency of 42, 171
Malton, James 6
Mansell, W. 8, Pls 1, 73
Mansfield, James, KC 31
Mansfield, William Murray, first Earl of 35, 36, 194
Marie Antoinette, Queen of France 16, 140, 143, 147, 159, 190, 194
Markham, Dr William 13, 35
Marshall, P.J. 53
Marsham, Charles, MP 63, 64
Mason (associate of Blood) 113
Maynard, W., publisher 195, Pl. 160
Melbourne, Elizabeth, Viscountess 85, 86
Middlesex election dispute 13, 15, 38
Midsummer Night's Dream, A 69
Milton, John 8, 39, 58
Mirabeau, Honore-Gabriel-Riquetti, Comte de 156, 204(n.31)
Mitchell, L.G. 70, 72, 103
Monro, Dr John 5, 155, 156, 204(n.30)
Montgomery, Richard 75
Montgomery sisters 46, 47
Moore, William, publisher 195, Pls 74, 91, 94, 96
Moritz, Carl Philip 38
Morning Chronicle 37, 118, 177
Morning Herald 123
Morning Post 67, 68
Morris, Captain Charles 87, 201(n.98)
Mortimer, John Hamilton 20, 91
Mountmorres, Hervey Morres, second Viscount 67, 201(n.45)

Nagle, James 11–12
Nandakumar, Maharajah 110, 133
Navy, sailors 20, 21, 25, 35, 51, 68–9, 75, 114, 128, 134, 176, 181
Nelson, Admiral Horatio 189
New and Complete Book of Martyrs 41
Newcastle, Thomas Pelham-Holles, first Duke of ix, x, 37, 40–41, 203(ch.6, n.1)
Newgate Gaol 6, 136
Newmarket 118, 120
Newton, Richard 6, 162, 171, 186–87, Pls 4, 175, 196
Nicholson, Margaret 169, 170
Nill, George, publisher 195, 202(n.35)
Nixon, John 56, 110, 150, 166, 167, Pls 42, 112, 158, 180
Nixon, President Richard M. 192
Nollekens, Joseph 160
No-Popery riots 20, 21, 38, 41, 68
Norfolk, Charles Howard, eleventh Duke of 113, 167, 184, 194
North Briton 14, 17
North, Frederick, Lord ix, 8, 12, 15, 25, 26, 35, 41, 73, 86, 87, 194, 198(n.68), 200(ch.2, n.24)
    and America 8, 20, 75, 91, 98, 99, 192
    coalition with Fox 44, 46, 47, 50, 51, 52, 53, 73
    and East India bill 53–6
    and impeachment of Hastings 89–93, 98, 99, 102–103, 106
    and Ireland 75–7, 78

North's administration 20, 28, 29, 34, 35
    Prince's secret marriage 83, 85, 89
    and Regency crisis 122, 123
    represented as sleepy 29, 83, 84, 99, 202(n.49)
    taxes on soap and small beer 35, 47, 48
    Westminster election 1784 69, 70, 72, 203(n.74)
Northumberland, Hugh Percy, Earl (later Duke) of 23
Norton, Sir Fletcher, KC 15, 19, 31
Nullum Tempus, Act of 13, 15
Nundocomar, see Nandakumar
Nunn, J., publisher 195, Pl. 69

Oak, as symbol of Britain 22–3, 152, 189
Observations on the Reflections 144
Onslow, George 15
Orléans, Louis-Philippe-Joseph (Egalité), Duc d' 118, 120, 180, 194, 203(n.3)
Oudh, Begums of 53–5, 93, 101, 106, 109, 110, 127, 202(n.58)
Owen, R., publisher 195, Pl. 19
Owl, symbol of mock wisdom 136, 140 (and in Pl. 34)
Oxford, University of 165–66, 204(n.490)

Paine, Thomas, 146, 155, 157, 162, 169, 187, 194
Palinurus 202(n.49)
Palmer, Samuel 139
Paradise Lost 38, 39, 58
Parliamentary History, The 149
Perceval, Spencer 189
Phillips, R., publisher 195, 199(n.5), 202(n.39)
Phillips ('W.G.'), caricaturist 66
Philosophical Inquiry into the origin of our Ideas of the Sublime and Beautiful, A 10–11, 181 (and see 'Sublime and Beautiful')
Physiognomy 7, 8
Pindar, Peter, see Wolcot, John
Pitt, William the elder 16, 22, 28, 57, 179
Pitt, William the yonger ix, 8, 28, 29, 38, 56, 62, 79, 81, 82, 93, 124–26, 139, 150, 151, 152, 157, 171, 187, 188, 189, 194
    and Chatham 28, 57, 179
    and Hastings 93, 94, 95, 105, 107
    Irish Propositions 75–8, 202(n.38)
    Pitt's East India bill 57, 58, 155, 176
    Prince's marriage and debts 84, 85–6, 87–8
    Regency crisis 118, 122–23, 124, 125, 126, 127, 128–29, 130, 203(n.30), 204(n.53)
    'rewards' Burke 146, 149, 150, 156, 157, 159, 160–61, 175
    and revolutionary France 159, 162, 166, 167, 169, 173, 174, 177, 181, 184, 185, 205(n.6)
    and Sayers 34, 104
    and Sheridan 49
    and Thurlow 161
    Westminster elections, 1784, 1788 66, 68, 72, 117
    1784 struggle 57–66
Pius VI, Pope 140
Place Act, 1707 111
Polyphemus the cyclops 25, 26, 32, 33
Porter, I. Or J. Pl. 37
Portland, William Henry Cavendish Bentinck, third Duke of 11, 15, 20, 44, 52, 56, 58, 63, 75, 87, 113, 137–38, 152, 166, 167, 190, 194
Powell, John 44, 82, 83
Pownall, B., publisher 195, 200(n.44)
Powys, Thomas, MP 37, 63, 64, 78, 79, 81, 194
Prattent, ?T. Pl. 92
Presbyterians 20, 139, 140
Pressly, William 32
Price, Dr Richard 10, 25, 139, 140, 144, 147, 152, 156, 194, 199(n.5), 204(n.8, n.19)
Price, William 7
Pridden, J., printseller 18–19
Priestley, Dr Joseph 25, 139, 152, 194, 199(n.5)
Print publishers 1, 2, 3, 5, 6, 7, 18, 70–72, 190, 195

advertisements by 5, 6, 7, 18, 167, 199(n.111)
     print shops windows 1, 2, 5, 7, 72
Prior, James 12, 41, 121–22
Propaganda 1, 2, 4, 17–19, 34, 55, 111–13, 117, 123, 192
Public Advertiser 2, 11–12, 13, 17, 18, 26, 67, 68, 82
Punch 197(n.2), 200(n.33)

Quakers 10, 41, 42
Quebec Act, 1774 41
'Queen Rant', *see* Siddons, Sarah
Queensberry, William Douglas, fourth Duke of 176

Ramberg, Johann Heinrich 97, 197(n.31), Pl. 93
Rambler's Magazine 44, 52
Ramsay, Allan 3, 197(n.14)
Real or Constitutional House that Jack Built, The 189
Reflections on the Revolution in France 10, 139–40, 146, 147,
     156, 157, 159, 161, 162, 165, 173, 177, 186, 187,
     204(n.31)
Rembrandt 20
Revolution Society, The 139, 147
Reynolds, Sir Joshua 7, 9, 20, 29, 30, 32, 36, 46, 47, 81,
     88, 199(n.80)
Rich, E., publisher 195, 201(n.63)
Richardson, W., publisher 195, Pl. 37
Richmond, Charles Lennox, third Duke of ix, 8, 29, 30,
     35, 37, 43, 44, 57, 63, 66, 88, 89, 123, 124, 162, 184,
     190, 194, 200(n.18)
Ridgway, James, publisher 133, 195, Pl. 54
Rigby, Richard, 35
Robespierre, Maximilien 204(n.16)
Rights of Man 146, 152, 154, 155, 157, 162, 166, 187
Rivals, The 49
Robinson, G. & Co., publishers 195, Pl. 92
Robinson, John, Dissenter 139
Robinson, John, MP 60–62, 200(ch.3, n.30)
Robinson, Mary 'Perdita' 56, 87, 194, 200(n.15)
Rockingham, Charles Watson-Wentworth, Marquis of
     11, 13, 17, 19, 20, 21, 25–6, 28, 29, 30, 35, 37, 38, 42,
     190
Rodney, Admiral George 27, 194, 199(n.72)
Rome, Beast of 147
Romney, George 190, Pl. 199
Rose, George 88, 117, 149, 150, 158, 160, 194
Rowlandson, Thomas 4, 5, 6, 20, 33, 43, 56, 60, 134,
     158, 169, 201(n.3)
     and Regency crisis 124, 125, 126, 127, 130–31,
     203(n.39)
     and Westminster election 1784 66, 70
     Plates 42, 129, 130, 131, 132, 136, 184
Royal Academy 6, 20, 32, 44, 46, 88, 177, 197(n.31,
     n.39)
Royal George 42–3, 44
Russell, *see* Bedford, Dukes of
Russia 159, 160
Rutland, Charles Manners, fourth Duke of 75

Sacheverell, Dr Henry 2
Sackville, Lord George 12, 35(as Germain), 194,
     198(n.17)
St Alban's tavern 63, 65
Saint-Albin, Abbé de 118
St Eustatius, Island of 27, 199(n.72)
Saint-Far, Abbé de 118
St James's Palace 85, 105, 107, 133, 134, 183
St Omer 16, 41, 68, 200(ch.3, n.20)
St Paul's Cathedral 32, 139
Sams, W., publisher 195, 205(n.43)
Sandby, Paul 66
Sandwich, John Montagu, fourth Earl of 19, 20, 29, 35,
     41, 43, 65, 194
Savile, Sir George 190
Sawbridge, John, MP 79, 81
Sayer and Bennett's Catalogue 7
Sayers, James (1784–1823) 4, 26, 32, 33–4, 38–9, 40, 50,

53, 55, 56, 60, 78, 79, 82, 83, 93, 95, 98, 99, 101, 105,
     106, 107, 110, 126, 127, 128, 152, 155, 158, 171, 173,
     181, 193, 202(n.33, n.48, n.68), Pls 22, 28, 39, 71, 72,
     75, 90, 95, 98, 134, 137, 161, 185, 192
School for Scandal, The vi, 49, 86
Schwellenberg, Mrs 124, 125, 145, 146
Scotland and the Scots 20, 69, 72, 94, 150
Scott, Major John, MP 81, 82, 93, 94, 105, 133
Scott, Dr W. 19
'Scratch, Annibal', *see* Collings, Samuel
Settlement, Act of 8
Shackleton, Richard 41
Shadrach, Meshach and Abednego 59
Shakespeare, William 8, 20, 50, 69, 81, 93, 94, 157, 159,
     167, 181, 189
Shelburne, William Petty, second Earl of 16, 20, 22, 25,
     26, 28, 35, 37, 38, 39, 40, 43–4, 46, 47, 57, 63, 77, 78,
     107, 184, 194, 199(n.1, n.5)
Sheridan, Betsy 115
Sheridan, Frances (*née* Chamberlaine) 49
Sheridan, Richard Brinsley vi, 5, 8, 9, 38, 49–50, 56, 93,
     158, 160, 188, 202(n.65), 204(n.49)
     breach with, and opposed by, Burke 135, 136, 137,
     139, 144, 149, 150, 152, 154, 155, 156, 157, 162–64,
     166, 167, 169, 187, 204(n.30)
     and French Revolution 135, 161, 171, 174, 183
     as imbiber 110, 150, 159, 166
     impeachment of Hastings 89, 93–4, 101–106,
     109–11
     personal finances 49, 86, 87, 123, 161, 164, 183
     Regency crisis 118, 120–22, 123, 124, 126, 127, 128,
     130, 131–32, 133, 134, 135, 136
     Westminster election 1788 113–116
Sheridan, Thomas (elder) 49
Sheridan, Thomas (younger) 49, 167
Sherlock, A., publisher 195, Pl. 79
She Stoops to Conquer 15
Shipley, Bishop Jonathan 70
Siddons, Sarah ix, 8, 81, 98
Sidebotham, James, publisher 7, 195, Pl. 5
Sidmouth, Viscount, *see* Addington, Henry
Slave trade 160
Smith, M., publisher 195, Pl. 56
Smith, 'Mr', publisher 18, 195, Pls 10, 11
Smithfield 106, 187
Smyth, Captain Hervey 177
'Sneer, Dicky' 5
South Sea Bubble 1
Spain and the Spanish 25, 27, 36, 37, 41, 124
Stamp Act 5, 17–19
Stanhope, Charles, third Earl 147, 184, 194
     as Lord Mahon 57
Steele, Thomas 88
Sterne, Laurence 57, 203(n.17)
Stormont, David Murray, seventh Viscount 113, 194
Strafford, Thomas Wentworth, first Earl of (*d.* 1641) 101,
     173
Stubbs, George Towneley (1756–1815) 84, 85, Pls 78, 80
'Sublime and Beautiful' 10–11, 12, 26, 51, 56, 58, 65, 70,
     73, 75, 87, 93, 101, 136, 137, 139, 140, 145, 147, 159,
     181, 188, 189, 190, 193, 198(n.66)
Sutherland, Lucy 31
Swift, Jonathan 49, 193
Sydney, Thoms Townshend, first Viscount 57, 66, 184,
     194
Symonds, H.D., publisher 195, Pl. 156

Tattersalls, 86
Taxation 35, 93, 150, 152, 162, 175, 184, 185
     and America 16, 17–19, 192
Taylor, Michael Angelo, MP 162, 184, 194, 205(n.21)
Tegg, Thomas, publisher 7, 189, 195, 205(n.42)
Tegg's Prime Jest Book 189
Temple, George Nugent, second Earl 55, 64, 66, 194,
     201(n.39)

Temple, Richard Grenville, first Earl 18, 19
Tertellus 95
Test and Corporation Acts 139, 140, 159
Theatre Royal, Dublin 49
Thelwall, John 184
Thoughts on the Cause of the Present Discontents 11, 28, 36
Thrale, Mrs Hester 24
Three Ladies adorning a Term of Hymen 46, 47
Thurlow, Edward Lord Chancellor 7, 8, 35, 36, 63, 89,
     93, 109, 113, 136, 176, 187, 201(n.62), 202(n.65)
     and George III 43, 60, 64, 106, 161
     and Hastings 96, 101–102, 104, 105, 106, 107, 171,
     173
     and Pitt 161
     and Regency crisis 121, 127, 131, 132, 154,
     203(n.30)
Todd, E., publisher 195, Pl. 66
Tooke, Revd John Horne, *see* Horne Tooke
Topham, Edward 5, 117, 123, 194
Tower of London 113, 155
Town and Country Magazine 15–16, 52
Townshend, George, fourth Viscount (cr. Marquis 1786)
     1, 2, 49, 57, 72, 150, 197(n.13), 198(n.65), 200(n.18),
     201(n.71, n.81), 203(ch.6, n.1), 204(n.29)
Townshend, Lord John 72, 111, 113–14, 116, 117
Trevelyan, Sir George 7
Trinity College, Dublin 10, 12, 41, 204(n.52)
Tristram Shandy 57, 202(n.17)
'Twitcher, Jemmy', *see* Sandwich
Tyler, Wat (*d.* 1381) 65, 146, 147

Ulysses and a Companion fleeing from the Cave of Polyphemus
     32, 33, Pl. 32
'Uncle Toby', *see* Richmond, Duke of
Ushant, Battle of 51, 58

Vaughan, General Sir John 27, 199(n.72)
Velasco Isla, Luis Vicente de 199(n.71)
Verres, Gaius 82, 83, 93
View of the Court sitting on the trial of Warren Hastings Esqʳ in
     Westminster Hall, A Pl. 92
Vindication of Natural Society, A 10
Vindication of the Rights of Man 157
Virgil, *Aeneid* 88, 202(n.49)
Voltaire, Francois-Marie Arouet 10

Wales, Prince of, *see* George
Wales and the Welsh 69
Walker (initials unknown), publisher 195, 205(n.41), Pl.
     198
Wallis, J., publisher 195, 201(n76), Pl. 61
Walpole, Horace 30, 41, 50, 70
Walpole, Sir Robert 1, 103, 158, 159
Walter, John, publisher 203(n.42), Pl. 142
Walwyn, B., publisher 195, 200(ch3,n.17,n.22,n.23), Pls
     57, 59
Warren, Dr Richard 129, 130
Warwick, Earl of 24–5
Washington, General George 28, 75
Watson, Brook, MP 160–61, 194
Watson, Bishop Richard 70
Watson, Thomas 46
Wedderburn, Alexander, *see* Loughborough
Wedgwood, Josiah 75
Wellington, Arthur, first Duke of 189
Wells, W., publisher 105, 200(n.16), Pl. 50
Weltje, Louis 68, 84, 85, 86, 128, 130, 194
Wendover 11
West, Benjamin 9, 56, 176, 177
Westminster elections
     1784 66–73
     1788 66, 72, 111–17, 123
Westminster Hall 59, 96, 97, 101, 104, 173, 200(ch.3,
     n.21)
Westminster Magazine 28

Wheatley, Francis 186
Whig Club, The 167
Whitaker, J., publisher 195, Pl.65
'Whiteboys' 11–12, 78
White Horse of Hanover, *see* Hanover
White's Club 183, 184
Whitworth, Richard 15
Whole Duty of Man, The 46
Whyte, F.F.X, Count Whyte de Melville 144
Wiggins, T., publisher 195, 20(n.8)
Wigstead, Henry 43
Wilberforce, William 174
Wild, Jonathan 65
Wilkes, John 13, 14, 16, 17, 18, 20, 93, 187, 194

William III, of England 152
William V, of Orange 194
Williams, Charles 188, Pl. 198
Williams, Helen Maria 144, 204(n.16)
Williamson, T., publisher 195, 205(n.33)
Willis, Revd Dr Francis 129–30, 203(n.39)
Willis, Bishop Richard 48–9
Wilson, Benjamin 17–20, Pls 10, 11
Windham, William, MP 102, 113, 184, 188
Windsor, 'Mother' 116, 132–33
Wolcot, John 169–70
Wolfe, General James 25, 26, 56, 176, 177
Wollstonecraft, Mary 157
Women in public life caricatured 70, 71

and *see* Devonshire, Duchess of, Hobart, Mrs Albinia
Woodward, George M. 6, 159
World, The 5, 117
Wraxall, Sir Nathaniel 53, 86, 128
Wray, Sir Cecil 66, 67, 70, 71, 194
Wright, J., publisher 195, 205(n.15)
Wright, Paul 41
Wright, Sir Sampson 115, 116
Wright 34, 177
Wycombe, Baron, *see* Shelburne

York, Frederica, Duchess of 159, 194
York, Frederick Augustus, Duke of 129, 159, 184, 194
Young, Edward 202(n.48)

Pubd May 20th 1788. by S W Fores N.3 Piccadilly

Gillray

O Liberty! O Virtue! O